THE COLOR
REVOLUTIONS

THE COLOR REVOLUTIONS

LINCOLN A. MITCHELL

PENN

UNIVERSITY OF PENNSYLVANIA PRESS

PHILADELPHIA

Copyright © 2012 University of Pennsylvania Press

All rights reserved. Except for brief quotations used for purposes of review or scholarly citation, none of this book may be reproduced in any form by any means without written permission from the publisher.

Published by
University of Pennsylvania Press
Philadelphia, Pennsylvania 19104-4112

Printed in the United States of America on acid-free paper
10 9 8 7 6 5 4 3 2 1

Library of Congress Cataloging-in-Publication Data
Mitchell, Lincoln Abraham.
  The color revolutions / Lincoln A. Mitchell.—1st ed.
    p. cm.
  Includes bibliographical references and index.
  ISBN 978-0-8122-4417-5 (hardcover : alk. paper)
  1. Protest movements—Former Soviet republics. 2. Opposition (Political science)—Former Soviet republics. 3. Regime change—Former Soviet republics. 4. Democratization—Former Soviet republics. 5. Former Soviet republics—Politics and government. 6. United States—Foreign relations—Former Soviet republics. 7. Former Soviet republics—Foreign relations—United States. I. Title.
JN6531.M57   2012
947.0009′049—dc23   2011043927

Contents

1. Introduction — 1
2. Pre-Color Revolution Regimes — 17
3. Electoral Breakthroughs — 44
4. The U.S. Role — 73
5. Russia — 92
6. Democracy After the Color Revolutions — 115
7. Exporting Color Revolutions — 141
8. Misreading Democratic Breakthroughs: U.S. Policy After the Color Revolutions — 167
9. The End of an Era — 187

Appendix. Studying Color Revolutions — 200

Notes — 211

Bibliography — 221

Index — 237

Acknowledgments — 245

CHAPTER 1

Introduction

ROUGHLY FIFTEEN YEARS after crowds of peaceful demonstrators from Prague to Tbilisi brought down Communist regimes that had denied hundreds of millions of people their freedom for more than half a century, the excitement of the late 1980s and early 1990s had given way, at least in much of the former Soviet Union, to a grim reality: building free and prosperous countries was not easy. This was true even after toppling a Communist system that had become economically, spiritually, and politically bankrupt. From Kiev to Astana, former Soviet republics were defined by kleptocracy, fraudulent elections, widespread corruption, and, for many people, poverty and a declining quality of life.

Beginning in 2003, on Rustaveli Avenue in Tbilisi, Georgia, and spreading over the next two years to the Maidan in Kiev and the Kyrgyz capital of Bishkek, this began to change. Hope, a commodity that had been in short supply in the Caucasus, Central Asia, and the Slavic countries of the former Soviet Union, returned. Again it took the form of peaceful demonstrators demanding their rights and showing the world that they could only be pushed so far. These peaceful protests—labeled the Rose Revolution in Georgia, the Orange Revolution in Ukraine, and the Tulip Revolution in Kyrgyzstan—brought an end to governments that had tried to steal one too many elections and sought to replace them with freely elected leaders.

For about thirty months, from late 2003 to mid-2005, these protests—which collectively came to be known as the Color Revolutions—looked as if they might possibly reshape the political terrain of the former Soviet Union. All had their origins in attempts by corrupt post-Soviet governments to steal an election. All brought to power a new government that was, at least initially, viewed as pro-democracy and pro-Western in orientation. All were almost immediately hailed as victories for democracy and as changing the balance between Russia and the United States.

By 2010, however, the democratic promise of the Rose Revolution had fizzled out in Georgia. That same promise disintegrated in Kyrgyzstan, when Tulip Revolution leader Kurambek Bakiev was forced to flee the country, and it suffered a setback in Ukraine with the election of Viktor Yanukovich as president—the same man who had sought to steal the 2004 election. These events raised fears that the democratic advances of the post-Orange Revolution period were being halted or even reversed.

Today, the Color Revolutions are all but forgotten by people who do not follow the region closely. For many they are little more than a footnote to the complex politics of the former Soviet Union. The Color Revolutions were not the paradigm-shifting events they seemed to be at first. Instead, they turned out to be further chapters in the post-Communist evolution of Georgia, Ukraine, and Kyrgyzstan, whose overall impact—while not the same in each of these countries—was, in general, significantly less than first thought and, indeed, hoped. Yet relegating the Color Revolutions to footnote status is a mistake because there are valuable lessons, such as the dangers of conflating democratic breakthroughs with democratization, to be learned from these events. Additionally, the Color Revolutions had a significant impact on both U.S.-Russia relations and Russia's relationships with the former Republics of the Soviet Union—perhaps more so than they did on democratic development in any of the countries where they occurred. By examining these events together it is possible to get a better sense of what the Color Revolutions were and what similarities they shared. This approach also allows us to place all these events in the broader context of political development in the former Soviet Union and the U.S. role in that development.

The Color Revolutions also provide a valuable perspective on the events in the Middle East and North Africa that occurred in early 2011 and saw longtime authoritarian leaders such as El Abidine Ben Ali in Tunisia and Hosni Mubarak in Egypt leave office following large public demonstrations. These countries now face long and difficult roads ahead as they seek to move toward democracy. The failure of democracy in post Color Revolution Kyrgyzstan and Georgia and the substantial backsliding in Ukraine underscore both how the hard work begins when the authoritarian kleptocrat leaves power and the dangers of confusing dramatic moments with democracy. Observers of North Africa would do well to keep this in mind.

The Color Revolutions

The term Color Revolution is ambiguous with regard to both definitions and cases. Clearly the Rose and Orange Revolutions qualify as Color Revolutions while the Tulip, Bulldozer, and Cedar revolutions in Kyrgyzstan, Serbia, and Lebanon respectively are in something of a gray area. This book will treat only the Rose, Orange, and Tulip Revolutions as Color Revolutions because they share temporal proximity and a post-Soviet context. I will also draw on the Bulldozer Revolution in Serbia at times because, even though it occurred more than three years before the Rose Revolution, it was an important model for the Georgians who went on to lead the Rose Revolution. I will also look at failed efforts to reproduce Color Revolutions in other countries of the former Soviet Union, most notably Azerbaijan and Belarus.[1]

The Rose Revolution occurred between November 2003 and January 2004 in Georgia. The government party, the Citizens' Union of Georgia (CUG), led by President Eduard Shevardnadze, committed massive and widespread fraud in a parliamentary election held on November 2, 2003. The fraud continued for several days following the election as the government party continued to increase vote totals for itself and allied parties through fraudulent counting. In the days following the election, two opposition parties, the National Movement, led by speaker of the Tbilisi city council Mikheil Saakashvili, and the Burjanadze Democrats, led by Nino Burjanadze, speaker of parliament, and Zurab Zhvania, Burjanadze's predecessor, led demonstrations and vigils in front of the parliament building in the center of Tbilisi. The central demand of the demonstrators was the resignation of President Shevardnadze.

After several weeks of demonstrations ranging in size from a few thousand to as many as a hundred thousand on the final days, Shevardnadze resigned on November 23. At that time, speaker of parliament Burjanadze, in accordance with Georgian law, became acting president. A few weeks later on January 4, 2004, in a snap presidential election, Mikheil Saakashvili, who had emerged as leader of the opposition and of the demonstrations following the election, was elected president in an election broadly assessed as free and fair but in which he faced no serious opposition.

Ukraine's Orange Revolution was in tone and style similar to the Rose Revolution. In this case, however, it was a presidential rather than a parliamentary election that preceded the revolution. The two major candidates in the 2004 election for Ukraine's presidency were Viktor Yanukovich and Viktor Yushchenko. Yanukovich was the candidate of Ukraine's corrupt outgoing president, Leonid Kuchma; he also enjoyed substantial backing from Russia and its president, Vladimir Putin. Yushchenko, the leading opposition candidate, ran on a pro-Western and pro-democracy platform.

The first round of the election was held October 31. Because there were several other candidates in the race, neither Yanukovich nor Yushchenko was able to reach a majority, so a runoff was scheduled between these two candidates for November 21. Yanukovich's supporters, including many from the Ukrainian government, sought to steal the runoff elections; initial results were broadcast that he had won. This led to street demonstrations in Kiev, which lasted for weeks and drew hundreds of thousands of people to the center of the capital city. Eventually, it was agreed that the runoff would be held around December 26. Yushchenko won that election and after several weeks of appeals was sworn in as Ukraine's president on January 23, 2005.

The Tulip Revolution began, like the Rose Revolution, with fraudulent parliamentary elections, which were held in Kyrgyzstan on February 25, 2005. Widespread protests began shortly after pro-government candidates were announced as the winners in most districts. These demonstrations continued for about a month, spreading to many parts of the country. On March 24, amid calls for his resignation, Kyrgyz president Askar Akaev fled to Russia; he officially resigned on April 3.

For the next several months the question who would take over as president remained unclear. In June, positioning and politicking between Felix Kulov, a long-time Akaev opponent who had been released from jail in March, and acting president Kurambek Bakiev led to a determination that Bakiev would be the Tulip Revolution candidate in the July election. On July 10, Bakiev was handily elected president of Krygyzstan with over 90 percent of the vote.

There are, of course, broad similarities among these three events. All were political transitions rooted in stolen elections that saw a pro-Western, and, at least initially, more democratic president come to power. Street demonstrations of varying sizes, reports from both domestic and international election monitors, and relative nonviolence were all key components of the Color Revolutions as well. As will be discussed in later sections, the U.S. and Europe also played an important but unclear role in these events. Additionally, in all these countries the post-revolution path to democracy has been difficult, with many setbacks.

These similarities, however, obscure key differences among the Color Revolutions. Some of these differences are obvious: the election that led to the breakthrough in Ukraine was a presidential vote, while the elections in Georgia and Kyrgyzstan were for parliament. The Rose and Orange Revolutions were much less ambiguously led by young, reform, and western oriented politicians than was the case in Kyrgyzstan. Other differences are less obvious but equally important. For example, the election in Ukraine between Yanukovich and Yushchenko was competitive, with the Ukrainian electorate divided roughly evenly, while the parliamentary election in Georgia saw the party of incumbent president Eduard Shevardnadze soundly rejected by the voters. Similarly, the Tulip Revolution saw scattered incidents of violence while the Rose and Orange Revolutions were far more peaceful in this regard.

What We Can Learn from the Color Revolutions

The Color Revolutions raise a number of questions concerning not only political developments within Georgia, Ukraine, and Kyrgyzstan, but also the broader geopolitical context in which they occurred, how these events effected relations between competing political powers in Eurasia, and the extent to which they brought about enduring political change.

The first question is whether common political environments or conditions contributed to the Color Revolutions. The relative openness of the previous regime, the strength of civil society and degree of freedom enjoyed by citizens of that regime, the widespread unpopularity of the existing government—all are areas that need to be explored. Another set of explanations looks at the political opposition, the degree of unity, strength, and popularity of that opposition, and the extent to which the Color Revolution was part of an opposition strategy, or more the result of the way events unfolded at the moment.

A second question is the nature and extent of the role of the west, particularly the United States, in the Color Revolutions. There has been substantial debate and disagreement on this question in the three Color Revolution countries, the former Soviet Union in general, and western countries.[2] In the west, this question has become laden with partisanship as left critics of the Bush administration have suggested that U.S. organizations played a major role in these three Color Revolutions, and that the Color Revolutions were not about democracy at all, but about efforts of the U.S. to bring pro-western governments into power (MacKinnon 2007; Engdahl 2009). Others in the U.S. have argued that the Color Revolutions were homegrown political events in which the U.S. played a productive but modest supporting role (Mitchell 2008; Way 2008).

A third question is the extent to which the Color Revolutions represented meaningful democratic breakthroughs in these three countries. At the time, all three events were viewed by western governments as advances for democracy and even evidence of the ongoing spread of democracy throughout the world. However, in all these countries, the post-Color Revolution governments have struggled a great deal to deliver on the democratic promise of the Color Revolutions. As the new governments have struggled, western powers—again, most notably the U.S.—have not been able to successfully craft policies for these three countries that reflect the challenges of building democracy in a post-Color Revolution scenario. In Georgia, for example, the U.S. was largely uncritical as the country slipped away from the early democratic promise of the Rose Revolution. U.S. policy in Kyrgyzstan and Ukraine was quite not the same as in Georgia, but it also failed to help the consolidation of democratic gains as effectively as it might have, albeit in different ways and with different outcomes.

Fourth, were the Color Revolutions linked not just by temporal and spatial proximity and the broad similarities listed above, but by efforts by the leaders of each to build on the previous Color Revolutions? In the Georgian case, the model may have been the Bulldozer Revolution in Serbia. The Ukrainians consciously sought out a Georgian model, Georgians, and Georgian advice, while the Kyrgyz sought similar advice and guidance from both Ukrainian and Georgian Color Revolutionaries. In the months leading up to the Rose Revolution, several civic and political leaders in Georgia visited Serbia to work with their counterparts in that country while Serbian civic activists came to Georgia to work with Georgian ones. After the Rose Revolution, Georgians worked in a similar capacity with Ukrainians and Kyrgyz in the months preceding the Orange and Tulip revolutions.

A related point is that in addition to these Color Revolutions, as well as the Cedar Revolution, which very deliberately sought to model itself on the Rose and Orange Revolutions, efforts were made by democratic activists in Azerbaijan in 2005 and Belarus in 2006 to use fraud-ridden elections as the springboards to Color Revolutions. These efforts failed, but remain part of the larger Color Revolution story.

A fifth major question to explore, which increasingly seems like one of the most important issues, is how nondemocratic regimes, primarily but not exclusively in the former Soviet Union, responded to the Color Revolutions. In much of the region, Color Revolutions put a real fear in nondemocratic leaders. They sought to ensure that they would not fall victim to further Color Revolutions through a variety of tactics, including restricting the abilities of foreign and domestic nongovernmental organizations (NGOs) to function in their countries, changing election laws and election systems, and increasing domestic surveillance and harassment of members of the political opposition.

Last, how did the Color Revolutions have an impact on relations between the U.S. and Russia due to Moscow viewing the Color Revolutions as evidence of growing American influence and ambition in the region? Russian efforts to push back against a perceived wave of Colored Revolutions and the ascendance to power of pro-American leaders, notably in Georgia through the Color Revolutions, also raises important questions about these events.

The Yushchenko and Saakashvili governments immediately accelerated their country's quest to join NATO. These aspirations were initially met with strong support and encouragement by most members of the alliance. This contributed to even greater rancor in Moscow as the Russian leadership viewed NATO expansion as a threat to Russian influence in the region. Georgia and Ukraine's hopes of joining NATO were not successful, but are still alive, particularly in Georgia. In 2008, NATO decided not to offer a Membership Action Plan (MAP) to either country, but promised that at some point they would both become members. This ambiguous approach did not lessen Russian anger while keeping hopes in Tbilisi and Kiev alive. The 2008 Russia-Georgia war pushed Georgia's NATO membership farther into the future.

Revolutions Defined

The phrase "Color Revolution" itself is problematic. Although I will use this phrase throughout this book to describe the political events in 2003–2005 in Georgia, Ukraine and Kyrgyzstan, the term is stronger in terms of imagery and connotations than on descriptive or analytical accuracy. The media often use the term "revolution" because it is dramatic and exciting, but that is not enough on which to rest a serious claim that these events were truly revolutions.

The Color Revolutions were, to a great extent, neither colors nor revolutions. Roses and tulips are primarily flowers; an orange is a fruit as well as a color; and the question whether or not these three events qualify as revolutions is legitimate, not only important for academic purposes. The use of the term revolution in Georgia, Ukraine, and Kyrgyzstan has raised the expectation of change among domestic populations, contributed to a new narrative about the country's recent history, and given additional legitimacy to the actions of revolutionary governments. Calling these events revolutions implies that the changes were dramatic and substantial, although in many respects this assumption is debatable. Moreover, the word revolution makes it easy to overstate the initial political gains and significance of these events.

The term revolution suggests that the events of November–December 2003, November–December 2004, and spring 2005 in each of these countries constituted a distinct break with the past rather than simply being a part of a longer post-Communist continuum, but this is far from obvious. In Georgia, where the new leadership had very few ties to the Communist period, it can be argued that the Rose Revolution represented a decisive turning point, but this is a more contentious claim in Ukraine and Kyrgyzstan, where, for example, the new revolutionary leaders still seemed relatively clearly tied to the Communist era.

The Color Revolutions may be best understood in Georgia as the last phase of the post-Communist transition. In Ukraine and Kyrgyzstan the Orange and Tulip Revolutions may also be better understood as components of those country's ongoing post-Communist transitions. These attempts to place these events analytically, however, must be balanced against the almost universal assessment by policy makers in the west that these events were revolutions constituting a significant break with the past.³

The Color Revolutions do not meet the threshold set by Huntington (1968), Goldstone (1991), and others, nor do they qualify as what Skocpol (1979) refers to as "social revolutions," but this does not mean that they were in no way revolutions, or that analyzing them as revolutions is a fruitless endeavor. While these events are undoubtedly best understood in the context of the three countries' continued transition away from the Soviet period, they were, at least at first, more than just another step in the gradual transitions of these countries. Additionally, the change in leadership from Kuchma, Shevardnadze, and Akaev to Yushchenko, Saakashvili, and Bakiev respectively was brought about through street demonstrations, albeit of varying sizes and presence outside the capital, and precipitated by a stolen election.

Yushchenko, Saakashili, and Bakiev, at least initially, all saw themselves, and for the most part, were viewed by the Ukrainian, Georgian, and Kyrgyz populations more broadly, as representing a significant break from the immediate past. Although none of these leaders were driven by what could rightfully be called called "ideology," they all had a vision of moving their country in a new direction.⁴

Coming to power because of street demonstrations following a fraudulent election does not, however, in of itself, make a revolution. Neither does the stated desire to break decisively with the previous administration or reorient the country's foreign or domestic politics. Moreover, all three Color Revolutions overthrew regimes that were also relatively new without established means of political succession, and largely transitional in nature.

Another way to approach this question is to look at how revolutionary the regimes were once they came to power. The three countries look quite different when analyzed this way. The Rose Revolution in Georgia was a more singular event for that country than the Orange and Tulip Revolutions were for Ukraine and Kyrgyzstan. In Ukraine, the cleavages that divided society and the electorate into two separate camps in the hotly contested, initially stolen 2004 presidential election, did not by any means disappear following the Orange Revolution. Rather, they reappeared as the central divisions in several elections beginning in 2005. Additionally, Ukrainian society remained deeply divided on key issues, most notably orientation toward Russia and democracy, which were central to the vision of the Orange Revolution.

Bakiev's government began its tenure by making revolutionary promises but within a few years became mired in the same corruption and lack of democracy that had characterized Akaev's later years. Bakiev also leveraged U.S. need for access to the Manas Air Force Base for almost unlimited support for his regime.⁵ It is therefore hard to argue that the Tulip Revolution represented some revolutionary break with the first decade or so of post-Communist Kyrgyzstan.

The post-Revolution government in Georgia has been the most committed to pursuing a political course and implementing a set of policies that can be described as revolutionary. While the government has not succeeded in achieving all its goals or keeping all its revolutionary promises, it has sought to reorient Georgia's domestic and international policies. Saakashvili's commitment to the west, linking Georgia's future to that of the U.S. rather than Russia, has been unequivocal. Similarly, the government has pushed through a set of political and social reforms that have sought to sweep away the corruption and stagnancy of the Shevardnadze years and replace that with a free market economy. The government's enthusiasm in this area has won praise from the World Bank, the Bush administration, and other supporters of free market economies, quick privatization, and little government support or involvement in the economy.

The break with the past in Georgia and the change in the domestic and international and domestic priorities are distinctly political. These new policies have not always led to meaningful changes in the lives of ordinary Georgians. The quality of life for many Georgians has improved since the Rose Revolution but not in a revolutionary way that has changed social structures or anything of that nature. In this regard, the Rose Revolution could be, in Skocpol's framework, described as a political but not social revolution.

Defining Color Revolutions

The Orange, Rose, and Tulip Revolutions have distinct characteristics that make them stand out from other political developments in countries in transition. A good definition of Color Revolutions reflects that while thus far they have only occurred in a few countries, similar events could conceivably occur in other countries as well. While this might be unlikely, it helps ensure that the definition is analytical, as well as descriptive. Thus, a useful definition of Color Revolution must capture the commonalities that make it possible for this term to represent a discrete political phenomenon, but efforts to do this must also be tempered by recognizing the distinct characteristics and real differences between these political events.

The key elements shared by the three Color Revolutions can be summarized as follows:

- Color Revolutions leverage stolen elections into political breakthroughs.
- Color Revolutions, at least in the short term, are widely viewed as democratic breakthroughs.
- Consolidating post-Color Revolution democracy is very difficult, so Color Revolutions can more accurately be described as transitioning from one form of semidemocracy to another, rather than as an unambiguous step forward for democracy.
- Color Revolutions are largely nonviolent.
- Color Revolutions occur in countries where for a variety of reasons the state, and government, are weak.
- While civil society organizations and public activity of varying sizes

are present, Color Revolutions are political events in which politicians play the major role.
- The role played by the international democracy assistance community varies substantially, but in all cases it is pivotal, even if minor.

The third element has become clearer now that all the Color Revolutions are several years old. Nonetheless, it is an important and distinctive element of Color Revolutions. Continuing to examine these events solely as part of an exploration of the advance of democracy not only is misleading but obscures the more serious question of the difficulty of developing democracy in the non-Baltic former Soviet countries. However, at the outset, as noted in the second element, the Rose, Orange and Tulip Revolutions were all viewed as important steps forward for global democracy. Thus, a central aspect of Color Revolutions, which we can see now with the benefit of a few years hindsight, is disappointment. None have lived up to their initial democratic promise.

Defining the role of international democracy assistance in the Color Revolutions is challenging because, as overlooked by many, the impact of this assistance varied substantially depending on the country. In all cases—even if only, as in Kyrgyzstan, through funding and nurturing the civic organization Kelkel—western donors contributed something essential. However, it must also be borne in mind that there have been hundreds of elections around the world where international donors' involvement in democracy assistance was comparable to Kyrgyzstan, and even to Georgia, but where nothing dramatic at all occurred.

The definition I offer shares some of Way's (2008) observations. The weakness of the state is viewed by both of us as an indispensable attribute of Color Revolutions. Some might argue that this is a tautological approach because we can define weak states as those where Color Revolutions occur. Radnitz (2010) makes a notable contribution to the centrality of state weakness to Color Revolutions by fleshing out the economic causes of this weakness.

> Members of the business class (in Georgia, Ukraine and Kyrgyzstan) remained neutral or joined the opposition rather than support the incumbent, and critical members of the regime defected. The resulting weakness of the regime rather than 'people power' per se, gave the opposition legitimacy and undermined the ability of the regime to sustain itself by force. (135)

Silitski (2009) recognizes the relevance of state weakness to Color Revolutions butis also concerned about the potential for tautology. It is a mistake simply to define a regime as weak because a Color Revolution occurred in that country. He argues that Russia, for the first years of Putin's rule was, in fact, quite weak, but Putin's regime flourished nonetheless.

> It is hard to determine *ex ante* a regime's power or its repressive capacity. We can say with authority that a regime is strong only *after* it has succumbed to or survived challenges.... Such matters as political culture, institutional checks and balances on incumbents, and the self-restraint of rulers must also be taken into account. (88; emphasis original)

Silitiski's point is important, but not entirely accurate. It was not at all hard to see that Shevardnadze's Georgia, for example, was a weak state. There were many clear indicators of this, including heavy dependence on foreign assistance, limited control asserted by the central government over much of the territory of Georgia, extremely poor service delivery, and widespread corruption. All these indicators of a weak state were present in Georgia during the years immediately preceding the Rose Revolution. Moreover, they were considerably less apparent in neighboring Azerbaijan, where attempts to replicate a Color Revolution in 2005 proved unsuccessful.

My definition omits entirely two points that McFaul and Beissinger include in their definitions of Color Revolutions: opposition unity and youth activism.[6] I have deliberately left these out because they were not key components of Color Revolutions; and, moreover, it is certainly possible to have a Color Revolution without either of them. The role of youth has been at times overemphasized by scholars such as Bunce and Wolchik (2004) and Kuzio (2006) as well as many youth activists themselves, who have made something of a cottage industry of traveling around the region describing their role in Color Revolutions and writing pieces describing, and generally overstating, their role.[7] In this regard, I also draw on D'Anieri's (2006) focus on the impact of politicians as one of the overlooked components of Color Revolutions.

The roles and size of the four major youth organizations, Otpor (Serbia), Kmara (Georgia), Pura (Ukraine), and Kelkel (Kyrgyzstan) varied significantly. Otpor and Pura were the largest and most relevant, while Kmara and Kelkel played peripheral roles in the Rose and Tulip Revolutions. The youth organizations best encapsulate the diffusion model, as they were consciously modeled on each other, with youth activists from Serbia helping to train the Georgians, from Serbia and Georgia helping to train the Ukrainians, and from all three countries helping to train the Kyrgyz. However, the impact of these organizations seemed to defuse itself each successive election.

It is also very difficult to determine the relative import of various youth organizations with any certainty because these organizations have a clear interest in having people think they played a major role in the Color Revolutions. Additionally, they were far better positioned to advertise their role than other organizations. First, there is something exciting about a group of young people in Georgia, Ukraine, or anywhere else working nonviolently to change their country. It fits into a narrative from the U.S. Civil Rights Movement and other social movements that is very appealing to western scholars and journalists. Second, the leaders of these youth organizations often speak English and have extensive access to government and NGO leaders from the west and, therefore, are able to communicate well and appealingly with these scholars and journalists.

One example of this is the relative attention devoted in the scholarly media to Kmara as opposed to the International Society for Fair Elections and Democracy (ISFED), another Georgian civic organization working in domestic election monitoring.[8] It is very unusual to see any reference to this organization in the work Bunce and Wolchik, Kuzio, or anywhere else, yet ISFED played a far more important role in the Rose Revolution. The highly competent election monitoring work and parallel vote tabulation (PVT) ISFED did were essential to convincing the Georgian people, not only that the 2003 parliamentary election was stolen, but that the winner really was the National Movement. However, the mostly middle-aged non-English speakers who did a great deal of the work for ISFED were a lot less accessible to those writing about these events.

The question of opposition unity is somewhat more complex. To be certain, the Serbian opposition unifying behind Vojislav Kostunica helped make the Bulldozer Revolution possible; the emergence of Yushchenko as the candidate of the opposition in Ukraine similarly made the Orange Revolution possible. However, in Georgia and Kyrgyzstan the situation was quite different. To look at the Rose Revolution and see opposition unity as a key factor is to largely miss what happened in Georgia in 2003. Unity among the opposition was late and weak. The weeks immediately following the stolen election, when demonstrations were occurring and there was something of a vigil in front of parliament, was as much a struggle between the leading opposition parties, the National Movement and the Burjanadze Democrats, as it was an effort to get rid of Shevardnadze and make radical change in Georgia.⁹ The opposition forces in Kyrgyzstan remained similarly disunified throughout the revolutionary period as supporters of Bakiev and Kulov vied for power during and after the demonstrations that led to Akaev's resignation.

Perhaps a more universal element of Color Revolutions has been the disunity of the leadership in post-Color Revolution governments. In Ukraine, the two major political leaders of the Orange Revolution, Yulia Timoschenko and her party BYT (Bloc of Yulia Timoschenko) and Viktor Yushchenko and his party Our Ukraine, continued to feud throughout much of Yushchenko's presidency. At one point, the tension between the two parties that led the Orange Revolution was so intense that in August 2006, President Yushchenko invited the Party of the Regions to form a coalition government with Our Ukraine. This arrangement meant that Viktor Yanukovich, who had tried to steal the 2004 presidential election, became prime minster of Ukraine within three years of his defeat. Continued strife between Timoschenko and Yushchenko contributed to Yanukovich's victory over Timoschenko in the 2010 presidential runoff.

In Georgia, the rivalry between Zhvania and Saakashvili, which had been one of the engines of politics for at least a year preceding the Rose Revolution, was initially resolved as Zhvania became prime minister and Saakashvili president. This proved only a partial solution as the two leaders had their own supporters in parliament and government, fought over policies, and blamed each other for various problems facing Georgia. This continued until Zhvania's untimely death in January 2005. Less than three years later, Nino Burjanadze, speaker of parliament and third major leader of the Rose Revolution, broke with Saakashvili and became a critic of the government amid speculation that she was preparing a presidential bid of her own in 2013. While she is no longer a serious candidate for major office, Burjanadze has remained a fringe radical political force in Georgia since leaving the government.

The Tulip Revolution and its aftermath were similarly characterized by disunity, including tension between President Bakiev and Prime Minister Felix Kulov as well as ongoing tensions between northern and southern Kyrgyzstan throughout much of Bakiev's presidency. Moreover, the Tulip Revolution regime was brought down by a group of former Tulip Revolutionaries led by Roza Otunbayeva who had played a key role in 2005.

Some degree of unity among the opposition is necessary for a Color Revolution, or any change of government, to occur. If the opposition is not unified, either the old government will remain in power or the country will fall into a period of political strife until some unity among political forces occurs or a single sufficiently strong leader or force emerges. Nonetheless, to identify unity of the opposition as a central element of Color Revolutions suggests that this unity occurred early in the process and remained strong. This was not the case in any of the Color Revolution countries.

Conclusion

The Color Revolutions were complex phenomena that, if understood properly, can contribute to our understanding of political transitions and regime development in the former Soviet Union, as well as the evolution of relations over the last decade between the U.S. and Russia. Examining them in a comparative and analytical context makes it possible to see trends and similarities as they emerged and had an impact on politics in the region. Ultimately, they are also a window into a brief, and optimistic, moment in post-Soviet but also American history. That moment has passed, but it is valuable to spend some time examining how that moment passed and how its potential impact dissipated.

Initially, and for several years after they occurred, the Color Revolutions were understood to be both democratic breakthroughs that would lead to greater democracy in the region and, perhaps more broadly, significant political events that would dramatically change the regime and overall political trajectory in each of the countries in which they occurred. In the years since 2003–2005, it has become increasingly clear not only that the Color Revolutions had a relatively modest impact on democratic development in the region, but that they also did not have an enormous impact on the political development of Georgia, Ukraine, or Kyrgyzstan. Although few suggested the events in North Africa in 2011 were analogous to the Color Revolutions, there remains a real possibility that semi-authoritarian regimes, not democracies, will consolidate power in North Africa in coming years, thus relegating recent events to having a smaller impact than initially thought.

The Color Revolutions have turned out to be at least as much about continuity as about change and, to some extent, at least as much about regime stability as regime change. They led to some immediate and even medium term change, but the number of things that did not change is also significant. Ukraine remained politically divided, hindered by widespread corruption; and, of course, Viktor Yanukovich, the man who sought to steal the 2004 election, was elected president in 2010. Georgia remained caught between authoritarianism and democracy with an economy that, in spite of reforms by the new government, remained largely stagnant. Kyrgyzstan under Bakiev was corrupt, violent, and impoverished, just as it had been under Akaev. Bakiev found himself fleeing the country only about five years after coming to power, demonstrating the unfortunately cyclical nature of Kyrgyz politics.

There were changes too. Ukraine became more liberal for awhile; Georgia, with more success in the early post-Rose Revolution years, rebuilt a state on the verge of collapse; while in Kyrgyzstan a new group of kleptocrats were in charge. It is difficult but nonetheless valuable to place these changes in some kind of comparative context and ask whether they meet a threshold of being revolutionary or signaling regime change. One way to address this is to compare the change in Georgia between the Shevardnadze and Saakashvili regimes, or the Kuchma-Yushchenko-Yanukovich presidencies in Ukraine and the Akaev-Bakiev-Otunbaeva periods in Kyrgyzstan to the changes that occur with national elections in western democracies.

Historic elections in the west, such as those that brought in Margaret Thatcher's conservatives in 1979, Ronald Reagan in 1980, or Franklin Roosevelt in 1932, probably introduced more change to the UK and U.S. than the Color Revolutions did to Georgia, Ukraine, or Kyrgyzstan, but these were not viewed as revolutions or changing regimes. Even the phrase "Reagan Revolution" was more a Republican slogan than a term of real analytical value. However, there are many elections in the west, such as that of George H. W. Bush in 1988, that bring about almost no change. The Color Revolutions, of course, brought about far more change than this. Accordingly, they may best be understood as mid-level change comparable to a shift in political parties in a western democracy, but not revolutionary by any means.

CHAPTER 2

Pre-Color Revolution Regimes

THE ROSE, ORANGE, and Tulip Revolutions occurred in three countries that have distinct histories, locations, and economies. Other than having once been part of the Soviet Union, they do not have a great deal in common. Although all have historical connections with Russia, thousands of miles separate Ukraine, Kyrgyzstan, and Georgia. Equally important, they have had links and ties with different countries and parts of the world as well. Ukraine and Georgia both view themselves as having historically been part of Europe, while Kyrgyzstan is part of Asia. However, due to its southern and eastern location, Georgia has also historically been part of the Ottoman, Persian, and Middle Eastern world as much as Europe. Ukraine shares a border with Poland, Georgia with Armenia, and Kyrgyzstan with China.

Ukraine and Georgia are primarily Orthodox Christian, but Georgian and Ukrainian Orthodoxy are not very similar. Christianity came to Georgia approximately six centuries before it was established in Ukraine. Accordingly, Georgian Orthodox Christianity draws on older strains of Christianity, so the two faiths have less in common than, for example, Russian and Ukrainian Orthodoxy. Kyrgyzstan is, of course, primarily Sunni Muslim. Although many in these countries speak Russian as a second language, the Kyrgyz, Ukrainian, and Georgian languages are not closely related. Ukrainians are Slavs, whose language and religion are quite similar to those of Russia. Neither Georgians nor Kyrgyz are Slavs. While Ukraine and Georgia have intermittent histories as independent states going back for centuries, the Kyrgyz state is, to a substantial extent, a Soviet creation.

Ukraine, Kyrgyzstan, and Georgia During the Soviet Period

Ukraine, Kyrgyzstan, and Georgia share a history of roughly seventy years, during which each of these now independent countries was part of the Soviet Union. This, naturally, is what links the countries and their recent political histories and makes it fruitful to examine them together. Still, even within the former Soviet Union, they played different roles. Ukraine was the second most populous republic in the USSR. Additionally because of its location on the western edge of the Soviet Union, it shared a strong cultural bond with Russia and strong historical ties to Eastern Europe. Moreover, Ukraine and Russia were the two largest republics in the USSR, comprising well over 60 percent of the Soviet Union's population. Georgia has had a long history with Russia as well, not as a fellow Slavic country but as part of a complex relationship where Russia served both as colonial ruler but also fellow Christian country able to provide support for Georgia against its Muslim neighbors.

During the Soviet period, Georgians struggled, with some success, to maintain their national identity. Georgian remained the official language of the Georgian SSR, the only republic where Russian was not an official language. Relatively far from Moscow, Georgia was able to play its comfortable and accustomed role on the fringes of somebody else's empire.

Kyrgyzstan, unlike Georgia and Ukraine, became a modern polity only under Soviet rule. The Soviet imprint is strong in the creation of both the modern Kyrgyz state and nation because there had been no real Kyrgyz state before the Soviet period. Before the Soviet revolution, Kyrgyzstan was populated largely by nomadic peoples and ruled by Mongols, Chinese, and finally Tsarist Russia. Additionally, Kyrgyzstan during both its Soviet and post-Soviet incarnations remained far more ethnically diverse than either Ukraine or Georgia. According to the last Soviet census in 1989, Kyrgyzstan was 52.4 percent Kyrgyz, 21.5 percent Russian, and 12.9 percent Uzbek, with the remaining 13 percent divided among many different groups. By 2009, the proportion of Kyrgyz had risen to 70.9 percent, still lower than Georgia, where ethnic Georgians constituted 70.7 percent of the population in 1989, 83.8 percent in 2002, and even more today. There was no strong Kyrgyz nationalist movement during the Soviet period or even immediately following the breakup of the Soviet Union.

Ukraine, Kyrgyzstan, and Georgia all experienced the Soviet Union differently and were differently affected by its collapse. Accordingly, the nationalism that constituted one of the core reasons for the Soviet collapse played itself out differently in these three countries. In both Georgia and Ukraine, nationalism and the desire for independence were present throughout most of the Soviet period, while nationalist feelings were considerably weaker, if they were present at all, in Kyrgyzstan.

The point of these cursory observations is not to provide a comparative history of the three countries but to demonstrate that the Color Revolutions were not a case, even initially, of democracy spreading to a particular small region such as Eastern Europe in the 1990s or Southern Europe in the 1970s. Instead, the revolutions were an example of countries thousands of miles apart, but with similar recent political histories, undergoing similar political changes at around the same time. However, several other countries, also newly independent former component parts of the Soviet Union, followed different trajectories and did not have Color Revolutions during these years. What then were the similarities shared by these three countries in the late 1990s and early 2000s that contributed to the occurrences of Color Revolutions?

Ukraine

Although Ukraine is a Slavic country considered by many to be the wellspring of Slavic culture, relations between Ukraine and Russia, the other Slavic giant, have always been complex. Obviously, Ukraine was central to the agricultural, mineral, and industrial wealth of the Soviet Union. It was also the adopted home of one of the Soviet Union's most prominent leaders, Nikita Khrushchev, and, of course, a major battleground of World War II, the seminal episode in, and triumph, of Soviet history. Ukraine was where the Nazis were fought to a standstill by the Red Army, before the Red Army pushed the Germans out of Soviet territory and all the way back to Berlin. Ukraine was unambiguously central to the economic, military, and cultural life of the Soviet Union. Moreover, because of the cultural and historic bond between the two countries, relations between Ukraine and Russia have been almost taken for granted, not unlike the relationship between the U.S. and Canada.

Nonetheless, a strong Ukrainian nationalist movement opposed Soviet power well into the 1950s. The division between western Ukraine, which is more independent and oriented toward Europe, and eastern Ukraine, more oriented toward Russia, did not begin with the election of 2004.[1] It was a constant theme throughout the Soviet period and the early years of Ukrainian independence. Not surprisingly, Ukrainian nationalists were strongest in western Ukraine. During World War II some even supported the Germans rather than the Soviet army.

Ukraine's position in the Soviet Union was also defined by the Holodomor, the genocide of the early 1930s in which millions of Ukrainians were killed by a manmade famine, victims of a Soviet collectivization effort that caused starvation in the midst of some of the world's most fertile agricultural land. The genocide devastated Ukraine, making many people there deeply hateful and angry toward the Soviet regime.

Throughout the Soviet period a substantial Russian minority lived in eastern Ukraine. They spoke Russian and identified as strongly with Russia as with Ukraine. The Russian minority and influence in Ukraine grew after World War II when the Crimea, which had a large Russian population, became part of the Ukrainian SSR in 1954. Since the birth of independent Ukraine in 1991, the continued presence of this Russian-identified minority has slowed Ukrainian nationalist urges to reorient the country westward and has opposed policies such as making Ukrainian the only official language of the country.

Georgia

Georgia's role in the Soviet Union was different from that of Ukraine. Georgia is an ancient nation with a long, albeit intermittent history as an independent state. Georgian nationalism remained strong through the Communist era: the hope of an independent Georgia was never far from the Georgian consciousness. For approximately a century preceding the Soviet revolution, Georgia was at the southern end of the Tsar's empire. By 1921, Georgia found itself at the southern end of another empire, this one belonging to the Communists. The transition between these two empires was not altogether smooth for Georgia: the country was briefly independent beginning in 1918 until Soviet troops moved into Georgia in 1921, destroying hopes for independence for another seventy years.

Georgia's experience on the fringes of foreign empires served the country well, since it was able to adapt to Soviet domination without fully abandoning its culture and identity. The Georgian language remained central to Georgian identity; and Georgian leaders, particularly in the postwar period, enjoyed more than the usual autonomy from Moscow. As one of the few warm weather climates with decent coastline in a northern empire, Georgia remained a desirable place for the Soviet Union's political and cultural elite. Georgia's role and visibility in the Soviet Union were also heightened because several prominent Soviet leaders were Georgian. Stalin, of course, was

Georgian, as was Lavrenty Beria, his longtime NKVD chief, who held other high-ranking Soviet positions as well.² In the last days of the Soviet Union and during the final days of the Cold War, Eduard Shevardnadze was the foreign minister of the Soviet Union and, after Mikhail Gorbachev, probably the most famous Soviet citizen in the world. Needless to say, Shevardnadze was also Georgian.

During the late Soviet period, Georgia was one of the most prosperous republics in the USSR. Its attractive climate and beautiful countryside, its ski slopes and, by Soviet standards, beautiful beaches made it a major vacation destination for Soviet citizens. Because Georgia was one of the warmest areas of the Soviet Union, it was able to produce fruits and vegetables that were in scarce supply in the rest of the country, further generating revenue. Additionally, Georgian wine and mineral water were well known throughout the region and another major source of export revenue. The relative wealth of Georgia made the economic collapse of the 1990s all the more precipitous and tragic.

During the late 1980s, Georgia had a strong independence movement, comparable to those in the Baltic republics. Underground political movements and parties sought independence, and ultimately a successful referendum in 1991 called for independence. In fact, Georgian independence was one of the causes of the breakup of the entire Soviet Union. By contrast, the independence of Kyrgyzstan and the other Central Asian states came as a *result* of the breakup. This fundamental difference between Georgia and Kyrgyzstan can be seen in, among other places, the two countries' different relationships with Russia.

Kyrgyzstan

Kyrgyzstan was even more on the periphery of the Soviet empire than was Georgia. Not only geography, but also culture and even climate separated it from the more western and European parts of the Soviet Empire. Collectivization, which led to widespread famines in Ukraine, had far less impact on the mountainous, nomadic populations of Kyrgyzstan. Throughout the Soviet period, the mainstays of the Kyrgyz economy remained agriculture, and to a more significant extent, animal husbandry. The remote mountainous landscape made industrial development less practical. Throughout the Soviet period, Kyrgyzstan remained one of the poorer republics, and while a Kyrgyz Soviet elite developed, many of the management, leadership, and academic positions were occupied by Russians and others from the western parts of the Soviet Union.

There were, of course, anti-Soviet sentiments throughout Kyrgyzstan during these years, but nationalist movements were very weak in the Central Asian parts of the Soviet Union for much of the twentieth century. In short, the Soviet regime, while still at times devastating, had less negative impact in Kyrgyzstan than in either Ukraine or Georgia. Collins (2006) describes the seeming paradox of the Soviet presence in Central Asia generally, saying "Central Asia incessantly felt the heavy and destructive hand of Soviet rule. And yet by 1980, as the Soviet grip began to relax Central Asia remained at best, only haphazardly penetrated by the Soviet system" (xi). Accordingly, Kyrgyzstan did not agitate for independence in the late 1980s and early 1990s, nor did it seek to secede from the USSR once the Soviet Union began to crumble. Instead, Kyrgyz independence followed the end of the Soviet Union.

Nonetheless, because of the relative absence of a pre-Soviet Kyrgyz state, the Soviet experience had a greater effect on the political contours of post-independence Kyrgyzstan than in Georgia and Ukraine. The division between north and south in Kyrgyzstan is as sharp as the division between east and west in Ukraine.[4] However, while the latter has long roots in Ukraine, the former stemmed more from Soviet, and before that Russian, efforts to reduce the influence of older identities and forge new ones that would preclude a unified and troublesome Kyrgyzstan. By the end of the Soviet period, these regional identities were stronger among the Kyrgyz people than any older clan-based identities (Luong 2002: 56). The rift between north and south has continued to frame Kyrgyz politics throughout the last two decades and helped create geographical loyalties, which have often been a barrier to democratic development. Importantly, as Luong (78) points out, the division between north and south does not entirely reinforce older clan affiliations as many clan populations are divided between the two regions.

After Communism

Although Georgia, Ukraine, and Kyrgyzstan were emerging from the same authoritarian system and seeking to build functioning institutions and modern economies, each confronted a different set of challenges at the dawn of the post-Communist period. Ukraine faced the challenge of turning its industrial, agricultural, and mineral potential into concrete economic development in a country that was increasingly, and perhaps inevitably, divided between a western region that looked to Europe and an eastern region that looked to Russia. A large number of ethnic Russians in the Crimea and other parts of eastern Ukraine remained in Ukraine after the breakup of the Soviet Union, contributing to strong and enduring ties between the two newly independent Slavic states. At the same time, in western Ukraine, independence activists picked up where their forebears had left off in the middle of the twentieth century, calling for a Ukraine that was independent of Russia and more oriented toward Europe. More than ever, Ukraine began to feel like a country where the western half was Poland, the eastern half was Russia, and Kiev was pulled in both directions.

During Ukraine's first years of independence, the country encountered severe economic problems as it proved extremely difficult to modernize the Soviet era industrial base. Ukraine's steel and coal industries found themselves poorly equipped to compete with those industries in western and other countries. This led to unemployment, underemployment, poverty, and a substantial economic downturn. As the economy worsened, the potential for instability grew, and consolidating the newly independent state became increasingly difficult.

Upon achieving independence, Kyrgyzstan did not have the industrial, mining, or agricultural wealth Ukraine enjoyed. Moreover, unlike some of its post-Soviet Central Asian neighbors, such as Turkmenistan and Kazakhstan, Kyrgyzstan had no oil or gas wealth beneath its soil. Thus, the challenges of building a functioning economy were different, since many people still relied on animal herding and sustenance agriculture for survival. However, this also meant that the deindustrialization Ukraine experienced following the collapse of the Soviet Union did not hit Kyrgyzstan in the same devastating way in the early 1990s.

For Kyrgyzstan, the end of the Soviet period meant the emergence, for the first time, of a modern, independent Kyrgyz state. Kyrgyzstan, therefore, had to wrestle with building not just a modern state and economy, but a nation as well. The Kyrgyz Soviet Republic had been created in the 1920s in a region populated primarily by different, but related, largely nomadic peoples. In addition, there were people from the western part of the Soviet Empire, primarily Russians, but also Ukrainians, Jews, and even Germans living in Krygyzstan when the Soviet Union came to its end. Many of these, among them a disproportionate number of Kyrgyzstan's educated and professional class, left in the early 1990s, going to Russia, Germany, Israel, and elsewhere. It was the slightly less diverse group of people who remained from which the modern Kyrgyz state had to try to create a nation.

The challenges of building a functioning state and economy were at least as severe in Georgia as in Ukraine or Kyrgyzstan. Georgia had been one of the most prosperous parts of the USSR during the late Soviet years, with strong tourism and agricultural sectors. This prosperity was linked to the broader Soviet economic system as vacationers were essentially assigned vacations in various parts of Georgia, and the largest shares of wine, mineral water, tea, and other agricultural products were exported to other parts of the Soviet Union. Once the economies in the rest of the region and the economic, social, and other links between the different parts of what had been the Soviet Union broke down, the Georgian economy began to collapse as well.

The Georgian state itself teetered on the edge of collapse for much of the early 1990s. The first leader of independent Georgia, Zviad Gamsakhurdia, proved erratic and incompetent, and in the eyes of many, something of a dangerous Georgian nationalist. His rhetoric and leadership contributed to secessionist wars in Abkhazia and South Ossetia, which put pro-Moscow forces, supported by Russian peacekeeping troops, in charge of both regions until the war between Russia and Georgia in August 2008 pushed South Ossetia and Abkhazia even more out of Tbilisi's orbit. In the rest of Georgia, rule by warlords in Ajara, gangsters in western Georgia, and breakdown of the state throughout most of the country characterized the first half of the 1990s.

The first years of the post-Communist period thus saw each of these countries wrestling with a different set of problems, albeit with some overlap. A shorthand way to understand this is that Georgia had to build a state and a democracy, but not a nation. Ukraine had to build a democracy, and to some extent a nation, given the divisions between the east and west parts of the country, but it did not have to build a state in the way Georgia did. Kyrgyzstan was faced with the challenge of more or less having to build a state, a nation, and a democracy.

The Regimes of Akaev, Kuchma, and Shevardnadze

By the late 1990s, Kyrgyzstan, Ukraine, and Georgia were all governed by former Communist leaders. Leonid Kuchma, who had spent the last years of the Soviet Union involved in Ukrainian heavy industry, was president of Ukraine; Askar Akaev, a former member of the Soviet Congress of People's Deputies, was president of Kyrgyzstan; the Georgian president was Eduard Shevardnadze, well-known former Soviet foreign minister during the Cold War. Shevardnadze and Kuchma had been in power since 1994, while Akaev had been the only president of independent Kyrgyzstan. All three had eventually succeeded, particularly during the middle and late 1990s, in bringing at least a modicum of stability to their countries following the initial upheaval caused by the ending of Soviet rule.

These former Communists differed in style, experience, and political skill, but all three served as a bridge between the Communist and post-Communist eras for their countries. Their longtime service to the Communist Party and the Soviet Union as well as their network of supporters and colleagues both inside and outside their respective countries meant that while the Soviet Union was dissolved in 1991, important parts of it lived on in capitals from Kiev to Bishkek. To a significant extent, the Soviet system survived in these countries until the Color Revolutions brought down this generation of Communist leaders of post-Communist countries.

Shevardnadze had been first secretary of the Communist Party in Georgia from 1972 until he became foreign minister of the Soviet Union in 1986, giving him a deep network of connections and relationships throughout the fifteen countries that came into existence at the time the Soviet Union collapsed. Shevardnadze did not, however, become the leader of newly independent Georgia in 1991. That position was taken by a prominent Georgian nationalist and opposition political leader who, after being active in the Georgian independence movement and seeing his party win a majority of seats in the 1990 legislative elections, won almost 65 percent of the vote for the presidency of the soon to be independent Georgia in May 1991. Zviad Gamsakhurdia, although popular among Georgians when he first took office, was unable to effectively steward Georgia through the first years of independence. During the years he was president, the bottom fell out of Georgia's economy. At the same time, minorities in Abkhazia and South Ossetia, two regions that had been autonomous republics (Abkhazia) and oblasts (South Ossetia), became concerned over Gamsakhurdia's aggressively nationalist rhetoric, eventually seeking support from Russia in their efforts to break away from Georgia. Moreover, various gangsters and local thugs took control of parts of the country as fighting often spilled over into the streets of Tbilisi and other cities. Gamsakhurdia himself was increasingly unpredictable, even paranoid and seemingly overwhelmed by the challenge of governing Georgia.

Beginning in 1992, a broad group of Georgians sought to replace Gamsakhurdia with somebody who was more stable and dependable. As the world's most famous Georgian, respected throughout the west, Shevardnadze was a natural person toward whom to turn. He was brought back to Georgia in 1992. His supporters helped depose Gamsakhurdia before seeing that Shevardnadze was elected president in 1995. In the west, Shevardnadze was viewed as a familiar and friendly face in a very difficult neighborhood, someone trusted in the U.S. and western Europe. These feelings only became stronger as Shevardnadze, at least initially, was able to help stabilize Georgia.

Ukraine's Kuchma, like Shevardnadze, was his country's second post-Soviet president. Kuchma served as a member of the Ukrainian parliament and as his predecessor, Leonid Kravchuk's, prime minister, before being elected president of Ukraine in 1994 in an election in which he defeated incumbent President Kravchuk in a runoff by a 52–45 margin. In that election, Kravchuk, due to his role in the early period of Ukrainian independence, was viewed as the more nationalist candidate, while Kuchma was seen as leaning more toward Russia. As Kuzio (1997) argues, however, this was an oversimplification. As is frequently the case in post-Soviet countries, both candidates tried to be all things—pro-west, pro-Russia, pro-independence, pro-business, pro-labor—to all people, while their critics accused them of having many, often contradictory, faults, such as being too nationalist and not nationalist enough or too close to Russia and not close enough.

The perception of Kuchma as the pro-Russia and Kravchuk as the pro-Western candidate nonetheless clearly framed the election for the voters of Ukraine. Kuchma's electoral base was in southern and eastern Ukraine, regions that were and remain more oriented toward Russia than is the case in western Ukraine, where voters supported Kravchuk. In the runoff between the two candidates, Kravchuk won all twelve oblasts of western Ukraine, including Volyn (84 percent), Ivano-Frankivsk (94 percent), Lviv (94 percent), Rivna (87 percent), and Ternopil (95 percent). Kuchma won all the remaining oblasts, including Crimea (90 percent), Donetsk (80 percent), and Sevastopol (92 percent).[5]

Ukrainian independence and statehood were issues in this election, with some Ukrainians fearing that a victory by Kuchma would lead the country back to Russia and weaken Ukraine's nascent independent statehood. However, the severe economic crisis that had characterized the first few years of independence could not be ignored either. Kuchma sought to use this issue to his advantage, presenting himself as, uniquely among the seven candidates for the presidency, able to fix Ukraine's broken economy.

Like Shevardnadze, Kuchma was seen as taking over from a president who was outmatched by the challenges of the office, but Kuchma did not enjoy the fame and international goodwill Shevardnadze did. The initial fears from the west that Kuchma's victory would lead to closer Ukrainian ties with Russia and mark a step backward for Ukraine dissipated somewhat when Kuchma indicated he would have a pragmatic approach and that his priorities would be economic reform and continuing to build relations with the west.

Unlike Shevardnadze or Kuchma, Akaev was his country's first president. He was a scientist who became a deputy to the Supreme Soviet in 1989. During his time in Moscow, Akaev aligned himself with Mikhail Gorbachev's reformers. He became chair of the Kyrgyz Supreme Soviet as a compromise candidate in October 1991, after Kyrgyzstan declared its independence. Although he had been a member of the Supreme Soviet, Akaev was still relatively unknown when he won this position in the second round of balloting. A year later, he was elected, without opposition, to the presidency of the newly independent Kyrgyzstan.

Although Akaev had been a high ranking Communist leader, he was able to win support in the west because he seemed open to political, and particularly economic, reform and had been supportive of similar reform during the last days of the Soviet Union. As president, Akaev initially pursued a course of "radical reform," with Kyrgyzstan becoming the first Central Asian state to create its own currency, in 1993, and to join the World Trade Organization, in 1998 (Spector 2004). The hope many in the U.S. felt regarding Akaev's administration was summarized at a congressional hearing after the Tulip Revolution as Senator Sam Brownback (R-Kan.) described how Akaev was viewed in the U.S. in the early days of his presidency: Akaev's presidency "shouldn't have ended this way from where it started.... This was clearly the case of the one that was moving forward the fastest, the rhetoric was right, the setting seemed to be right, was sizing up . . . 'you know, this really should be the model country moving toward democratic, open, stable society development.' And then it careened off wrong, badly" (CSCE 2005).

Senator Brownback's words were grounded in widely held perceptions of Kyrgyzstan dating to the 1990s. Luong (2002) points out that, "according to most observers, Kyrgyzstan embarked on a rapid transition to democracy immediately after independence. As a result, during its first five years of independent statehood, Kyrgyzstan made more progress toward political liberalization than any of its regional neighbors" (15). Luong also points out, however, that by the turn of the century both "Kyrgyzstan and Kazakhstan [had] retreated from earlier democratic reform paths and moved instead toward a more restrictive political system" (17).

A broader post-Soviet context can help explain the regimes in Georgia, Kyrgyzstan, and Ukraine as well. As the twentieth century drew to an end, so did the excitement and hope that had characterized western views during the early years of the post-Soviet period. By the turn of the century it was reasonably clear that some of these countries, including Eastern European nations like Poland and Hungary and the three Baltic states—Estonia,

Latvia, and Lithuania—which had previously been part of the Soviet Union, were on a path that would lead to democracy and more or less full integration into European institutions, such as the EU and NATO. What was happening in the remaining countries of the former Soviet Union was less positive. Throughout the region, in countries such as Azerbaijan, Belarus, and Turkmenistan, it was clear that democracy was in retreat as authoritarian or semi-authoritarian regimes began to settle into power.

Georgia, Ukraine, and Kyrgyzstan, along with some other countries, including, at that time, even Russia, were in a gray area. Strong, functioning democratic states still seemed to be, at best, on the distant horizon, but none of these countries could be described as genuinely authoritarian, particularly in light of some of their neighbors. Ukraine, Georgia, and Kyrgyzstan looked quite liberal when compared, for example, with Belarus, Turkmenistan, and Azerbaijan. Georgian civil society was viewed as the strongest in the non-Baltic former Soviet Union, with a broad range of opinions represented in the media and numerous civic organizations and think tanks highly critical of the government. Ukraine had a far more competitive political party system in the first years of the twenty-first century than Belarus or Russia, while Kyrgyzstan was often described, apparently not in jest, as the "Switzerland of Central Asia." Akaev himself had first used this term, but gradually it caught on, somewhat.

This absurd moniker was seemingly meant to suggest that Kyrgyzstan was an island of tranquility and liberalism, as well as beautiful mountains and, presumably, cuckoo clocks, in the midst of a less democratic region. While this was an overstatement to be sure, it was not wildly inaccurate. In a testimony to Congress shortly after the Tulip Revolution, Martha Brill Olcott, a specialist on the region, argued that the strength of civil society was the key factor that made Kyrgyzstan stand out from its neighbors: "The critical factor in Kyrgyzstan was that NGO groups were so deeply rooted that there was no prospect of keeping them out of the election campaign, even though their life was made miserable oftentimes."[6] Spector (2004) described Akaev's Kyrgyzstan as having "a vibrant civil society, including independent media outlets and non-governmental organizations, flourish[ing] despite 70 years of Soviet rule" (3).

Despite their being more liberal than their increasingly less liberal neighbors, the picture was far from entirely positive in Georgia, Kyrgyzstan, and Ukraine. Shevardnadze, Akaev, and Kuchma all presided over regimes steeped in cronyism, corruption, and electoral fraud. All three governments were semidemocratic in nature with a few trappings of democracy, such as varying levels of freedom of speech, assembly, and the like, and elections that, while not free and fair, did allow for some degree of contestation and some possibility of peaceful transitions of power.

All three countries were also characterized by weak state institutions, although to a greater degree in Georgia and Kyrgyzstan than in Ukraine, and all faced difficulty delivering basic services, enforcing laws, collecting revenue, and maintaining domestic tranquility. To some extent, the weakness of these states was linked to their semidemocratic status. As Holmes (2006) points out, authoritarian regimes, like democracies, are not easy to consolidate. Poverty of the state, particularly in Georgia; failure to solidify control over the entire country, particularly in Georgia and Kyrgyzstan; and failure to develop more than a few functioning government institutions were barriers not just to full democracy, but to genuine authoritarianism as well.

Economic Development and Corruption

The inability of Kuchma, Shevardnadze, and Akaev to build strong functioning states was exacerbated by the continued weakness of the economies of the countries during the late 1990s. Georgia, following the defeat and chaos of the years immediately after the collapse of the Soviet Union, had not been successful in efforts to rebuild its economy. The tourist industry did not return to anything approaching its Soviet era strength, while exports of foodstuffs did not generate the previous levels of revenue. Kyrgyzstan, unlike Georgia, had not been one of the wealthier republics during the Soviet era, so the continued decline during the late 1990s was less precipitous and extreme, but it continued to slide into poverty nonetheless. As a small, somewhat isolated independent country without substantial national resources, Kyrgyzstan faced a difficult economic challenge, one the Akaev regime was unable to overcome. The weakness of the Ukrainian economy during this period was due to a range of factors, including the collapse of the Russian economy, to which Ukraine had been closely tied; the difficulty of modernizing a Soviet-era heavy industry-oriented economy; and the collapse of the market and linkages the Soviet system had provided for Ukraine.

The economic problems facing the three countries were also due to the absence of rule of law and presence of widespread corruption. The breadth of corruption was another identifying characteristic of the semidemocracies of all three pre-Color Revolutionary regimes. Paying bribes for the most basic services, constant harassment of ordinary citizens from low ranking government officials seeking payoffs, and foreign assistance stolen by government ministers were the rule not the exception, particularly in the later years of the pre-Color Revolution regimes.

This high level of corruption was both a cause and a sign of the weak states in each of these countries. Corruption is often very pronounced in weak states, where people are more open to looking outside the state to solve problems and secure services. The state has little ability to crack down on corruption, and poorly paid state employees find that they depend on outside income, including bribes and payoffs, to survive. Corruption also leads to weaker states as money, which could be used to build state institutions, ends up being stolen, and citizens begin to see positions in state institutions as opportunities to steal money, not to work hard and serve their country. Citizens, if possible, also seek ways to ensure service delivery from outside the state such as private schools and private security agencies. Thus, corruption and state weakness became a difficult cycle out of which to break.

Table 1, drawing on data from Transparency International's (TI) Corruption Perception Index (CPI) puts corruption in Georgia, Ukraine, and Kyrgyzstan in some comparative context. These data, while reflective of the degree of corruption in each country, are not ideal because TI does not sample every country every year. However, the overall findings are relatively unambiguous. Corruption remained a major problem throughout the presidencies of Akaev, Kuchma, and Shevardnadze as demonstrated by the low scores by these countries for each year when data were available. The best year for any of these was Ukraine in 1999, when it was only the 75th least corrupt country of the 99 sampled by TI that year. By 2004, based on data from 2003, the year before the first Color Revolution, all three countries were in the lowest quintile of TI's sample.

Table 1. Corruption Perceptions Index:
Georgia, Kyrgyzstan, Ukraine

	1998	1999	2000	2001	2002	2003	2004
Georgia	X	84	X	X	85	124	133
Kyrgyzstan	X	87	X	X	X	118	122
Ukraine	69	75	87	83	85	106	122
N		85	99	90	91	102	133	145

Data from Transparency International (TI), www.transparency.org. TI does not rank every country every year and did not rank any of the three Color Revolution countries before 1998.

Politics and Democracy

In the years leading up to the Color Revolutions, Georgia, Kyrgyzstan, and Ukraine were characterized by dysfunctional states, showing poor economic performance and widespread corruption. Accordingly, as they remained in office over the years, the initial hope that had greeted Kuchma and Shevardnadze, and to a lesser extent, Akaev, began to dissipate, albeit in some respects surprisingly slowly. Gradually their countries evolved into kleptocracies, where the primary purpose of government was to enrich senior office holders and virtually every governmental and economic transaction was viewed as an opportunity to steal money. Understanding the extent of the corruption and state weakness in these countries is essential to understanding the Color Revolutions. It is not, however, sufficient.

The state of democracy and development of political and civic institutions is also a central aspect of the conditions that led to the Color Revolutions in these three countries rather than other countries in the region. The initial assessment that Ukraine, Kyrgyzstan, and Georgia at the turn of the millennium were characterized by weak states, vibrant civil societies, and enough political space for opposition forces to emerge and organize is, in a broad brush and relative sense, accurate. It does not, however, reflect the nuance needed to get a more complete picture. It is too easy to lump the three regimes together, but there are significant differences between them.

In general, all three countries had relatively strong civil society organizations (CSOs) that were able to draw attention to corruption, human rights violations, and other government shortcomings. The regimes were not sufficiently strong or authoritarian to stop this kind of activity and may, at least at first, have viewed allowing some critical CSOs as a way to shore up foreign support and demonstrate the essentially democratic and progressive nature of their governments. While these governments were far from democratic or progressive, the bar for demonstrating this was not very high, as these governments simply sought to show that they were more open and liberal than their neighbors.

The relative strength of civil society in these three countries was the product of somewhat open political systems where basic rights of assembly and speech were not systematically repressed and some degree of political competition was permitted. The strength of civil society and degree of government tolerance for dissent, however, should not be overstated.

Elections During the Akaev, Kuchma, and Shevardnadze Years

The comparatively strong civil societies that existed in Kyrgyzstan, Ukraine, and Georgia during the years preceding the Tulip, Orange, and Rose revolutions suggest that some democratic foundations had developed in these three countries. The state of elections during the later years of the Akaev, Kuchma, and Shevardnadze regimes, on the contrary, make this picture more complex. Not only were elections generally bad during this period, but in many cases they got worse over time, culminating in the extreme fraud that characterized the 2003–2005 elections contributing directly to the Color Revolutions.

Elections are not the only, or even necessarily the most important, defining characteristic of democracy. However, it is hard to imagine a country that is genuinely democratic that does not have free, fair, and competitive elections. The ability and willingness of all three pre-Color Revolution leaders to tolerate dissent and criticism with regard, in varying degrees, to media and civil society, disappeared when it came to elections. The poor quality of elections during this period clearly demonstrates the severe limitations of the democratizing impulse of Kuchma, Shevardnadze, and Akaev.

The elections immediately preceding the Color Revolutions will be addressed in substantial detail later. However, those elections were part of a trend of worsening elections in all three countries. A look at the major balloting preceding the Color Revolution elections, specifically the presidential and parliamentary elections of 2000 in Kyrgyzstan; the presidential election of 1999 and parliamentary election of 2002 in Ukraine; and the presidential election of 2000, parliamentary election of 1999, and, to a lesser extent, local election of 2002 in Georgia, provide insight into politics, democratic development, and elections in these countries.

The presidential elections of 1999 and 2000, which saw Shevardnadze, Akaev, and Kuchma elected to their final terms in office, were characterized by widespread fraud despite the outcome never really being in doubt. This confirmed the corrupt nature of politics in the three countries and suggested that the regimes would be severely tested if reasonably competitive elections ever occurred. The parliamentary elections of 1999–2002 were, in some respects, more important because in these elections voter fraud was instrumental in determining the partisan makeup of the parliament during the last days of these regimes. All these elections were bad, but to paraphrase Tolstoy, they were bad in different ways. These differences between the kinds of bad elections, and election violations, fraud, and other problems provide insight into the types of regime as well.

In 2000, Kyrgyzstan held three national elections, two rounds of parliamentary elections, and one presidential election. Viewed together, these provide reasonably clear evidence that, as the new century dawned, that country was no longer an island of democracy in Central Asia; nor was it the Switzerland of that region, as supporters of President Akaev still asserted. Instead, Kyrgyzstan had become another country dominated by a strong president willing to commit election fraud and other illegalities, if not widespread human rights abuses like some of his neighbors, to stay in power. The result of these elections was a Kyrgyzstan where power was more concentrated in the hands of Akaev and his supporters and there was decreased confidence in the country's democracy both domestically and overseas.

The OSCE/ODIHR (2000a) report on the parliamentary elections, which occurred on February 20 and March 12, made this point very clearly:

> Both rounds of the 2000 parliamentary elections in the Kyrgyz Republic were characterized by a series of negative trends that ultimately prevented a number of political parties and candidates from competing in the election on a fair and equal basis . . . marred by a high degree of interference in the process by state officials, a lack of independence of the courts . . . and a bias in state media . . . the opportunity for particular political parties and candidates to be represented in the new parliament was systematically undermined.

The presidential election occurred a few months following the second round of the parliamentary elections, on October 29, 2000. The OSCE/ODIHR (2001) assessment of the presidential election bluntly claimed that "the 29 October 2000 presidential election in the Kyrgyz Republic, despite some positive features, failed to comply with OSCE commitments for democratic elections and failed to reverse the negative trends identified during the parliamentary elections." This was essentially a polite way to say that while the parliamentary elections were bad, the presidential election was worse.

To ensure victory in this election, Akaev ordered the arrest of several opponents including, Daniyar Ussenov, Felix Kulov, and Topchubek Tuganaliev. Spector (2004) claims that Akaev also "used the language law to disqualify eight challengers." The result was a resounding victory for Akaev in which he received 74.4 percent of the vote and defeated runner-up Omurbek Tekebayev by a margin of almost 5–1.

The Ukrainian presidential election that saw Kuchma elected for his second and final term in 1999 was different from the 2000 presidential election in Kyrgyzstan. Unlike Akaev, Kuchma did not use legal machinations to clear the field of his most formidable opponents. Therefore he did not come close to winning in the first round. As shown in Table 2, 5 of the 13 candidates received significant electoral support. While these results suggest that Ukraine in 1999 was more politically competitive than Kyrgyzstan in 2000, it was not competitive enough for Kuchma to risk losing the runoff election, which he won decisively by 56.25 to 37.8 percent.

Importantly, the major opposition that emerged from this election was not a western looking or democratic opposition but Petro Symonenko, a Communist candidate likely buoyed by poor economic conditions in much of the country, affinity toward Russia by many in eastern and southern Ukraine, and some degree of nostalgia for the Soviet Union.

Any analysis of the results for this election, like many in the region, must be done in the context of the degree to which the election was conducted fraudulently. While Kuchma allowed serious opponents to run against him, he also used state resources to ensure they would not defeat him. The OSCE/ODIHR report (1999b) describes "allegations of obstruction, illegal arrests of campaigners, illegal seizure of campaign materials, the circulation of vast numbers of anonymous and defamatory materials, falsified versions of newspapers, biased media coverage and involvement of state officials in the campaign," as "true" (11). This type of election fraud suggests the need for the government to become more involved as the election approached, indicating a more open, if far from democratic system, than Akaev's Kyrgyzstan.

Kuchma also took more serious steps "such as students and hospital staff voting under the supervision of their superiors, instances of multiple vot-

Table 2. Results from 1999 Ukrainian Presidential Election, First Round

Candidate	Votes	Percentage
Leonid Kuchma	9,598,672	36.49
Petro Symonenko	5,849,077	22.24
Oleksander Moroz	2,969,896	11.29
Natalia Vitrenko	2,866,972	10.97
Yehven Marchuk	2,138,356	8.13

ing and proxy voting, and state officials bussed around to vote more than once" (OSCE 1999b) to ensure his victory in the second round. Kuchma's final election victory was clearly tainted and demonstrated that Ukrainian democracy had, to say the least, stagnated during his time in office.

Another Ukrainian election after 1999 preceded the Orange Revolution. The parliamentary election of 2002 had a much greater impact on Ukrainian politics, was the most important in laying the groundwork for the Orange Revolution, and breathed new life into the opposition and democratic forces there. In this election, a plurality of seats (110) was won by the Our Ukraine coalition, led by Viktor Yushchenko. Yushchenko had been Kuchma's prime minister before being fired by Kuchma in April 2001. The Our Ukraine Coalition included the two Rukh parties, which were strong nationalists, as well as other parties such as Reforms and Order, Solidarity, Forward Ukraine, Liberals, and Congress of Ukrainian Nationalists. The bloc led by Yulia Timoschenko did less well, but still managed to win 22 seats in the new 450-member parliament.

The result of the 2002 parliamentary election was certainly not that democracy had come to Ukraine, but it was a big step forward from the 1999 election and helped create the context that made the Orange Revolution possible. Unlike in 1999, when the strongest opposition to the regime had come from the Communist Party, these parliamentary elections saw the emergence of a strong, viable western leaning opposition force in Ukraine.

Georgia held three national elections in the late Shevardnadze years: the 1999 parliamentary election, 2000 presidential election, and 2002 local elections. These helped set the stage for the parliamentary election of 2003, which precipitated the Rose Revolution. The local elections sought to elect local governments throughout Georgia so they were, perhaps oxymoronically, national local elections. The 1999 parliamentary election was instrumental in setting the events in motion that would end with the Rose Revolution. The OSCE/ODIHR (1999a) report was not extremely critical of that election, asserting "In the areas where elections were held, voters were mostly able to express their will and, despite some irregularities, were generally able to vote without interference in an atmosphere largely free from intimidation. However, some instances of intimidation and violence observed during the pre-election period and on election days, raise concern."

This assessment of the election understated the problems associated with the counting and tabulating of the votes resulting in the strongest opposition party, the Labor party, being kept below the 7 percent threshold while pushing the weaker, semi-opposition Industry party above the threshold.

The result was a three-party parliament with little genuine opposition to President Shevardnadze.

The new parliament was dominated by Shevardnadze's Citizens' Union of Georgia (CUG). The CUG was a dominant single party that included reformers, old Communists, corrupt businesspeople, and technocrats. Its membership in 1999 included all three Georgian politicians who would go on to lead the Rose Revolution in 2003. The other two parties in the parliament were the Revival Party, which was based in the southwestern province of Ajara and usually was able to work cooperatively with the CUG, and the Industrialists Party. While the CUG remained the only truly relevant party in the parliament, the heterogeneity within it meant there would be some excitement and room for political advance and change in the new parliament.

The Georgian presidential election of 2000 was, not unlike the Kyrgyz presidential election of 2000, dominated by the incumbent. However, in this case President Shevardnadze did not rely on administrative resources or legal pyrotechnics to eliminate the possibility of a strong challenge. Instead, he employed his superior political skill. Shevardnadze's victory over another former Georgian Communist leader, Jumbar Patiashvili, by 80–17 percent in the election's first, and only, round demonstrated his mastery of the Georgian political environment.

After his easy reelection, which was described by OSCE/ODIHR (2000b) as one where "fundamental freedoms were generally respected during the election campaign and candidates were able to express their views," Shevardnadze was poised for a successful last term in office to cap off a remarkable political career which had spanned decades. This, of course, is not how events played out as Shevardnadze was unable to hold the country together and stop its slide toward increased corruption and economic failure.

The elections in 1999 and 2000 were not democratic, but because the outcome of the presidential election was never in doubt, and because at the time of the parliamentary election, Georgia was still largely a one-party state, the extent of fraud and abuse of administrative resources in the election was understated. Shevardnadze's reputation in the west may have contributed to possible political pressure to keep election reports from being as negative as they might have been, but in Georgia there was a broad sense that the parliament that emerged from the 1999 election did not accurately represent the will of the people.

For evidence of Shevardnadze's rapidly declining popularity following his reelection, one need look no farther than the 2002 local elections, during which city and village councils were elected throughout Georgia. The

Tbilisi city council was the most visible local election in Georgia and was also both a referendum on Shevardnadze and a practice run for the 2003 parliamentary elections. The Tbilisi elections were won by the two most radical opposition parties, the Labor Party with 26 percent of the vote and the National Movement party with 24 percent. The latter, led by former CUG MP Mikheil Saakashvili, campaigned on the unambiguous slogan "Tbilisi without Shevardnadze." These elections, it is also worth noting, were conducted relatively fairly, presumably because the CUG thought they were not very important.

Parliaments and Political Parties

In both Ukraine and Georgia, although to a substantially lesser extent in Kyrgyzstan, the years leading up to the Orange and Rose Revolutions saw the emergence of national legislatures that, while not equal partners of the executive, played an important role in the governance, and more significantly, democratic dialogue and opening. These two parliaments, which emerged from imperfect and flawed, but not completely fraudulent elections in 2002 in Ukraine and 1999 in Georgia, evolved into institutions where issues could be debated, criticism of the president could be articulated, and opposition figures could gain notoriety nationally.

The existence of this type of parliament should not be overlooked as a factor in what became the Orange and Rose Revolutions. These parliaments demonstrate both that Georgia and Ukraine were far from authoritarian regimes and that they were a political compliment to the role that civil society played in the Orange and Rose Revolutions. Both events had a substantial political as well as civil society component. In each case, that political component largely originated in parliament.

In Ukraine, the process by which opposition figures emerged in the parliament, and thus on the national political scene, was reasonably straightforward. They, or the parties they led, as described above, won seats in the 2002 election. In Georgia, the process was somewhat different. The parliament that emerged from the 1999 election only had three parties: the CUG and two parties that were neither democratic nor strongly oriented toward the opposition. Thus, the parliamentary opposition that emerged, and eventually developed into the leadership of the Rose Revolution, came from within the governing CUG. This occurred because the CUG, while a dominant single party during the last years of the Shevardnadze era, was not cohesive.

The different factions began to emerge clearly in the new parliament and more formally in 2001 and 2002, when three different opposition factions emerged from the CUG.

In Kyrgyzstan, the parliamentary election of 2000 did not provide a political opening. Instead, it further consolidated Akaev's rule and contributed to the weakening of the democratic advances made in that country in the mid-1990s. In this regard, Kyrgyzstan was on a different cycle than Georgia or Ukraine. The Akaev regime had been in place longer, and its democratic promise had begun to erode more unambiguously by the time of the 2000 elections.

In Georgia and Ukraine, while the legislatures played important roles, defined some democratic elements, and provided platforms for democratically oriented opposition figures, clear limits emerged on just how significant these legislatures were, or could have become. Although the legislatures provided an opportunity for prominent politicians to address issues and criticize the government in Georgia and Ukraine, power in these two countries, and in Kyrgyzstan as well, remained centralized in the presidency. The parliaments appeared to be peripheral to questions of governance, so poor governance and corruption continued in spite of reform elements in the parliament. Additionally, because none of the three regimes were, as demonstrated by widespread election fraud, about to allow themselves to be defeated through elections, a decent parliament, while clearly helpful, would, on its own, be limited in its democratic impact.

In Georgia and Ukraine, the new party system, which eventually displaced Shevardnadze and Kuchma's parties, grew, albeit differently, out of the parliamentary elections and the nature of the parliament. During the 1990s, none of these countries succeeded in developing anything approaching a cohesive, functioning, and competitive political party system. In all three countries, parties were dominated by one or more individuals, did not have a clear or shared vision for their country or anything close to an ideology, and tended to operate in a centralized top-down fashion.

Each of these countries developed their own form of dysfunctional political parties and party systems. Georgian politics was dominated by the CUG during the last half of the 1990s; between 1995 and approximately 2001 it is perhaps best described as a one and a half party system.[7] The CUG was the only power with true bearing on actual governance, but other parties were allowed to participate in politics and engage in, but not win, elections.

Kyrgyz politics during Akaev's years in office developed differently with regard to political parties. Akaev did not have a party he controlled and that played a role in Kyrgyzstan comparable to the one played by the CUG in Georgia. Notably, in the 2000 elections, 73 members of the new parliament, a total of 70 percent, were elected as independents OSCE/ODIHR (2000a). Most of these people were in no real way independent. Nearly all supported President Akaev and rarely took a position different from his or sought to pursue a political initiative of their own. Through manipulation of the electoral process and encouragement of independent candidates and satellite, pseudo-opposition parties, Akaev created a semidemocratic system that was dominated by one office, and one man, to a much greater extent than in Georgia or Ukraine.

Ukraine during the Kuchma years came closer to a multiparty system than either Georgia or Kyrgyzstan. This should, however, not be interpreted to mean that Ukraine was a multiparty democracy during this period.[8] Following the 2002 parliamentary elections, ten parties were represented in the legislature. Although it would be inaccurate to describe any of these parties as having a cohesive vision or ideology or as being democratic, they formed groupings that defined politics in Ukraine. The Our Ukraine and Motherland parties were western-looking opposition parties. The Communists were also in opposition but with a different orientation, while parties such as the Union of Social Democrats (USDP) supported President Kuchma. Of course, given the enormous problems of party unity, Kuchma was able to create a working majority on many issues.

Foreign Policy in Pre-Color Revolution Georgia, Kyrgyzstan, and Ukraine

In the early years of independence following the collapse of the Soviet Union, balancing Russia and the west was at the center of the foreign policy challenges facing Georgia, Ukraine, and Kyrgyzstan. Russia is, of course, a large and powerful neighbor of all three countries and still has a great deal of influence in the economic and security questions facing them.[9] Kuchma, Shevardnadze, and Akaev brought different experiences and outlooks to this challenge.

The nature of this challenge changed over the course of the 1990s and the early twenty-first century as Russia's relative strength in the region changed. Throughout most of the 1990s, due to its weak economy and many internal problems, Russia was not in a position to influence political outcomes in the other former Soviet countries or assert its will in the region. By the time of the Color Revolutions this had begun to change. With the ascension to power of Vladimir Putin, who sought to rebuild the Russian state—at a time when rising oil prices made this fiscally possible—Russia began to reclaim its position as a dominant power in the region. Had this process started a few years earlier, the Color Revolutions would have been much less likely.

Georgia

Shevardnadze obviously had more experience in foreign policy than either Kuchma or Akaev, but his relationship with Russia was nonetheless complex. He had supported Georgia's efforts in Abkhazia and South Ossetia against Russian-backed secessionists, but had failed in these efforts. Moreover, Shevardnadze's failure to consolidate any of the early progress in building the Georgian state ensured that Georgia would remain weak and unable to challenge Russia in the region. Shevardnadze, as former foreign minister of the Soviet Union, had strong relationships throughout the Russian foreign ministry, especially in the early days of his presidency. This network of personal relationships was balanced, however, by residual anger at Shevarnadze from some Russians who viewed him, not entirely inaccurately, as the Georgian who lost Russia's empire.

Throughout his presidency, Shevardnadze realized the need to balance the United States and Russia. He was successful in doing this throughout most of his time in office, at times even seeming to play the two more powerful countries off against each other. For example, shortly after the terrorist attacks on the U.S. on September 11, 2001, when Russia began to once again voice concern about potential terror nodes in the northern Georgian region of Pankisi, with the goal of increasing Russian security presence in that area as a means to fight terrorism, Shevardnadze responded by recognizing the threat and allowing increased security presence in the area—but by U.S. Special Forces followed by marines rather than Russian security forces.

During the last year or so of his administration, as American pressure for fair elections and political reform was, if not quite strong, then certainly stronger than before, Shevardnadze increased Georgia's economic cooperation with Russia, agreeing on an electricity project and other Russian investments in Georgia. This helped send a message to the U.S. that if it pushed too hard, Shevardnadze could always seek support elsewhere. It is not clear to what extent Shevardnadze was bluffing in this regard; and it soon became irrelevant.

In general, Shevardnadze steered a cautious and relatively successful course, securing increasingly close relations with the U.S., particularly when the Baku-Tbilisi-Ceyhan (BTC) pipeline was agreed upon and begun. The BTC pipeline, which brings oil from the Caspian Sea from Azerbaijan, through Georgia, and then on to Turkey, where it is distributed to Europe and elsewhere, was part of an attempt by Shevardnadze to link Georgian interests irrevocably to those of the west by raising Georgia's import as an energy, and, more generally, transportation corridor. This project was somewhat successful, but has never really been the engine of Georgian economic growth for which some had hoped. Shevardnadze sought to pursue these goals, while being careful never to anger Russia too much. This was easier in the 1990s when Russia had still not found its post-Soviet strength.

Kyrgyzstan

Kyrgyzstan's strategic challenges were different from Georgia's. Like Georgia, Kyrgyzstan was not rich in natural resources, but unlike Georgia, it did not have a location that made it of strategic value in the transportation of natural resources. Kyrgyzstan's location, at least initially, made it of less central import to Europe and the U.S. than either Ukraine or Georgia. Additionally, Kyrgyzstan not only had to determine its relationship with Russia, but also had another regional power, China, on its southern and eastern border. This was particularly important during the period in the 1990s when China's economy and global influence were growing, while Russia's was not.

Geographical realities made it considerably more difficult for Kyrgyzstan to pursue the westward leaning policies of Ukraine and Georgia, nor is it clear that is what Akaev wanted to do. During the 1990s, Kyrgyzstan remained quite close to Russia, particularly at first. Akaev made his intentions clear in a 1992 interview: "No matter what new ties we establish in the west and east, no matter how great our urge to merge into the eastern, western or worldwide economic community, our ties with Russia . . . will always be special and we will give this priority."[10]

This comment and initial direction of Kyrgyz foreign policy should be viewed in the context of the early 1990s when Russian and American aims were not as clearly different as they have come to be in the twenty-first century. It was certainly possible for a Central Asian state to maintain a special relationship with Russia while seeking greater integration into the west, east, and international political and financial world.

Kyrgyzstan's role in international politics changed early in the new century not primarily because of the influence of a newly resurgent Russia but because of the American security concerns that grew out of the attacks in New York and Washington on September 11, 2001. These attacks raised the importance of Kyrgyzstan as a Muslim (albeit reasonably secular) country, but also as a Central Asian country less than 750 miles from Afghanistan and Pakistan. Akaev's cooperation with the Bush administration on a number of security issues, primarily the opening of Manas Air Force Base, not far from Bishkek, in late 2001, shortly following the attacks on the U.S. became the central issue in U.S.-Kyrgyz relations during the last years of Akaev's presidency.

Ukraine

Ukraine under Kuchma gradually retreated from its initial interest in the west, moving closer to Russia over the years. As Ukraine's industry and economy began to recover in the late 1990s, and especially after 2000, these ties were strengthened as several major industries were largely controlled by Russian businesses. The two countries also remained strong trading partners throughout the late Kuchma years.

Although Ukraine enjoyed a warmer relationship with Russia than Georgia did, the Ukrainian government during the 1990s had to balance Russia with the west. As Kuchma's term went on, the new borders of the EU and NATO grew closer to Ukraine. Additionally, Ukraine received a substantial amount of foreign assistance from western countries and multilateral organizations during this period. As Russia's economic and political strength increased it was probably inevitable that the longstanding divisions in Ukrainian society and political life would make it extremely difficult to maintain this balance.

Following the 2002 election, the division in Ukraine between western and Russian leaning politicians once again became clear. By that time, Russia certainly understood that victory by pro-western reformers in 2004 would be a blow to Russia's influence in the region while a victory by a pro-Kuchma candidate would maintain or increase Russian influence. In this regard, Ukaine was quite different from Georgia where even late in the Shevardnadze years, virtually all the major political figures saw Georgia's future as primarily with Europe and the U.S. rather than with Russia.

Conclusion

The regimes of Eduard Shevardnadze, Leonid Kuchma, and Askar Akaev had broad similarities. They were all relatively liberal and tolerant though far from democratic. All three regimes were initially greeted with hope from the west, but political conditions and hope of democratic advances weakened during the three leaders' time in office. The positive views of the early days of these regimes led many in the west to be reluctant to confront just how corrupt and undemocratic these regimes had become by 2003–2005. Ultimately, of course, they were all pushed out, relatively peacefully, when they attempted to steal one too many elections. In all three countries the regimes proved unable to consolidate initial democratic gains.

The reasons for this "democratic erosion" as Fish (2001) calls it, while not identical, were similar in all three countries as the transition to a modern economy and to a deeper consolidated democracy proved difficult. All were dogged by a level of corruption so high that it all but precluded a functioning state or economy. While all three countries granted a reasonable, but varying degree of media and political freedom, this freedom was never fully useful within the existing regimes because the governments were committed to resorting to whatever means were necessary to ensure that they never lost an election.

Kuchma, Akaev, and Shevardnadze presided over semidemocratic hybrid regimes that were transitional in nature. In the first decade of independence, the Soviet legacy was still extremely strong and, unavoidably, penetrated all level of politics. The Color Revolutions represented, among other things, efforts to make a final and more decisive break with the old Soviet regime. It remains unclear how decisive those breaks were.

CHAPTER 3

Electoral Breakthroughs

THE IMAGES OF the Color Revolutions, of young, peaceful demonstrators solemnly standing in the cold, rain, and snow, demanding their voices be heard and that stolen elections not be allowed to stand, of old Communist era rulers being, shuffled in the case of Shevardnadze, literally, off the political stage, and of new energetic regimes replacing moribund kleptocracies, are very powerful, but only tell part of the Color Revolution story.

The 2003 parliamentary election in Georgia, the 2004 presidential election in Ukraine, and the 2005 parliamentary election in Kyrgyzstan all occurred in the context of regimes that had been growing weaker and moving away from whatever democratic possibilities had once existed. These regimes were also characterized by increasing corruption, a history of election fraud, and economies that, while slightly improved from the late 1990s, were still characterized by widespread poverty and joblessness. The leadership of all these regimes, however, continued to cling to power, seeking to do whatever was necessary to hold on to that power.

The three Color Revolutions followed a similar pattern. In the months preceding each of these elections, a great deal of concern was raised from civil society organizations (CSOs), opposition political parties, and some international organizations that the upcoming elections would not be conducted fairly. In all three elections, the opposition was, at first, dispersed and disunified, but in each case at least a modicum of cooperation between the parties was eventually achieved. However, none of this was enough to stop the government from seeking to commit widespread, obvious, and blatant election fraud.

After the elections, relatively peaceful demonstrations of varying sizes were held for periods of days or weeks, culminating in either the resignation of the corrupt president and recognition of the new political order or the overturning of election results and recognition of the new political order. These broad similarities should not be left unexamined, but the differences among these cases also help us to understand better the causes of the Color Revolutions, the post-revolutionary developments in each of these countries, and the extent to which Color Revolutions can be treated as a discrete political phenomenon.[1]

The Color Revolutions themselves were surprisingly brief events. The length of time between the day of the stolen election to the day of the swearing in of the new president ranged from roughly two to six months, but having a sound, if only general, understanding of the events during this period, as well as in the months immediately preceding the election is essential for understanding the Color Revolutions.[2]

Georgia

The 2003 parliamentary election in Georgia promised to be an important test of Georgia's democratic development as well as of its increasingly unpopular president, Eduard Shevardnadze. The campaigning for these elections, scheduled for late 2003, began almost immediately after the local elections occurred on June 2, 2002. Equally important, the parliamentary elections, while significant in their own right, were also understood as a warm-up or even a primary for the next presidential election, scheduled to occur sometime in spring 2005, in which Shevardnadze would almost certainly not run. The leader of the opposition party that did the best in the 2003 parliamentary election would emerge as an early frontrunner in the presidential campaign. The local elections had demonstrated the broad dislike of Shevarnadze among the Georgian people as well as his political vulnerability. These elections did not, however, winnow the number of opposition parties.

As 2003 dawned, several opposition parties planned to compete in the parliamentary election that would determine the makeup of the entire 235 member parliament.[3] The majority of these members, 150, would be elected through a single national list system with the seats divided among those parties that met or exceeded the 7 percent threshold. The remaining seats were single mandate seats with one MP being elected from each rayon.[4] These rayons ranged substantially in size so that some MPs would represent districts with well over 50,000 people while others would represent less than 20,000.

Because the majority of parliament would be chosen through the party list system with a not insurmountable threshold of 7 percent, the structural incentives for the opposition to unify were not strong. With regard to the single mandate districts, cooperation and coordination rather than unity were needed to ensure that opposition candidates did not campaign against one another and help the government. Moreover, the nature of the parliamentary election and its relationship to the presidential elections, expected in spring 2005, meant that the various political parties wanted to test their strength independently of each other to get a sense of who would be strongest candidate in 2005. This lack of unity was a central aspect of Georgian politics in 2003, continuing until only a few days before Shevardnadze resigned.

Throughout most of 2003, seven political parties had a realistic chance at breaking the 7 percent threshold and winning party list seats in parliament. Additionally, numerous other minor parties either joined with the larger parties or failed to make much of an impact on the election. The major parties can usefully be broken into three groups: pro-government parties, opposition parties with roots in the CUG, and opposition parties that had never been part of the CUG.

The three pro-government parties were the CUG, renamed For a New Georgia (FNG) and joined by several small coalition partners for the election; the Industrialist Party, an independent but generally pro-government party, and the Revival Party, which was based in Ajara and loyal to Ajaran strongman Aslan Abashidze.

The second group, made up of opposition parties with roots in the CUG, also consisted of three parties: the National Movement (NM), the United Democrats and the New Rights (NR). The NM was the most radical, in politics and style of the three parties. The NM was led by the speaker of the Tbilisi City Council, Mikheil Saakashvili, who had at one time been a protégé of Shevardnadze and, as recently as 2001, an MP from the CUG. The United Democrats were more moderate in style and substance and were led by the former speaker of parliament, Zurab Zhvania. Zhvania had been a leader in the CUG and also close to Shevardnadze, causing many ordinary Georgians, as well as more radical opposition leaders to question the veracity of Zhvania's commitment to reform. The United Democrats became the Burjanadze Democrats (BD), when Nino Burjanadze, the sitting speaker of parliament who, like Saakashvili and Zhvania, had also been elected as an MP from the CUG, joined the party and took the top spot on the list in August of 2003. The NR was another breakaway faction of the CUG, led by a physician turned businessman named David Gamkrelidze. The NR was a moderate opposition party with a reasonably clear right of center ideology and a cautious political style.

The third group was not really a group. It consisted of only one significant party, the Labor Party, a radical opposition party calling for a more social democratic government, thereby further differentiating itself from the other three opposition parties, which all presented themselves as center-right, although at times appearing less than certain of the meaning of that term. Labor was closely identified with its leader, Shalva Natalashvili, and had been kept out of parliament in 1999 due to manipulation of the vote count. Natalashvili frequently described Labor as the only true opposition, decrying the other three parties as the "new CUG."

For the most part, these parties differed in style and personalities more than substance. The exception was the Labor Party, the only one with an explicitly left of center platform. Moreover, Georgia, unlike Kyrgyzstan and Ukraine, does not have any strong regional divisions. Although there are regional identities, and no small amount of elitism from old Tbilisi families, Georgians do not view themselves and make political decisions based on being from, for example, the north, west, or south. Accordingly, the election was likely to be retrospective, with voters basing their vote on their appraisal of the CUG. However, the extremely low level of support for the CUG meant that most voters would also have to decide between at least four seemingly similar opposition parties.

While election fraud had been widespread in Georgia for years, this kind of political analysis was still possible in Georgia in 2002–2003. In three regions, Ajara, Samskhe-Javakheti and Kvemo Kartli the situation was quite different. Elections in Ajara were dominated by the Revival Party. In this respect, Ajara functioned more like a one party state, with voters having little opportunity even to learn about other parties and where voter fraud was on a much greater scale than in the rest of Georgia. Samskhe-Javakheti and Kvemo Kartli, both in Southern Georgia, were populated by ethnic Armenians and ethnic Azeris respectively. In these two regions CUG domination was greater, so elections were much worse than in the rest of Georgia. Most of the discussion that follows is about the remaining 70 to 80 percent of the country.

For most voters in Georgia, the decision about which opposition party to support was not clear, There were not only very few substantive policy differences between the parties, but rumors that each party was actually pro-government abounded. All the parties including the CUG, but not always Labor, wanted a reinvigorated economy, democracy, territorial integrity,[5] close ties with the West, and an end to corruption. The election was largely about which of the parties could persuade the voters that they were best able to achieve these goals.

Because this was a parliamentary and not a presidential election, the CUG did not need to win the election to remain in power, but a loss would certainly not have boded well for the near future. The CUG could not have hoped for a majority in parliament, but it did not want to be marginalized in the new legislature. However, given its extremely low popularity, the CUG had few options other than resorting to vote fraud. For much of 2003, the key political question in Georgia was not whether the CUG would seek to steal the election, but how many votes the CUG would try to steal.

The vote fraud began with a failure to produce a decent and usable voters list and efforts to bribe and intimidate state employees as well as ordinary voters. As Election Day approached, the fraud increased. On Election Day, in most of Georgia, some polling places opened late, some were disrupted, some ballot boxes were stuffed, and some people voted more than once. The election was worst in Ajara, where election observers were intimidated, a shooting occurred in front of a major polling place in Batumi, the region's capital, and ballot box stuffing and multiple voting were very widespread. Although Election Day was messy, the worst fraud was still to come.[6]

Although the election had gone poorly, the will of the Georgian people was still discernible. An exit poll by American and Georgian polling firms released shortly after the polls closed showed a clear majority for the opposition parties, with the NM winning a plurality of the party lists seats. The parallel vote tabulation (PVT) made public the day after the election confirmed these findings.[7] The counting continued well into November as protests and vigils in the capital grew.

Ukraine

The Orange Revolution was the only Color Revolution sparked by a stolen presidential election. The presidential election scheduled for November 2004 in Ukraine promised to be important because Leonid Kuchma was not planning to run for a third term. Thus, the election was sure to be a test of the Kuchma regime's ability to transfer loyalty, in the highly personalized political context of Ukraine, from one leader to another. This was particularly difficult given the failure of Kuchma to develop a strong and unified political party or to cultivate any obvious successors. Moreover, Kuchma's regime had little internal stability; during his less than ten years in office, he had run through seven prime ministers, some serving as little as one or two months.

Whereas the election in Georgia was, to use the common hackneyed expression applied to many elections in transitional countries, a test of

Georgian democracy and an opportunity for democratic reform, this was not initially the case in Ukraine. For most of 2002 and 2003, the upcoming presidential election was more of a last chance for Ukraine's bid to move toward democracy. One more stolen election in Ukraine would have sealed its fate as a failed democratic experiment, not like its neighbors Belarus and Russia.

Although several prominent politicians had pockets of support in various parts of Ukraine, the election quickly narrowed to a two person race. There was little doubt that the first round, scheduled for October 31, 2004, would produce a runoff between the two leading candidates, Viktor Yanukovich and Viktor Yushchenko. This is precisely what happened as Yushchenko and Yanukovich finished first and second in the first round.[8] In the disputed second round, Yanukovich won by a slim margin of 49.42 percent to 46.69 percent, a result viewed by many as fraudulent and led directly to the demonstrations and ultimately a rerun of the second round which Yushchenko won. Yanukovich and Yushchenko had more in common than their first names. Both were political insiders who had served in various high level governmental positions. Yushchenko had served as Kuchma's prime minister from December 1999 to May 2001, while Yanukovich had become prime minister in November 2002 and still occupied the post at the time of the election.[9]

Yanukovich was the candidate of the outgoing Kuchma regime and enjoyed all the administrative and financial support that came with that status. Additionally, Yanukovich benefited from the increasingly close ties between the Kuchma and Putin regimes. The leader of the Russian Federation strongly supported Yanukovich, traveling to Ukraine on several occasions to show his support, channeling resources to Yanukovich's campaign and ensuring very positive coverage of the sitting prime minister on Russian television, which quite a few Ukrainians still watched, particularly in the eastern part of the country. Yanukovich did not, however, possess strong political skills. He was a poor speaker and campaigner who also did not have a strong and independent base of support other than his strength in the east.

Yushchenko emerged as the consensus but not sole opposition candidate relatively early in the campaign. The success of his Our Ukraine party in the 2002 parliamentary election positioned him as the strongest of the opposition forces. With the support of Yulia Timoschenko, who agreed to support Yushchenko with the understanding that she would be appointed prime minister in a Yushchenko government, and of numerous small parties, Yushchenko was clearly the biggest obstacle to Yanukovich's bid to extend, and perhaps even institutionalize the Kuchma regime.

Yushchenko was, as noted earlier, far from a wild-eyed revolutionary. He had a background in finance and had served as director of Ukraine's central bank from 1997 to 1999 before taking over as prime minister, a position from which parliament removed him by a vote of no confidence in May 2001. Yushchenko's base had naturally always been in western Ukraine. He was an economic liberal who believed in strong ties to the West. He also was married to a Ukrainian American woman. All these things contributed to Yushchenko's popularity in the west, while having the reverse effect in eastern Ukraine.

Unlike Yanukovich, Yushchenko had some charisma and political skills. He was an energetic campaigner whose style contributed to the growing popularity of Yushchenko and his party. He was not, however, radical in either style or substance. By the time he sought the presidency, he had been an insider for roughly a decade and had been a supporter of Kuchma for much of the president's term.

The presidential campaign of 2004 was partially a referendum on Kuchma's years as president. Yanukovich was the candidate of continuity, promising to keep the country on the course of continued economic growth, closer relations with Russia and little democratic reform. Yushchenko said he wanted to take the country in a different direction forging closer relations with Europe and the U.S and continuing or accelerating economic and political reform. These substantive differences were reinforced by Ukraine's existing regional cleavage with the west supporting Yushchenko and the east, Yanukovich.

Long before the election took place it was clear that it was unlikely that the election would be conducted in a free and fair manner. No recent election in Ukraine had been free and fair; and there was little reason to believe the 2004 presidential election would be any different. Unlike in 1999, when a relatively popular Kuchma used administrative resources and election fraud to increase his margin of victory in an election he would have won anyway, by early 2004 it seemed apparent that Yanukovich would not be able to win if the election were conducted fairly. Even the enormous structural advantages, legal and not, which were tied to his almost de facto incumbency would not be enough to ensure a Yanukovich victory.

There are three phases in the election cycle—before, during, and after the election—when fraud can be committed. Yanukovich, like the CUG in Georgia, ended up having to pursue all three. For most of 2004, there was a sharp disparity in financial and administrative resources as well as media coverage between the two leading candidates. Yanukovich was given access to all the resources of the presidency to ensure that he won the election. This included not only the ability and means to claim credit for various government accomplishments and projects, but also for providing government largesse to various parts of the Ukrainian population. It also, however, meant that an uglier side of administrative resources was accessible to Yanukovich, particularly in the eastern half of the country. Accordingly, state employees were threatened with being fired, physically beaten, or subject to other forms of intimidation if they did not support Yanukovich. This was the case not just with those who, like teachers, police, and others, worked directly for the state, but for employees in, for example, large privately held mines and factories, whose owners were supporters of Kuchma and Yanukovich.

Additionally, for most of 2004, both Ukrainian and Russian media consistently gave Yanukovich visibility and positive coverage, while either casting Yushchenko in a negative light or not covering him at all. State controlled media was much more powerful in Kuchma's Ukraine than in Shevarnadze's Georgia. Ukraine also had fewer independent media sources, although this began to change as the election and subsequent street demonstrations occurred. Nonetheless, the high level of press freedom enjoyed by the Rose Revolutionaries was not available to Yushchenko and his supporters in Ukraine. Furthermore, because the Kremlin considered the election important, the Russian media, especially television stations Ukrainians watched, made coverage of it a high priority.[10]

This kind of pre-election fraud continued up until Election Day. During this period, supporters of other candidates were intimidated and threatened; state controlled, or influenced media, did not give equal time to all the candidates; and the election commissions dragged their feet and otherwise made it difficult for a fair election to be implemented. In short, Yanukovich and his supporters worked to ensure that there was no chance that he would lose the election. This fraud occurred during the first round of balloting but resumed, with even greater enthusiasm, after that first round yielded the expected runoff between Yanukovich and Yushchenko.

By 2004, Kuchma did not preside over a regime in which elections could easily be fixed in advance. While the regime was far from liberal, there had been too much reform in recent years for an opposition coalition such as the one led by Yushchenko to be easily silenced or marginalized. Moreover, the corruption and perceived failures of the Kuchma government, combined with the poor candidacy of Yanukovich, helped make Yushchenko, and the movement he led, formidable opponents to the government candidate. Therefore, the pre-election machinations from the Yanukovich camp were not enough to secure victory for their candidate so they had to engage in further fraud on Election Day. The Election Day fraud, in both the first and second round included the gamut of post-Soviet election shenanigans. People voted more than once, ballot boxes were stuffed, state authorities intimidated voters, and other efforts, such as multiple voting by supporters of Yanukovich, were made to ensure that he would win. In the first round, this election fraud was not of great consequence because the field had narrowed to the two leading candidates months before the first vote was cast. However, in the second round, the stakes were much higher: the fraud continued during the vote counting period, as returns were held up, numbers were changed, voters for Yushchenko were thrown out, and all efforts were made to ensure a victory for Yanukovich.

After the second round, it was clear that the 2004 presidential election had been stolen. The fraud was widespread and rampant, although concentrated in eastern Ukraine, where support for Yanukovich was strong to begin with, making it easier to tag on a few votes as needed—and where large business concerns controlled by backers of Yanukovich made it possible to use those resources, that is to say intimidate employees, who worked in those businesses.

There were also reports of abuse and fraud committed by supporters of Yushchenko in western Ukraine. This is not too surprising because in many semidemocratic countries, all political candidates and parties that can do so engage in some level of electoral fraud. However, two points should be borne in mind with regard to this issue. First, the extent of election fraud was not the same on both sides; significantly more was committed by supporters of Yanukovich. Second, while supporters of Yushchenko may have added extra ballots in some polling places or leaned on their employees to support Yushchenko, access to media and government resources was not equal, so Yushchenko did not have the ability to commit fraud in these areas.[11]

When the second round results were released, showing a narrow 49 percent to 47 percent victory for Yanukovich, the Orange Revolution began in earnest. Hundreds of thousands of ordinary Ukrainians went to the streets of Kiev to show that they would not allow a presidential election to be stolen and for a fraudulently elected president to be seated.

Kyrgyzstan

Like the Georgian election of 2003, the one in 2005 in Kyrgyzstan was a parliamentary rather than a presidential election. A critical difference between the two is that while in the 2003 Georgian election the parliament was to be mostly chosen through a party list system, in Kyrgyzstan the parliament would be elected from 75 single mandate districts.[12] This was the result of a 2003 constitutional referendum and was to be the first time that the parliament would be chosen entirely from single mandate districts. Like the Ukrainian election, the Kyrgyz election had a two round structure. In districts where no candidate succeeded in getting a majority there would be a runoff. The first round of the election was held on February 27, the second two weeks later on March 13.

In 2005, the population of Kyrgyzstan was roughly five million, meaning that each district would have, on average, approximately 67,000 people. These districts were smaller than city council districts in many major American cities. While this may have meant that Kyrgyz would have the opportunity to know and work closely with their MP, in practice it also meant that local business leaders or prominent local figures with strong ties to the president would be at an advantage.

More important, eliminating party list seats weakened parties and strengthened independent candidates. Party list systems mean that the campaign is waged on national issues. In a party list system, with apologies to Tip O'Neill, all politics are not local.[13] In a country like Georgia in 2003 a party list system made it very easy for leaders of opposition parties to emerge as national leaders and to engage with voters on national issues. The switch to a national legislature consisting entirely of small single mandate districts meant that local issues would again become more important, making it less useful and relevant for any one candidate to present himself as a national candidate. Correspondingly, this made it easier for candidates sympathetic to Akaev to offer solutions, or more realistically, bribes on the local level. It is not entirely clear whether or not this was Akaev's intention when he pushed through the constitutional referendum in 2003.[14] However, this change to the parliament was part of a broader set of amendments that aimed to help Akaev centralize power and lengthen his term in office (Toursunof 2003).

According to the referendum, Akaev could remain in office through 2005, since elections would be held in October of that year to choose his successor. Thus, the parliamentary and presidential elections would only be about ten months apart. In this respect, the Georgian and Kyrgyz cases share an important similarity, a disincentive for the opposition to unify because of the possibility of using the parliamentary election as an opportunity for prominent opposition figures to position themselves for the forthcoming presidential election.

The Kyrgyz election occurred in a more repressive context than either the 2003 Georgian election or the 2004 Ukrainian presidential election. By the time of the election Akaev had been in power for almost fifteen years. Although he was technically barred by the constitution from seeking a third full term as president of Kyrgyzstan, there was little reason to believe that he would allow himself to be replaced as the real power in Kyrgyzstan. Due to increasingly unfree media, restrictions on civil society, and harassment of political opposition figures, by 2005 Kyrgyzstan had come a long way from being the "Switzerland of Central Asia."

The increasingly repressive political conditions and the new electoral system contributed to an election that was substantially without meaningful political parties. Unlike Ukraine, where a coalition was built early and a single major opposition candidate was agreed upon, or Georgia, where there were distinct opposition parties and movements, in Kyrgyzstan the election was characterized by competition between individuals. In most cases, these individuals were elites. There was no opposition coalition, or even collection of identifiable opposition parties in Kyrgyzstan, comparable to Ukraine or Georgia.

As Radnitz (2006) indicates, a great deal of party activity and excitement took place among opposition political figures before the election. However, this did not result in the formation of a cohesive and identifiable opposition. According to Radnitz, the People's Movement of Kyrgyzstan (NDK) was the most important group that emerged in this period, but the party "had little in the way of a common platform . . . and was never able to unite around a single figure." However, the NDK was able to bring numerous opposition leaders together and begin to bridge the persistent division between north and south.

The NDK was far from being the only significant opposition party in the election. Ata-Jurt (Fatherland) was founded by veteran Kyrgyz diplomat Roza Otunbayeva. The party grew to include several other MPs disenchanted with Akaev. Two other former ministers formed Jany Bagyt (New Direction). Other older parties such as the Communists and Dignity also were prominent in the opposition. The latter party was led by Felix Kulov a former ally of Akaev who was, at the time, serving a prison term on what were broadly viewed as false charges.[15]

There were of course several pro-government parties as well, including Alga Kyrgyzstan (Forward Kyrgyzstan), led by Akaev's daughter, and Adilet (Justice). According to Abazov (2007), "although some dozen political parties and coalitions took part in the election campaign, parties did not play a significant role in the election. Instead some 400 candidates stood for the 75 seats in the Jogorku Kenesh (parliament) as at least officially 'independents'" (532).

Through several means, Akayev sought to ensure a favorable outcome in the parliamentary election, and thus keep the door open to remaining in power after his term expired. First, the media climate in Kyrgyzstan had grown gradually worse throughout the years leading up to the election, making it extremely difficult for political opponents to communicate with the Kyrgyz people. Second, the regime used legal machinations to eliminate potential rivals. For example, Felix Kulov, one of the most popular opposition figures, was imprisoned in 2001 and was therefore unable to run for parliament. The courts disqualified the candidacy of Roza Otunbayeva because she had spent so much time outside the country in the period leading up to the election. Otunbayeva had been outside the country serving as a diplomat in the U.S, UK, and other postings. Last, the regime used the normal battery of fear and intimidation to dissuade ordinary Kyrgyz from supporting or becoming involved with opposition candidates or parties.[16]

The authorities in Kyrgyzstan were adept at exploiting the repressive environment and electoral rules to create barriers for opposition candidates to succeed. Election Day, at least in the first round, went relatively smoothly. However, only 33 seats, less than half, were won in the first round. It is very difficult to measure precisely how many of those were pro-government, but the Kyrgyz people were dissatisfied with the outcome, raising tensions around the upcoming runoff. The demonstrations, which eventually led to the Tulip Revolution, began in the period between the first and second round of elections. The second round, in which more than half the members of parliament were chosen, did not go as smoothly as the first. Results from the second round indicated a clear majority for supporters and allies of Akaev. After the second round, the demonstrations continued, increasing in size.

After Elections

The election period in each of these countries was characterized by widespread fraud and administrative abuses resulting in a stolen election. In Georgia, the CUG and Revival Parties continued stealing votes well after the voting had ended, ensuring that they would continue to dominate the parliament. The exit poll and PVT, however, indicated that the voters had shown a preference for an opposition dominated parliament, led by Saakashvili's NM and the Labor Party. In Ukraine, a second round victory by Yanukovich was attributable to widespread fraud. In Kyrgyzstan, the announced winners of the 75 single mandate races were largely from pro-Akaev parties or independent candidates aligned with the president. Most of the winning candidates had benefited from a patently restrictive electoral environment and voter intimidation and harassment.

While none of these elections could be described as close to being free and fair, they were far from being the first bad elections in the former Soviet Union or even specifically in Georgia, Ukraine and Kyrgyzstan. Based on recent experience in these three countries, as well as the region more broadly, the governments committing the fraud may have expected a few days of relatively minor demonstrations followed by acceptance of results and the new parliament or president being seated.

In Ukraine and Kyrgyzstan, however, there were additional precedents to be considered. The reaction to the stolen election in Georgia set a new and different kind of precedent for Ukraine, while the reaction to the stolen elections in Georgia and Ukraine set new precedents for Kyrgyzstan. The demonstrations following the announcement of the fraudulent results in Georgia undoubtedly came as a surprise to the semidemocratic leaders in Georgia and throughout the region, but similar demonstrations in Ukraine and Kyrgyzstan were less of a surprise.

In all three countries, the fraudulent election results were met by demonstrations and other forms of resistance. However, even though the demonstrators in Ukraine consciously emulated the Rose Revolutionaries and demonstrators in Kyrgyzstan consciously emulated demonstrators in both Georgia and Ukraine, the post-election events in the three countries differed significantly.

Georgia

Because the election in Georgia was for parliament rather than for a new president, the issues at stake in the election fraud were somewhat less concrete. Even if the official numbers had been accepted, there would have been several opposition parties in the parliament who together would have had a presence, although not a majority within the legislature. Simply protesting the outcome of the election and the marginal difference in seat distribution would not have been a sufficiently motivating cause for most of Georgian society.[17]

Shortly following the election, however, two issues emerged that remained at the heart of the demonstrations. First, the NM demanded to be recognized as the true winner of the election and to receive the largest block of party list seats in the legislature. Second, the BD demanded that they be admitted into parliament since both the PVT and exit poll showed them passing the 7 percent threshold, while the official results kept them below this magic number. Needless to say, these two issues were of particular import to two opposition parties, the NM and the BD. Accordingly, these two parties took the leading role in the ensuing street demonstrations while the other two major opposition parties, Labor and the NR, did not participate.

The leadership of the Rose Revolution also came from these two parties. Saakashvili from the NM, as well as both Zurab Zhvania and Nino Burjanadze from the BD, were the most visible politicians leading and organizing the street demonstrations. However, the participants in the demonstrations, especially toward the end, came from a much broader swath of Georgian society. Participants included supporters of Labor, whose lower income and older voters were anxious for change, as well as the NR and ordinary people who had no strong partisan identity.

The central demands of the demonstrations, particularly in the early period, were to recognize the NM's plurality and to let the BD into parliament. These demands, particularly the latter, would still not have been enough to mobilize a meaningful number of demonstrators or to sustain any protests. The organizers knew this and opted for one central demand that, while somewhat unrealistic to many, was certain to excite and mobilize citizens of Georgia. That demand was for Shevardnadze's resignation. This demand became the dominant slogan of the Rose Revolution because it encapsulated all that frustrated and angered ordinary Georgians.

Significantly there was consistent tension between the NM and the BD throughout the early days of the demonstrations. Saakashvili and Burjanadze were still maneuvering for the position of leader of the opposition as both parties tried to steer the post-election scenario to their benefit. Unity between the two parties, and more important, among the three leaders of these two parties, did not occur until several weeks into the demonstrations.

For most of November, the two parties joined together for demonstrations while working against each other behind the scenes. Each party was deeply concerned that the other would agree to a deal with the government that would exclude them. This did not happen, largely because the government was so discredited that both parties feared being tainted by any association with the government. Ultimately, the three leaders were able to work together during the period immediately before, during and after Shevardnadze's resignation. However, even this unity was only brief.

The demonstrations outside the parliament building in Tbilisi lasted almost three weeks. For the most part, the demonstrations were not large. Some days, only a few thousand people gathered outside of the parliament, but judging the support for the Rose Revolution simply by the size of the demonstrations overlooks some important points. The demonstrations were only one manifestation of opposition to Shevardnadze. There was a great deal of passive support for the demonstrators throughout Georgia that made it possible for activists to easily mobilize, move, and communicate with people.

The failure of Shevardnadze to rally any geographic or demographic group of Georgians to support him speaks to his extraordinarily low popularity. Unlike, Akaev or Yanukovich, who had strong support in their respective bases, Shevardnadze did not enjoy a geographic base anywhere in Georgia. When Shevardnadze flew to Telavi in the region of Kakheti in eastern Georgia, once a stronghold of support, as part of a half-hearted attempt to resist the demonstrators on the streets of Tbilisi in November 2003, local people did not allow his plane to land. Ultimately, Shevardnadze turned to Ajaran warlord Aslan Abashidze for support. Abashidze sent several busloads of paid and unenthusiastic demonstrators from Batumi to Tbilisi, but they were outnumbered by what had become huge crowds of anti-Shevardnadze demonstrators. Abashidze's supporters ended up fleeing Tbilisi and returning to Ajara after only a few days, as Saakashvili and his supporters stormed parliament and forced Shevardnadze to resign.

The Rose Revolution set an impressively nonviolent tone for what became the Color Revolutions. The demonstrations in Tbilisi were not only nonviolent in nature, but, for the most part, confined to a few blocks in the middle of the capital. Not only were no guns fired, but life for many Georgians was hardly disrupted until the last few days before Shevardnadze resigned when the government sought, with little success, to create roadblocks to prevent supporters of the opposition from getting to Tbilisi to participate in demonstrations.

The nonviolence resulted from a commitment on both sides to avoid violence, but was made easier, because President Shevardnadze's regime was so weak that orders to shoot demonstrators, had they occurred, would very likely have been ignored by soldiers who were usually paid late or not at all and thus not particularly supportive of Shevardnadze. Additionally, the absence of any ethnic or geographical divisions among the Georgian electorate made it very difficult for the government to create a situation where one group of Georgians could have been pitted against another.

Ukraine

The widespread fraud in the second round of the Ukrainian election meant that Yanukovich was able to win narrowly, essentially stealing the election from Yushchenko. A presidential election, where there can be only one winner, is, of course, far more of a zero sum game than a parliamentary election. In both Georgia and Kyrgyzstan there was at least a possibility of compromise. The demand for Shevarndadze's resignation, for example, was a potent rallying cry in Georgia, but it was negotiable.[18] There was no similar possible settlement in Ukraine. One of these men was going to be president and one was not.

Yanukovich's supporters resorted to stealing votes to swing the election in favor of their candidate, but Yanukovich still had a strong base of support. In this respect the 2004 election in Ukraine was polarizing. Moreover, it was polarizing along the geographical lines that had been a constant in Ukrainian politics since 1991. In the runoff, the eastern parts of the country voted overwhelmingly for Yanukovich, while the west supported Yushchenko in similar proportions.

The geographic division in the election was stark, with Yanukovich winning virtually every region of eastern Ukraine and Yushchenko doing the same in western Ukraine. Yanukovich carried several eastern regions with enormous percentages of the vote. He won 82 percent of the vote in the Crimea, 96 percent in Donetsk, 93 percent in Lunansk, and 89 percent in Sevastopol, all of which are located in southern or eastern Ukraine. Yushchenko ran up similar numbers in the western part of the country, winning 76 percent of the vote in Vinnytsia, 86 percent in Volyn, 93 percent in Ivano-Frankvisk, 76 percent in Kiev region, 92 percent in Lviv, and 94 percent in Ternopil.[19] The capital, which in previous elections had been divided between east and west, also supported Yushchenko strongly, with 74 percent of the vote there.

The demonstrations in Ukraine began shortly after the results of the runoff were released. As in Georgia, the demonstrations occurred in the center of the capital city, Kiev, and had the feel of a vigil about them with demonstrators unwilling to leave without some kind of resolution to the dispute. The demonstrations in Kiev occurred in a central square known as the Maidan. The number of demonstrators on the Maidan was enormous, with estimates of up to a million people at its height and at other times numbering several hundred thousand. While Ukraine has roughly ten times the population of Georgia, and Kiev has at least twice as many people as Tbilisi, the differing sizes of the demonstrations were even greater than these proportions might suggest, so cannot be attributed to the population of the country alone.

As in Georgia, a clear leadership emerged during this time that was able to organize the demonstrations; communicate with demonstrators, the media, foreign observers, and diplomats; and negotiate with the government. Yushchenko was, predictably, one of the leaders. Yulia Timoschenko emerged as another important and dynamic opposition leader.

There was also real division in Ukraine, with at least 40 percent of the people legitimately supporting Yanukovich. In Georgia, according to the PVT and exit poll, roughly three quarters of the population had voted definitively against the government or any of the parties that loosely supported it. It is hard to imagine that a candidate aligned with Shevardnadze could have won as much of 30 percent of the vote even in a comparably flawed presidential election in Georgia in 2003. The demonstrations in Ukraine needed to be huge precisely because the demonstrators did not enjoy the enormous, almost even unanimous, reservoir of support that those in Georgia the previous year had enjoyed.

Moreover, the stakes were higher in Ukraine. Somebody had to win, and somebody would lose. There was no outcome that would have allowed one side to win with the other side being able to get something. The central demand of the demonstrators in Ukraine was to reverse the outcome of the stolen election and make Yushchenko president. Kuchma's government was not willing simply to admit it had been involved in widespread fraud, even though this was reasonably apparent, and just let Yushchenko win. There was also no clear legal or constitutional means to reverse the outcome of an election.

There were other political reasons not to overturn the results of the election. Yanukovich had supporters constituting almost half the population. These supporters believed that their candidate had won and if there had been election fraud, which was hard to deny, it was not only one side that had committed it. As was noted earlier, there had, in fact, been election fraud on both sides, but little evidence to suggest that Yushchenko's supporters had stolen as many votes in the west as Yanukovich's in the east. One measure of this difference from the OSCE/ODIHR report was that "There was a regional variation, with polling in western and northern regions being assessed negatively in 4 percent and 5 percent respectively. However, in central and eastern regions this figure was 11 percent and 9 percent respectively."[20]

The result was deadlock. Clearly, Yanukovich would have commanded little legitimacy as the president of Ukraine had he been allowed to take office. This outcome would not be acceptable to the hundreds of thousands of demonstrators who showed no signs of leaving the Maidan as November turned to December and the Ukrainian winter began to set in. The deadlock ended when an agreement was brokered calling for new elections, specifically a new runoff between Yanukovich and Yushchenko. This new runoff, a repeat of the second round, became known as the third round.

The agreement to conduct a third round of the election was only part of the deal that ended the deadlock. It was also agreed that the constitution would be revised so that the powers of the president would be reduced somewhat and power would be shared between the president and the cabinet of ministers. The latter would be presided over by a prime minister to be chosen by the parliament.

By the time the third round occurred, on December 25, the momentum had shifted unmistakably to Yushchenko. To the surprise of nobody, Yushchenko won the third round by a margin of 47–44 percent. The third round was still close, but with less fraud involved, Yushchenko was able to achieve a narrow victory as the country split along almost identical geographical lines as it had in November.

The events in winter of 2004 were, like those in Georgia a year earlier, nonviolent. The demonstrations were remarkably peaceful, almost celebratory in nature. Once the agreement had been made, Yanukovich and his supporters did not challenge the new arrangements or the new outcome. However, they did not slink away as a political force in Ukraine as the CUG did in Georgia.

Kyrgyzstan

The post-election scenario in Kyrgyzstan was markedly different from those in Ukraine and Georgia. The protests were less peaceful, less organized, and less centered in the capital. In some respects, it was not a post-election scenario at all since the uprisings started between the first two rounds of the election. There were two weeks between the first round of the elections and the elections in districts where no candidate had received a majority in the first round. Importantly, 42 of the 75 seats were not decided in the first round so that by the time the demonstrations started, the outcome of the election was still not fully, or even mostly, known. These demonstrations, therefore, were almost preemptive, seeking to stop the government from stealing more seats in the runoff.

The protest started between the two rounds because, based on the first round, it was clear that the government was poised to commit more fraud in the second round. A majority of individual parliamentary elections were not resolved in the first round, so the second round was important to the overall outcome of the election. Nonetheless, the second round occurred as scheduled and, as expected, sufficient fraud—including stuffing ballot boxes and intimidating voters—was committed to ensure a parliament that would be friendly to President Akaev.

After the second round, the protests began in earnest. As with the demonstrations in Georgia, the demonstrators felt that the primary person to blame was the president, so it was his resignation for which they called. Unlike in Georgia, however, strong and peaceful leadership did not emerge quickly in Kyrgyzstan so the demonstrations were less organized and more violent. Protests were scattered around the country with peaceful demonstrations occurring at the same time as takeovers of government buildings, minor acts of looting, and the like.

There was no figure in Kyrgyzstan during this period comparable to Burjanadze, Saakashvili, and Zhvania in Georgia or Yushchenko and Timoschenko in Ukraine. This not only created obstacles for organizing the demonstrations, but it made negotiations more difficult as well. It was not clear with whom Akaev could negotiate and whether negotiating partners would have been able to deliver had they made an agreement with the authorities. The Kuchma and Shevardnadze governments, on the other hand, knew precisely with whom they needed to talk and that agreements with opposition leaders would almost certainly be binding.

The geographical division also played itself out differently in Kyrgyzstan and Ukraine. Unlike Ukraine, where most of the government fraud occurred in the region where the government was strong, Akaev's supporters in Kyrgyzstan stole votes in parliamentary districts throughout the country. However, because Akaev was from the north, this fraud was felt acutely in the south where the election was seen, not entirely inaccurately, as an attempt by a northerner to retain control over the whole country rather than share that power with a southerner or group of southerners. Not surprisingly, the demonstrations started, and were strongest, in the south. Bishkek, of course, is in the northern part of the country, so the protests were less significant there than in southern cities such as Osh and Jalalabad.

Unlike in Ukraine and Georgia where the opposition presented a unified post-election visage and direct cohesive demands, the demonstrators throughout Kyrgyzstan were protesting different concerns. Youth groups such as Kelkel demonstrated against bad elections.[21] Some demonstrators in the south opposed the perception of continued dominance by northerners while many rural Kyrgyz seemed to be protesting against corruption and poverty.

As the days passed and the demonstrations did not abate, it became clear that the events in Kyrgyzstan were playing out differently than those in Georgia and Ukraine had. Occasional episodes of violence broke out including looting and destruction of property. While most of the violence was against property, there was a real possibility that Kyrgyzstan would end up in civil war rather than the peaceful transitions that had characterized the Orange and Rose Revolutions.

During this period, the ambiguity around the election results continued. For a brief time there were two competing parliaments in Bishkek, both claiming to represent the people of Kyrgyzstan. The first was led by opposition figure Kurambek Bakiev, the other by supporters of Akaev. By March 28, however, Bakiev's parliament was recognized by the Kyrgyzstan's Central Election Committee (CEC). This was a major blow to the old regime and definite indicator that Akaev was likely on his way out. A few days later, on April 4, Akaev fled to Moscow, where, on April 11 he signed a resignation letter, bringing to an end fifteen years as leader of Kyrgyzstan.

Akaev's resignation may have solved one immediate problem, but it created others. Again, unlike Georgia, where Saakashvili had solidified his position as the leader of the opposition during the demonstrations, or Ukraine, where Yushchenko had been the preeminent opposition political leader for months, there was no easily identifiable opposition leader in Kyrgyzstan. Therefore, when Akaev resigned, there was contention about who should replace him.

This dispute was reinforced by the geographical cleavage in Kyrgyz society. Akaev was a northerner; and the demonstrations had been largely fueled by southerners wanting a bigger share of power in Kyrgyzstan. However, the most well known political opponent of Akaev, Felix Kulov, was also a northerner. Kulov had been freed from jail in March and assumed a leadership role in the opposition. As a northerner, Kulov was automatically unacceptable to most Kyrgyz from the south of the country. However, the Kyrgyz from the north who had opposed Akaev and joined in the demonstrations and would not be content with a leader who was a relatively unknown southerner.

Kurmanbek Bakiev, the leader of the new parliament, was a southerner with some credentials on the national level, so he became the candidate with the strongest base of support in the south. For a few weeks it was not clear what would happen. A presidential campaign between Kulov and Bakiev had the potential to tear the country apart on regional lines once again. Eventually, Kulov agreed to serve as Bakiev's prime minister, eliminating the possibility of a divisive election between the two of them.

New Leadership

In all three countries, shortly after the demonstration, vigils, and other forms of public activism ended, the new regimes appeared to consolidate quickly. In Ukraine the results of the third round, although quite close, were not challenged, and Yushchenko assumed the presidency early in 2005 without incident. In Georgia and Kyrgyzstan, Saakashvili and Bakiev won elections by overwhelming, almost unanimous, margins, facing no serious opposition. In Georgia, Saakashvili's candidacy was supported by both Zhvania and Burjanadze while in Kyrgyzstan all the major opposition figures, including Kulov, supported Bakiev.

The elections that brought Saakashvili and Bakiev to power were much freer and more democratic than any others which had occurred in the recent past in Georgia or Kyrgyzstan. The OSCE/ODIHR report on the 2004 Georgian presidential election stated that "Georgia demonstrated notable progress over previous elections, and in several respects brought the country closer to meeting OSCE commitments and other international standards for democratic elections. . . . [T]he authorities generally displayed the collective political will to conduct a more genuine democratic election process."[22] The OSCE/ODIHR report from Kyrgyzstan reflected a similar sentiment. "The 10 July 2005 early presidential election marked tangible progress by the Kyrgyz Republic towards meeting OSCE commitments, as well as other international standards for democratic elections. This was the case in particular during the pre-election period and the conduct of voting. . . . Fundamental civil and political rights, such as freedom of expression and freedom of assembly, were generally respected throughout the election process."[23]

Although the Color Revolutions brought in new leaders, and in the case of Georgia and Kyrgyzstan, with overwhelming popular support, the degree to which the previous regime had been weakened or even overthrown by the events following the stolen elections varied and was not always clear. In Ukraine, the Orange Revolutionaries succeeded in overturning a stolen election and replacing the candidate who stole the election with the candidate who actually won it. While this should be lauded, it did not destroy, or even gravely weaken the Kuchma-Yanukovich forces in Ukraine. These forces lost power, but they by no means ceased to be major actors in Ukrainian politics.

Since the Orange Revolution, two parliamentary elections have taken place in Ukraine. In both of those elections, Yanukovich's Party of Regions won the most votes, with 34 percent in 2007 and 32 percent in 2006. More strikingly, Yanukovich served under Yushchenko as Prime Minister from August 2006 to December 2007. Yanukovich, of course, went on to win election as Ukraine's president in 2010 after Yushchenko had served only one term. Yanukovich's victory in that presidential election was another piece of evidence that many in Ukraine had never abandoned the losers of 2004. The notion that the Orange Revolution destroyed the old regime, a defining character of revolutions, is not accurate. However, the idea that the Orange Revolution destroyed the old system may be more accurate since Ukraine is no longer dominated by one party or group. It is also clear that the Orange Revolution ensured that more voices and opinions, representing a substantial plurality, if not majority, of the Ukrainian people would no longer be shut out of politics.

The Rose and Tulip Revolutions, at least on the surface, had a much more destructive effect on the previous regimes led by Shevardnadze and Akaev respectively. No candidate representing the old regime ran against either Bakiev or Saakashvili in the new presidential elections. In Georgia, most of the remaining senior figures in the Shevardnadze administration either slunk into political obscurity or pledged their support to the new administration. To a great extent, this was true in Kyrgyzstan as well. In neither country were supporters of either Shevardnadze or Akaev again a major force in national politics. Indeed, when Bakiev was ousted in April 2010, it was by disillusioned Tulip Revolutionaries, not Akaev loyalists.

The change in regimes may seem more acute in Kyrgyzstan and Georgia than in Ukraine, but it is worth remembering that in all three countries the new leaders had been entrenched in the old regime only a few years before the Color Revolutions. In Kyrgyzstan, the difference between Bakiev, who unlike Saakashvili or Yushchenko had never been a real reformer, and the old regime was as much about regional allegiances as orientation to democracy or the west.

Ukraine emerged from the Orange Revolution just as divided as it had been before the election. The third round between Yanukovich and Yushchenko revealed a division in the electorate between east and west that was almost identical to that seen in the second round. This division would remain at the heart of post-Orange Revolution politics in Ukraine. At first glance Georgia and Kyrgyzstan would appear to have emerged from the Rose and Tulip Revolutions with a far greater degree of political unity, but this proved to be an illusion. In the years following their elections, Saakashvili and Bakiev would be dogged, much like their predecessors, by a stream of senior officials, often allies from the revolution, leaving the government and joining, or forming, the opposition.

Summary

In a broad sense, the Color Revolutions followed a similar pattern. The decade or so before the Color Revolution began with a period of hope that the regime would move ahead with democratic reforms, but this hope withered away as all three semidemocratic regimes became weaker and less democratic over time. As this situation developed, a key national election was scheduled.[24] An opposition, although not a unified one, emerged in all three countries that was strong enough to at least pose a political threat to the government. The government responded by expanding voter fraud and stealing the national election. This led to the post-election events and concessions to key opposition demands such as the resignation of the president or new elections. New elections occurred in all three countries, leading to the election of a new president who had been the leader of the opposition.

Looking beyond the events themselves, other important similarities and contrasts are evident as well. For example, the evolution of the political and civic opposition in Georgia, Ukraine, and Kyrgyzstan is central to the Color Revolutions. As noted, the political opposition in all three cases had roots in the old regime. In none of these cases can the events be compared to Mao or Castro leading armies of peasants and outsiders to take over the capital.[25] The political leadership in all these cases were insiders familiar with the way power and politics worked in their country.

This may have been one of the reasons, particularly in Georgia and Ukraine, why the Rose and Orange Revolutions were so nonviolent. Yushchenko and Zhvania, in particular, were well liked and well respected by many in the Ukrainian and Georgian governments during and after the election. Although these two politicians had moved into the opposition, many in government viewed them as representing hope for the future and understood them to be capable administrators. It was not difficult for these two opposition leaders to open and maintain dialog with security forces during the post-election demonstrations and protests to reduce the chances of violence.

Importantly, there were also electoral foundations for the emergence of the major leaders in Georgia and Ukraine. In Georgia, Zhvania and Saakashvili had created their own parties and run in the local elections in June 2002. These elections demonstrated that opposition figures represented and were substantially supported by the people. This was truer for Saakashvili because his party did considerably better than Zhvania's in that election. Other parties, notably Labor and the New Rights, ran on opposition platforms and did well in the local elections, providing legitimacy for their opposition voices as well. Most of this opposition legitimacy dissipated when these two parties did not participate in the post-election demonstrations. In Ukraine, the parliamentary elections of 2002 provided a similar opportunity for parties led by Yushchenko and Timoschenko to emerge as the leading voices of the opposition.

After the election, Yushchenko emerged as the leader of the opposition for obvious reasons. The victory that had been stolen was his. However, the political leadership of the Orange Revolution was not limited to Yushchenko; other politicians, notably Yulia Timoschenko but also Boris Tarasyuk and Yuri Kostenko, who had been active in their support for Yushchenko, also emerged as leaders of the movement in November 2004.[26] These politicians had been part of the coalition that had supported Yushchenko against Yanukovich. In this respect, the Ukrainian case was quite different from the other two. In Ukraine, the political fault lines had been clear and coalitions were assembled months before the election, making for a more easily understandable and better planned post-election chain of events.

In Georgia, Zhvania, Burjanadze and Saakashvili were the leaders of only two of at least four opposition parties that had some opposition credentials based on their electoral history, but they emerged from a crowded field to become the clear leaders of the Rose Revolution. Immediately before the election, one could certainly have argued that Labor was Georgia's strongest opposition party. It had done extremely well in the local elections, essentially tying with the NM in Tbilisi and had a strong base among poor and elderly voters. This was a sharp contrast to the BD which continued to draw support from urban elites while resonating less with low educated and older voters. Moreover, Labor, unlike the other three opposition parties, had never been part of the CUG. Yet, within two weeks of the election Labor had become an afterthought to Georgian politics.

The failure of Labor to take a leading role in the opposition is even more puzzling when its strong showing in the November 2003 election is considered. According to the exit poll and the PVT, Labor finished a close second to the NM in the election and would have the second largest delegation in the parliament. The official results, however, bumped Labor down to 4th place, behind the CUG and Revival as well as the NM.

Labor's leader Shalva Natalashvili's decision not to participate in the demonstrations led to the severe weakening of his party. Natalashvili's decision likely sprang from his distrust of Saakashvili, and particularly Zhvania from his days with the CUG, as well as his view, which he reiterated to me every time we spoke in 2002 and 2003, that Zhvania and Saakashvili were not legitimate opposition. On this issue, Natalashvili was completely unable to read the pulse of the population, which no longer cared about political hair splitting and was just angry at the government.

The emergence of the political opposition occurred later and less clearly in Kyrgyzstan than in the other two cases. Kyrgyzstan's weaker party system and electoral structure made it difficult for a national leadership to emerge, or even for the election to be truly national in character. As a former Prime Minister who had broken with Akaev, Bakiev's profile was similar to that of Yushchenko, Zhvania, and other leaders of the Orange and Rose Revolutions, but Bakiev was not a national opposition figure in the same sense. Moreover, the post-elections scenario in Kyrgyzstan saw many isolated acts of protest, looting, and civil disobedience not under the leadership of one person or party.

The other primary leaders of the Tulip Revolution included Felix Kulov and Roza Otunbayeva. Kulov was the leader of Ar-Namys, an opposition political party, but he spent the months preceding the election in jail, so although a popular figure, he was not able to take a direct leadership role until the change was under way. Otunbayeva was an independent political force as well who sought to use her standing as a diplomat to create a base for herself.

The Role of Civil Society

All three Color Revolutions were rooted in civil society as well as in politics. CSOs were active in all three countries in the period leading up to the election as well as during the post-election period. CSOs were engaged in a range of activities including election monitoring, mobilizing activists, engaging in acts of protest, using the media, and planning and leveraging resources. These organizations played a key role in keeping society somewhat open and free and drawing attention to government corruption and other problems.

Much of the scholarly work on CSOs in the Color Revolutions has focused on youth activist groups. Bunce and Wolchik (2005, 2006) have been the leaders in discussing the roles of CSOs, specifically youth activist organizations, in Color Revolutions. Their research has evinced a depth of understanding that is not always apparent in more cursory descriptions of the Color Revolutions. The major youth organizations on which most scholarly attention is focused are Kmara in Georgia, Pura in Ukraine and Kelkel in Kyrgyzstan. There was a clear effort by the leadership of Pura to imitate Kmara and for Kelkel to imitate both Kmara and Kelkel. However, Kmara was not original either, borrowing and learning a great deal from Otpor, a youth organization that played an important role in Serbia's Bulldozer Revolution of 2000.

The similarities between these organizations are strong and seem even greater because they were, to a large degree, modeled on each other. All four organizations drew their membership largely from urban mostly educated youth and were primarily focused on weakening the old regime, claiming to be nonpartisan but having strong ties to the major opposition parties. Additionally, they all relied substantially on money from outside the country, either in one form or another from the U.S government or from George Soros' Open Society Institute (OSI).

There were significant differences among these organizations as well. In general terms, these four organizations could be divided into two groups, the first consisting of Otpor and Pora; the second consisting of Kelkel and Kmara. Otpor and Pora were significantly larger and played a greater role in the Bulldozer and Orange Revolutions. These were mass events in which many people came together to demonstrate against a stolen presidential election. Otpor and Pora were key actors in mobilizing, organizing, and monitoring the enormous crowds in Belgrade and Kiev. They also worked closely with the political leadership to ensure unity between the major opposition political parties and forces.

Kmara and Kelkel were more on the fringes of the less organized post-election demonstrations in Georgia, and particularly in Kyrgyzstan. Kmara was smaller than either Pora or Otpor and understood to be close to Saakashvili and the NM. In Georgia, the post-election events were more spontaneous and organized largely by the political parties and politicians, with

Kmara playing a clearly secondary role. Kelkel was involved in events in Bishkek, but the demonstrations, disorder, and even looting and occasional violence were more dispersed in Kyrgyzstan and not heavily driven by the youth activist organization.

In addition to these youth organizations, the other major domestic CSOs that played critical and immediate roles in the Color Revolutions were election monitoring organizations, the International Society for Fair Elections and Democracy (ISFED) in Georgia, Citizen Voters of Ukraine (CVU) in Ukraine and the Coalition for Democracy and Civil Society (CDCS) in Kyrygzystan.

ISFED, CVU, and CDCS played a key role in communicating the extent and nature of the election fraud to international organizations and shared information with the international observer missions. Perhaps more importantly, they played an absolutely central role in informing the populations of these three countries that their governments were seeking to steal the election. Domestic monitors in all three countries had the ears of the local population and, where possible, local media as well.

These domestic election monitoring organizations tended to have a lower international profile than some of the youth activists' organizations, but had a strong impact on all the Color Revolutions. In the cases of Georgia and Kyrgyzstan, ISFED and CDCS were clearly more important than the more studied Kmara or Kelkel. However, the extent to which these organizations can truly be considered domestic is questionable. While the leadership, board, and staffs of these monitoring groups were all domestic, all four of these organizations gained a great deal of financial, technical, and political support through their relationship with the National Democratic Institute (NDI), an American democracy assistance organization funded largely from the United States Agency for International Development (USAID) or other agencies in the American government.

The development of domestic monitoring organizations is a central part of NDI's work around the world. These organizations usually work closely with NDI in their early years before gaining varying degrees of independence. At the time of the Color Revolutions, CVU was more independent of NDI, but CDCS and ISFED both received most of their funding through sub-grants from USAID to NDI to the monitoring group. ISFED and CDCS also had close working relationships with technical and other experts from NDI, who helped them implement their monitoring and parallel vote tabulations (PVTs).

Another election monitoring organization that also helped identify and highlight election fraud in Ukraine and Kyrgyzstan was the European Network of Election Monitoring Organizations (ENEMO). ENEMO was a hybrid of domestic and international monitors. It consisted of network of domestic monitoring organizations from throughout the former Soviet Union and Eastern Europe. This network was able to bring election monitoring expertise and experience to the challenging election monitoring environments in Ukraine in 2004 and Kyrgyzstan in 2005.

Not surprisingly, ENEMO also benefited from a close relationship, including financial and technical support, from NDI. NDI had played a valuable role in strengthening domestic election monitoring throughout the region, and globally, so organizations working with NDI had access to some of the top election monitoring professionals in the world as well as ongoing political and financial support.

Conclusion

The Rose, Orange, and Tulip Revolutions occurred over a period of only a few months in Georgia, Ukraine, and Kyrgyzstan, but they were the products of years of political machinations, civil society development, and political maneuvering by faltering regimes. The increasingly corrupt and inefficient regimes of Kuchma and particularly Akaev and Shevardnadze created an enormous, and in the case of Georgia, virtually unanimous, desire for change. The weakness, but also the relatively free nature, of these regimes made the Color Revolutions possible. All three of these regimes were probably too weak to repress large post-election demonstrations, but they were also probably too liberal to call for violent suppression of demonstrators.

The Color Revolutions were all resolved quickly as new leaders were elected in presidential elections. These leaders and in fact most of the people around them had been part of the old regime. The leaders of the Color Revolutions did not espouse a radical or new ideology, but came to power through harsh criticism of the incumbent governments and claims that they could run the country better and more honestly. They promised change, but change in the form of better results, not in new world views or ideologies.

The Color Revolutions were not only domestic events, but occurred in a complex and evolving international context. All three countries have had to seek a balance between one global superpower, the U.S.A., and one regional power, Russia. In more general terms, they have had to balance Russia and the West. The Color Revolutions substantially affected this balance. Moreover, the politicians and civil society activists who led the Color Revolutions had strong ties to the west. For all three of these countries the tension between their relationships with the west and with Russia became central to politics after the Color Revolutions.

CHAPTER 4

The U.S. Role

THE COLOR REVOLUTIONS are almost a political Rorschach test for observers of international politics. How one views these events—as triumphs of the "freedom agenda," as twentieth-century U.S. imperialism in twenty-first-century nongovernmental bottles, as American-supported plots or events that were orchestrated by the citizens of Georgia, Ukraine, or Kyrgyzstan—reveals more about the observer than about the events themselves. This is especially true if that observer is Russia, which has sought to portray these events as part of an American conspiracy to ensure that friendly, pro-America leaders are in place in the countries surrounding Russia. The antiwar left in the U.S. and Europe has frequently taken a similar position, suggesting that Color Revolutions and electoral breakthrough strategies are part of a long history of American intervention around the world. The U.S. government tried to have it both ways in the years following the Color Revolutions, rebutting assertions of conspiracies and plots, but still claiming to have played an important role. The real story, not surprisingly, is more nuanced and complicated than any of these positions suggest.

U.S. Policy in the Former Soviet Union in Context

When the Color Revolutions occurred, the former Soviet Union in general was less important to the U.S. than it had been a few years earlier. The initial excitement and political adrenaline of the immediate post-Soviet era had worn off by the first years of the twenty-first century, when many of the former Communist bloc countries of Eastern Europe as well as the Baltic states appeared clearly headed toward full integration into Europe. However, it was equally apparent that the remaining countries of the Soviet Union faced difficult challenges with no guarantees whatsoever of becoming market oriented democracies. Some of these regimes, notably those in Belarus and Turkmenistan, had consolidated into nasty authoritarian regimes.

Not only were conditions more difficult in the region, but the attacks of September 11, and the subsequent wars in Afghanistan and Iraq, meant that U.S. policy was focused far more intensely in other parts of the world, making much of the former Soviet Union a secondary priority. This was probably a mistake, but may also have been unavoidable. Russian resurgence into the global stage may have been one of the most important global developments of the last decade, but was not sufficiently recognized by an administration that was focused elsewhere.

U.S. policy toward the former Soviet Union during that period was largely a product of the inertia caused by discouraging news in the region and more pressing challenges elsewhere in the world. The result of this was a regional policy during the Bush administration that, at least at first, seemed, in many respects, quite similar to that of the Clinton administration. The fundamentals of the Clinton era policy toward the former Soviet Union—for example, support for NATO expansion and democracy assistance, as well as an attitude that did not take Russia seriously as a competitor and assumed no consequences for the use of hard or soft power—remained the same for most of the Bush administration. It was in this context in which the Color Revolutions occurred and accelerated Russian hostility to American activities in the region.

As the Russian state and economy strengthened, and Russia returned as an important player and competitor of the U.S. in the countries of the former Soviet Union, a difficult challenge arose for Washington. The U.S. had to balance pursuing its own interests and relationships with new, but occasionally important allies, with the recognition that Russian interests had to be considered in a way that had not been true in the 1990s. Doing this successfully would have required the U.S. to chart a course that was sensitive to Russia's concerns while true to America's core interests. It is not at all obvious that such a course could have been charted, but there is not much evidence that the U.S. even tried.

Had the U.S. abandoned our post-Soviet allies and sent messages to Moscow that the region was now theirs again to do what it wanted, U.S.-Russia relations would likely be in a very different place right now, but this would also have meant a severe weakening of U.S. influence and power, not to mention greatly endangering the sovereignty and well being of numerous countries, such as Georgia and Ukraine, as well as other small post-Soviet states.

Even the U.S. policy of democracy assistance, which contributed to the Color Revolutions, was not a simple issue. While democracy assistance projects were a sore spot for Russian-American relations, it should be kept in mind that in all three Color Revolution countries, and most of the other countries in the region as well, Russia had never stopped being deeply involved in domestic politics. This was most evident during the 2004 election in Ukraine, in which Yanukovich received a great deal of Russian advice and support, but similar, if less dramatic, dynamics were at play in other countries as well. Thus, for the U.S. to walk away from democracy work in these countries would have created a situation in which Russian presence was permitted, but U.S. presence was not.

Perceptions as well as actions are also relevant for evaluating the effect Washington's involvement in democracy assistance and the Color Revolutions had on U.S.-Russia relations. In Georgia and Kyrgyzstan, in particular, where the case that the Rose and Tulip Revolutions were American plots is considerably weaker than comparable arguments for Ukraine or even Serbia, what happened after the Color Revolution probably had a greater impact on U.S.-Russia relations than the events themselves.

Following the Tulip and Rose Revolutions, the U.S. publicly took credit for those events, offering them as success stories and evidence of the efficacy of democracy assistance policy while seeking to build closer ties with those countries This contributed at least as much as the events themselves to the growing tension between the U.S. and Russia. Nonetheless, while the U.S. undoubtedly made some specific tactical mistakes and suffered from the absence of a bigger picture in the regions, it should be recognized that the strategic challenges facing the U.S. at the time were real with no easy answers. The U.S. role in the Color Revolutions should be understood in this context.

Debating the U.S. Role

The question of the U.S. role in the Color Revolutions is important for several reasons. First, the Color Revolutions are still held up as examples of how democracy assistance can be successful. They occurred in countries that had received substantial democracy assistance, but drawing a line from this to any real understanding of American intentions, or even impact, is less clear. Nonetheless, the perception that they were somehow an American plot is widespread, especially in the former Soviet Union, and extremely important, having had a good deal of influence on politics in the region.

Vladimir Frolov (2004) summarizes the Russian view of American involvement in elections and democracy assistance more broadly, so is worth quoting at some length:

> Today, Russia is facing a fundamentally new phenomenon in the post-Soviet space—one that is radically changing the role of election procedures in the formation of legitimate power. Elections in the CIS countries are turning from an instrument of the people's will into a convenient pretext for outside multilateral interference. This new environment is aimed at creating international legal conditions for changing a regime by challenging election results, claiming as illegitimate the existing constitutional procedures and provoking an acute political crisis. As a rule, the crisis either turns into a "color" revolution, that is, an unconstitutional change of power through a coup that is automatically recognized by the "international community," or else it leads to long-lasting political destabilization that is controlled from outside and which ultimately paralyzes the legally elected power.
>
> The outside factor—represented by an integrated network of Western nongovernmental organizations; mass media (above all television), international observation organizations, such as the Office for Democratic Institutions and Human Rights (ODIHR), OSCE and PACE; public opinion agencies and the political leadership of Western countries—now plays a crucial role in managing election results in the post-Soviet space. They have accomplished this role by claiming to know which elections are legitimate and which ones are not. Thus, an election is legitimate and corresponding to international standards if the results satisfy these organizations in terms of the makeup of the winning forces. If, however, the probable winner does not suit their needs, they portray the election as illegitimate, not free and unjust. Paradoxical as it may seem, same teams of "observers" declare election results as illegitimate in some countries of the former Soviet Union and legitimate in others despite the almost mirror-like coincidence of claims (as was the case during the March parliamentary elections in Moldova that were conducted with considerable violations). (Frolov 2004)

Frolov's view not only nicely summarizes the Russian perspective, but also highlights some of the difficulties associated with U.S. involvement, even if not at the level Frolov imagines, in elections in the former Soviet Union. While Frolov's analysis is not always accurate, it is built on enough accurate information to be reasonably convincing, particularly to people who may already be suspicious of American activity and democracy assistance. For example, he points out that the U.S. and Europe use the term "international community," which suggests consensus and cooperation, to refer specifically to themselves and their allies. While his assertions about election assessments may be overstated, it is often not difficult to find a political agenda behind western election evaluations, particularly if one is looking for evidence of that agenda.

MacKinnon (2007), for example, offers a western view of the Color Revolutions as American plots, highlighting the role of the NED in funding democracy work in the region:

> Funding political turmoil is not a new business for NED . . . While NED is now more restricted in how it meddles in the politics of other countries, it skirts these rules by funding what it calls "civil society": nongovernmental organizations and media outlets that are nonpartisan on paper, but whose activities work to the benefit of a favoured candidate or party. (30)

MacKinnon continues to argue that "NGOs (i.e., IRI and NDI) could use the same models (as those used in the early 1990s in Bulgaria and Romania) in other countries where the United States was interested in ousting a misbehaving regime" (31). MacKinnon's analysis is suffers from only looking at selected parts of the story. The NED's long history of projects that were not meant to lead to revolution and the equally strong history of NDI and IRI working to strengthen governments do not fit into MacKinnon's narrative, so are left out.[1]

The notion that the Color Revolutions were an American plot is appealing in its simplicity. In all three countries, heavy American involvement led to a similar political process and outcome and to the seating of a new, pro-American president. This notion, however, does not hold up well under further scrutiny. The American involvement in these countries varied significantly in both size and nature. It is also clear that many other countries with a similar level of American involvement saw nothing like Color Revolutions during this period. The political processes were similar in these countries, but factors other than U.S. involvement, such as post-Soviet countries learning from one another and sharing experiences, could have contributed to what happened.

Last, it is worth mentioning that if the Color Revolutions were an American plot, they were not a very well thought out one. In late 2005, it might have been possible to see the Color Revolutions as succeeding in securing pro-American regimes in Tbilisi, Kiev, and Bishkek, but within a few years even this assumption about the motives for the Color Revolutions as American plots needs to be revisited. In Ukraine, Viktor Yanukovich and the Party of the Regions had stymied efforts by Yushchenko and Timoschenko to move the country toward the west before returning to power with Yanukovich's election in 2010. Bakiev's government continued to provide the U.S. access to the Manas air force base, but not without extracting a great deal of money in return before being ousted in April 2010. Beginning in 2008, Saakashvili's government in Georgia, while continuing to profess strong ties to the U.S., was on several occasions perilously close to drawing the U.S. into a broader conflict with Russia in the South Caucasus.

In addition to questions of whether or not the Color Revolutions were American plots, these events also raise questions regarding the efficacy of American democracy assistance programs. While the Color Revolutions, on balance were not an American plot, American democracy assistance clearly played a role in all these events. Thus, understanding the American role in the Color Revolutions requires some ability to look at the question with nuance. Before turning to address these issues in greater depth, it is useful to take a closer look at what is meant by U.S. involvement in the Color Revolutions.

Defining U.S. Involvement

Determining the extent of the U.S. role in the Color Revolutions depends on how the U.S. role is defined. In each of these countries, from the early 1990s until the Color Revolutions, the U.S. was involved, through foreign assistance, in a range of activities including programs aimed at economic development, better health care, modernizing various government agencies, military exchanges and, of course, democracy assistance. Looking at the impact of democracy assistance programs outside this broader context tells only part of the story.

Foreign assistance was only a part of overall U.S. involvement in these countries in the years leading up to, and since, the Color Revolutions. Other U.S. actions including official statements, unofficial dialogue with both the old regimes and the color revolutionaries, exchange and educational programs, and last, but of extreme import, the actions of private foundations all contribute to what can be understood, in the bigger picture, as U.S. involvement in Georgia, Ukraine, or Kyrgyzstan.

If the U.S. role in the Color Revolutions is defined at its narrowest as simply U.S. support for democracy assistance programs, domestic CSOs, and election monitors, then the character of U.S. involvement can more easily be seen as oriented toward inciting political change and even revolution. Therefore it is possible, and probably easy, to identify U.S. funding for election fairness projects, conferences, and workshops for opposition political parties, as well as funding for anti-government CSOs and make a plausible argument that there was a U.S. conspiracy afoot. However, funding for anti-government CSOs seems considerably less nefarious when balanced against far greater assistance for the government itself. Similarly, political projects with opposition parties also seem less significant when balanced against similar U.S.-supported work with government parties and political leaders. Additionally, focusing the analysis too heavily on programs that are explicitly oriented around democracy assistance also makes it possible to overlook the import of other, less politically oriented programs that often have significant, if indirect, political impacts, such as exchange and education programs.

The tendency by some to see conspiracies where they do not exist and dramatically overstate the role of U.S. actions[2] must be balanced against the tendency by others to claim the U.S. played no role in the Color Revolutions.[3] This is further complicated by the fact that the U.S. involvement, and intentions, were different in each of these countries, making it foolish to generalize too broadly about Georgia, Ukraine, and Kyrgyzstan.

To understand the impact of the U.S. in an appropriately nuanced way, it is necessary to define U.S. involvement in these countries reasonably broadly and to consider aid to the governments, diplomatic statements, and foreign policy considerations in addition to democracy assistance and election related work. Additionally, an understanding of U.S. interests in the region generally, and in each of these countries in particular, during the period leading up to the Color Revolution helps provide a fuller picture of the U.S. role.

U.S. Interests

Even without a cohesive regional strategy, U.S. relationships with Georgia, Ukraine, and Kyrgyzstan shared important similarities in their pre-Color Revolution periods. These were all countries where the initial post-Soviet excitement had given way to something of a malaise, or even a fatigue, as it became clear that the road to democracy and prosperity would not be easy for any of these countries.

They had all had become stuck in the middle. Their advance toward democracy was clearly stalled, but they were not experiencing famine, ethnic cleansing, war, terrorism, or any of the other major issues which tend to get the attention of Washington policy makers, politicians, and even the media. Georgia, Ukraine, and Kyrgyzstan had also joined the ranks of countries that had become neither major economic partners nor competitors for the U.S.

Additionally, the governments of Georgia, Ukraine, and Kyrgyzstan were, in varying degrees, American allies and, even more important, cooperated in what was then the relatively new Global War on Terror. Even before the Rose Revolution, Georgia was among the most pro-American countries in the world, as its president was a beloved figure in the west welcoming U.S. marines into his country after the attacks of September 11, and even supported the U.S. by sending troops to Iraq in 2003. Kyrgyzstan became an increasingly important ally of the U.S. during this period, particularly as the Manas air force base was opened outside Bishkek at the end of 2001, only a few months after September 11. Although the Kuchma regime in Ukraine moved closer to Russia in its later years, Ukraine continued to cooperate with the U.S. on many security and other foreign policy matters.

In reality, there was no compelling reason for the U.S. to seek a change in government in any of these three countries. This had, of course, not been the case in Serbia in 2000 when an electoral component was part of a multipronged strategy to oust Slobodan Milosevic. Georgia, Ukraine, and Kyrgyzstan, however, were not Serbia and were not governed by leaders who were guilty of widespread human rights violations or who had brought their countries into conflict with the U.S. They were governed by weak but relatively benign regimes which, while not able to meet the needs of their people, were also not able to create real problems for the U.S. Accordingly, there were no immediate strategic reasons why the U.S. might have initiated, or even supported, regime change in Georgia, Ukraine, and Kyrgyzstan in 2003–2005.

There were, however, secondary issues that helped frame American policy during this period. The first was Russia. By 2003, Russia was reasserting itself in the region and increasingly competing with the U.S. for political influence. Supporting democratic breakthroughs was one way to weaken Russia's influence.

This issue resonates reasonably clearly in Ukraine where the election of 2004 pitted two candidates with very clear, and clashing, views toward Ukraine's global political orientation. However, the context regarding Russia is much less clear in Kyrgyzstan and Georgia. In both of these countries the pre-Color Revolutionary regimes generally, although not always, enjoyed good relations with the U.S. While these relationships never were, and never could have been, perfect, they certainly were not problematic enough that the U.S. would have sought to overthrow the Shevardnadze and Akaev governments.

U.S. Programs and Support

One of the challenges to determining the U.S. role in the Color Revolutions stems from the breadth of government agencies, American and domestic NGOs, private foundations, and other programs involved in each of these countries. These agencies rarely were able to speak with one voice and often disagreed with one another over key issues, such as the state of democracy or prospects for fair elections. Herein lies a particularly acute challenge because for many outside these organizations, it is hard to believe that NGOs funded by the U.S. government would aggressively and actively disagree with that government, or that various branches of the U.S. government might have strong disagreements regarding politics in a particular country.[4] This is a particularly difficult concept for people who are not familiar with how large and heterogeneous the world of U.S. government supported actors often is.

Nonetheless, the breadth, and frequent ambiguity, of U.S. involvement in all three of these countries makes it difficult to identify a unified voice or goal of the U.S. There certainly were people in all three of these countries who drew their salaries either directly or indirectly from U.S. taxpayers and who sought the overthrow of the Kuchma, Shevardnadze, and Akaev regimes, but that alone does not augur an American plot, because it must be weighed against the people, also drawing their salaries from the U.S. taxpayer, who did not want to see these governments overthrown. Clearly, if one looks carefully and with a sufficiently jaundiced eye, it is possible to find the conspiracy, but if one takes a broader view it is inevitable that the conspiracy is lost in the broader morass of U.S. policy.

At the time of the Color Revolutions, democracy assistance had been a component of U.S. policy in the post-Soviet region for roughly a decade. It remains a constant in much of the region. Understanding this is important because it weakens the argument that the U.S. was doing something unusual or special in Georgia, Ukraine, and Kyrgyzstan. Democracy assistance programs continue for years in many countries yielding far less dramatic results. These programs are, in the context of broader foreign policy projects, cheap and, often quite modest in their goals and methods. The notion that the mere presence of democracy assistance programs in a particular country is evidence of a U.S. attempt to change the regime cannot be taken seriously because these programs are in place all over the world in countries with governments that are supportive of the U.S.

While the existence of even extensive democracy assistance programs in a given country cannot be taken as evidence of any revolutionary American plans, these programs vary in size, scope, and approach. Not all democracy assistance portfolios are the same, so to understand the role of U.S. democracy assistance programs in the Color Revolutions, it is useful to look more closely at the details of the programs.

Much of what is classified as democracy assistance in countries like Georgia, Ukraine, and Kyrgyzstan in the years leading up to the Rose Revolution consists of programs seeking to strengthen local governance or help the national legislature function better. While these programs are valuable for a range of reasons, particularly for countries seeking to consolidate democratic gains, they are not the stuff from which revolutionary plots are hatched.

The more politically sensitive components of democracy assistance, which has drawn the attention of critics of U.S. policy from both within the region and in the west, are what might be called special election related projects. These include political party campaign workshops and support for domestic election monitors of the sort described in Chapter Three. These projects were supported in all three countries. The Committee of Voters of Ukraine (CVU), International Society for Fair Elections and Democracy (ISFED), and Coalition for Democracy and Civil Society (CDCS) were all helped enormously by the material and technical support provided by NDI, which for the most part was paid for with U.S. taxpayer dollars. Political party workshops, in practice, consist of a range of activities including training sessions on various aspects of political campaigns or party organization. Such workshops were done in all three countries. These programs are implemented regularly in many post-Soviet countries at election time. Funding of domestic election monitoring groups is done by USAID and NDI all over the region, often in countries where fraudulent elections do not lead to any major political changes. The same is true of political campaign trainings which are held in most countries and are open to a broad range of parties as elections approach.

These ordinary democracy assistance activities had been ongoing in the former Soviet Union for years, contributing to democratic consolidation in the Baltic States, while showing fewer unambiguous successes in the rest of the region. If this were the extent of U.S.-funded involvement in democracy related activities during the period immediately preceding the Color Revolutions, the notion that the U.S. was behind these events would not be taken seriously by anybody. However, in addition to these projects, there were other U.S. supported programs which were more contentious and political, although not quite revolutionary in nature.

These more political programs were different in each of the three countries and were supported by varying degrees within the U.S. democracy assistance community in each of the three cases. In Georgia, the other important democracy assistance programs which contributed to the Rose Revolution were efforts by NDI to nurture a coalition of the major opposition parties. This included facilitating numerous meetings between the leadership of the National Movement, Burjanadze Democrats, and New Rights, as well as between middle level and regional leaders of the three parties. Other higher profile parts of this program consisted of study tours for the leadership of the three parties to Poland and Serbia. While these efforts helped build some important relationships that contributed to the coordination between two of these parties after the election, it should be remembered that this program also failed to deliver any concrete results before the election since there was no coalition and only the faintest outline of coordination among these parties during the election itself. Other than that, while the battery of democracy assistance programs in Georgia during 2003 was substantial, that was more due to the openness the Georgian government felt toward the west than to any unusual election related projects.

Nonetheless, the nature of these political programs cannot be easily dismissed. By 2003, donor countries and democracy NGOs had grown accustomed to a degree of political access and involvement in the countries where they work that would never be tolerated in their own countries and, from the vantage point of the Kremlin or any other nondemocratic regime in the region, could easily be described as conspiratorial, or at the very least, an extremely high level of involvement. In the Georgian case, major opposition leaders, including Zurab Zhvania and Mikheil Saakashvili, traveled to

Poland and Serbia as part of programs supported by USAID, NED, and OSI, where they made contact and had valuable interactions with democracy activists in those two countries. The inter-party meetings that sought to help develop coalitions were not just facilitated by NDI, but were almost attended by NDI staff who prepared the agenda, helped broker deals, and advised all the parties involved. There were also efforts to strengthen the embryonic youth group Kmara by having study visits to Serbia to learn from Otpor and by bringing Otpor activists to Georgia to work with Kmara. Similar meetings and exchanges occurred in both Kyrgyzstan and Ukraine. Whether this constitutes a conspiracy, and the corollary of whether involvement of this kind is justified as part of an effort to help people seeking their freedom, are subjective questions. However, governments throughout the region on seeing this were not unreasonable in drawing attention to what they viewed as, at best, an inappropriate degree of American involvement.

In Kyrgyzstan, efforts to support coalition building among the Kyrgyz opposition, a far greater challenge given the dispersed and weak political party system as well as the single mandate electoral system, were not supported as actively by the U.S. government. Although in spring 2005, as the Kyrgyz elections approached, the memory of the Orange and Rose Revolutions was still very fresh, there was little additional support given to election processes in Kyrgyzstan to help facilitate another Color Revolution. With its far weaker ties to Europe, less developed civil society, largely unfree media, and government that seemed very attuned to the threat of a Color Revolution, Kyrgyzstan did not really garner much additional attention until after the election. There were, of course, a handful of democracy NGOs who believed the Color Revolution momentum was real and could spill over to Kyrgyzstan, but these organizations, notably NDI, were not provided sufficient program money to act on this belief in a serious way.

On the question of U.S.-supported activities in the election year, Ukraine looks different from either Georgia or Kyrgyzstan. While not nearly as pronounced as was the case in Serbia in 2000, the U.S. had a clear preference in the 2004 election in Ukraine and, moreover, following the Rose Revolution in Georgia, increased and broadened its election-related work in Ukraine. Because the presidential election of 2004 came on the heels of the Rose Revolution, as well as the stark nature of the choice between Yushchenko and Yanukovich, the Ukrainian election seemed an important and viable opportunity to explore the possibility of a similar breakthrough in Ukraine.

Special U.S. election-related programs in Ukraine included increased funding for CVU, which was not too different from the increased funding

ISFED had received in Georgia in 2003. While the need to nurture coalitions was not as great in Ukraine, where the emergence of Yushchenko as the candidate of the relatively unified opposition occurred early in the election cycle, more of an effort was made both to help Yushchenko win the election and to plan a post-election strategy.

According to McFaul (2007), organizations funded by the U.S. government such as Freedom House and the German Marshall Fund facilitated "significant contact" between the Ukrainian activist group Yellow Pora and "civic resistance activists from Slovakia, Serbia and Georgia." Additionally, "Freedom House organized and funded a summer camp for Ukrainian youth activists and invited trainers from the Serbian youth movement Otpor to attend" (78). These are just some of the ways the U.S. was involved in putting together the infrastructure for the Orange Revolution.

Obviously, any efforts to help Yushchenko win qualify as being involved in the process in a more serious way, but these also are different from crafting a revolutionary plot. It should also be kept in mind that U.S. assistance in this regard, primarily through workshops, trainings and consultations by NDI and IRI, was initially offered to all participants, but it was the Yushchenko candidacy that had both the capacity to take advantage of this offer and a political approach that relied more on winning, than, for example, buying votes. A workshop on campaign strategy is less useful to a party that plans to steal the election and intimidate voters anyway.

The United States and Europe were not the only, or even most significant, outside powers who sought to play a part in the 2004 election in Ukraine. Russia provided an enormous amount of formal and informal support to Yanukovich. So, if this election was a proxy fight between the U.S. and Russia, it was somewhat one-sided in favor of Russia. Estimates of how much financial support Russia provided to Yanukovich's campaign range from $5–10 million to $600 million, according to Russian political consultants.[5] Ryabov and Petrov argue that "an estimate of $50 million for the 'Russia project' is more probable," but make the more general, and important point that "Yanukovich did not lack funds and could afford any projects or proposals he wanted to pursue."[6] Yanukovich also benefitted by a pre-election campaign appearance in Ukraine by Russian president Vladimir Putin and by ample positive coverage of his campaign on Russian television.[7]

The post-election developments in Ukraine differed from those in Georgia and Kyrgyzstan because they were both larger and better planned. The demonstrations in Kyrgyzstan were scattered and disorganized. Those in Georgia were sufficiently small that they did not require a great deal of advance planning. The demonstrations on the Maidan in Kiev in November and December of 2004 were different: they were enormous and lasted for weeks.

Bringing hundreds of thousands of people to the center of the capital in the beginning of the Ukrainian winter and keeping them there for weeks cannot happen by accident. It requires the political work involved in mobilizing demonstrators, as well as the logistical work of making sure these people are kept warm, are fed, have access to toilets, and so on. Therefore, planning for the post-election demonstrations began in the summer of 2004 as Ukrainian activists attended camps and workshops where they acquired the skills necessary for such a large undertaking. The financial resources for these workshops came primarily from wealthy Ukrainians who were no longer supportive of the Kuchma-Yanukovich block. This included people like David Zhvania and Petro Poroshenko. While not the major funder of these activities, the U.S. did, through foreign and domestic NGOs, lend technical expertise in areas such as mobilizing people, planning demonstrations and logistics, and offering the usual support for domestic election monitoring. While NGO, rather than government involvement, and technical rather than political financial support, are important distinctions in Washington, it is not hard to see how these can be seen as distinctions without differences in Moscow and elsewhere.

This perception is exacerbated by the way the U.S., and George Soros, the other key American player, have sought to both claim a major role for themselves, while almost simultaneously minimizing that role. OSI is, of course, independent of the American government as it is a private foundation funded by Soros with no input or guidance from the U.S. government. In 2004, Soros commented "I'm delighted by what happened in Georgia and I take great pride in contributing to it."[8] Less than a year later, while still actively supporting the Rose Revolution and its leadership, Soros said "the role of the foundation and my personal [role] has been greatly exaggerated."[9] Comments like these send a confusing message making protestations that OSI played a relatively small role less than believable.

A special USAID publication, *Democracy Rising*, which sought to highlight USAID's support for democracy in the Color Revolutions and beyond, attempted both to take partial credit for these breakthroughs and downplay the U.S. role. "The colorful revolutions were created by citizens from Ukraine to Lebanon, with U.S. and other support." However, the same article also stated "The United States was the main supporter of democracy around the world. . . . The fallen rulers in some countries may blame 'outside interference' for their defeat. But U.S. and other democracy aid only serves as a source of ideas and inspiration." Making all these claims in the space of only six paragraphs is confusing; although not entirely illogical to Americans familiar with USAID and its programs, to others it seems like a clumsy and implausible attempt by the U.S. to have it both ways (USAID 2005: 2–3).

Another element of the U.S. role in the Ukrainian election is the advisory and consultative capacity diplomats, NGO leaders, and others filled in Ukraine. This is probably impossible to quantify, but nonetheless significant. The sharing of experience, provision of sound advice, convening power and strategic input which a skilled democracy operative can offer can have substantial value and is not particularly expensive. It does not cost an NGO or the U.S. government much to have an experienced person working for NDI, Freedom House, or IRI who can serve this role. Such people exist in the NGO community in most nondemocratic countries. One difference between Ukraine and Krygyzstan and Georgia is that the people who played that role in Ukraine received more support and encouragement from official U.S. channels.

Although they often received less encouragement from the U.S. government, the people working on democracy assistance programs in Georgia and Kyrgyzstan sought to offer similar advice to the key leaders of the Rose and Tulip Revolutions. In Georgia, where deep and longstanding relationships existed between the democracy assistance community and the political opposition, this advice fell on more receptive ears. In Kyrgyzstan where democracy programs had never gotten traction comparable to similar programs in Georgia, these voices were less effective.

Diplomatic Efforts

Democracy assistance projects were only one of the components of U.S. foreign policy relevant to the Color Revolutions. There was a diplomatic component to this as well. In all three countries, ambassadors, State Department officials, and others became involved, in various degrees in trying to facilitate greater democracy and better elections. Focusing on specific programs only provides a limited view of U.S. activities in a country like Ukraine. The broader diplomatic position of the U.S. as well as the informal relationships between the two countries is also important. Clearly the U.S. had a preference for free elections and did not want to see Yanukovich steal the presidential election. Neither the U.S. nor any of its European allies made any effort to conceal this preference. On the other hand, they did not do a great deal about it in a diplomatic sense. The views of the U.S. were clear, but it was equally apparent that Ukraine did not face global ostracism, trade sanctions, substantially reduced aid, or any other penalties if they did not have good elections. A fraudulent victory by Yanukovich would certainly have set back Ukraine's integration into European and Euro-Atlantic multilateral organizations, but because opposing this integration was part of Yanukovich's platform, it is likely that a legitimate victory would have had the same effect.

Nonetheless, as the Kuchma regime wound down and became more corrupt and less democratic during the first years of the new century, the U.S. became increasingly focused on the elections of 2002 for parliament and 2004 for the presidency. While the U.S. did not precisely see these as opportunities for regime change, these elections were viewed as central to the future of U.S.-Ukraine elections.

Testifying before Congress during the Orange Revolution, but before the redo of the runoff, U.S. ambassador to Ukraine John Herbst commented:

> The primary focus of United States-Ukrainian relations over the past year has been on the Presidential election. Over a period of many months, the United States and our European allies repeatedly advised Ukrainian authorities, both publicly and privately, that we were watching, watching very closely, and consider it a test of Ukraine's commitment to democracy.
>
> The United States-funded assistance to independent media, political party development, voter awareness and education, training for election officials and observers and more. Our election-related assistance to Ukraine was approximately $13.8 million. Of particular note, the United States funded what we believe was an unprecedented election observer effort. (Herbst (2004: 25)

The clichéd rhetoric about tests of commitments to democracy notwithstanding, this statement indicates the extent of American commitment to using the elections as an opportunity to make change. $13.8 million is more money than a government would spend if it just had a passing interest in election fairness in a given country, even in a big country like Ukraine.

During the time the Orange Revolution was moving forward, the U.S. redoubled its diplomatic efforts in Ukraine. In late November 2004, Senator Richard Lugar (R-Ind.), a leading foreign policy voice in the U.S. Senate, respected on both sides of the political aisle traveled to Kiev as a personal representative of President Bush to evaluate the developing situation. His finding that "It is now apparent that a concerted and forceful program of Election Day fraud and abuse was enacted with either the leadership or cooperation of governmental authorities," made it clear what the American position on the election was. Lugar also reminded the Ukrainian leadership and people of a letter Bush had written to Kuchma, stating that "you play a central role in ensuring that Ukraine's election is democratic and free of fraud and manipulation. A tarnished election, however, will lead us to review our relations with Ukraine." Lugar's message, and the support it had in Washington, was clear.[10]

In Georgia, the diplomatic messages were more mixed. Through spring, summer, and early fall 2003, civic and political leaders of the Georgian opposition traveled to the U.S. on several occasions to make their case to allies and supporters in various positions in the American government. These people, including, for example, future prime minister Zurab Zhvania, had developed strong relations in Washington, ironically under Shevardnadze's tutelage, which they drew on as they sought to influence American policy toward Georgia and the elections.

Additionally, numerous high level U.S. political figures, from both parties, including senator John McCain, former deputy secretary of state Strobe Talbott, former chair of the Joint Chiefs of Staff John Shalikashvili, and former secretary of state James Baker came to Tbilisi in late summer and fall 2003 to demonstrate to the Georgian government the import with which the U.S. viewed fair elections. Baker was, like Lugar, a special representative of President Bush, but Baker's visit came months before the election, and the recommendations he made were either ignored or manipulated by the government once he left Tbilisi.

Ambassador Richard Miles in Georgia was more cautious about the 2003 elections than Ambassador Herbst was in Ukraine. This was partially because the election in question was a parliamentary election that, even as the election approached and it became difficult to ignore the likelihood that there would be widespread fraud, was viewed as only a first step toward the transition to post-Shevardnadze Georgia. Most expected this to happen in 2005, the year of the presidential election in which Shevardnadze had already indicated he would not run. Thus, the desire for democracy needed to be balanced against the hope for stability during the remainder of Shevardnadze's term in office.

American diplomatic efforts did not play a similar role in the Tulip Revolution. There was considerably less pressure on the Akaev government to conduct fair elections in 2005 and little effort by senior U.S. officials outside Kyrgyzstan to become more involved in the election. Even after the events in Georgia and Ukraine, the U.S. maintained a substantially more cautious approach in Kyrgyzstan.

It is possible to describe fairly clearly the money, programs, and diplomatic efforts that the U.S. invested in democracy assistance in each of these countries, and relatively easy to dismiss the accusations that the Color Revolutions were American plots, but it is more difficult to accurately and realistically assess the real impact of these programs and the broader democracy assistance strategy. It is particularly difficult to do this without an unambiguous understanding of U.S. goals in the region with regard to democracy.

A commitment to strengthening democracy in the former Soviet Union is an important goal, but one that can take many forms and certainly does not automatically translate into a desire to change governments or ruling regimes. For most of the years preceding the Color Revolutions, U.S. democracy assistance actors worked comfortably with the governments of Georgia, Ukraine, and Kyrgyzstan, as well as with the governments of other semidemocratic regimes in the country. The short term goals such as more responsive legislatures, more empowered local governments and stronger advocacy organizations were all important, but not exactly revolutionary in nature.

The question of U.S. intentions is complicated; and varies from country to country. By 2003, just as working with these semidemocratic governments was no longer likely to yield much progress with regards to democracy, working for democracy increasingly meant thinking about changing governments. What precisely did it mean to support fair elections, strong and very anti-government NGOs, coalitions of opposition leaders, and independent media in the run-up to the any of these elections, if at least some did not think about changing governments?

Accordingly, something shifted in democracy assistance strategy in the months leading up to the Color Revolutions in these countries. These relatively harmless seeming programs continued but were complemented by a more aggressive approach. The programs that for years had helped to make parliament more open, NGOs more aggressive, and local governments more representative of the people's needs quietly contributed to the emergence of strong opposition blocks, effective civic activists, and ultimately the Color Revolutions. These contributions were underscored by a collection of special election year projects that were more expressly political in nature. While these factors and the subsequent Color Revolutions do not add up to conspiracies, it is equally certain that they do not simply make a happy coincidence. Just as it is reductive and overly simplistic to call the Color Revolutions conspiracies, it is equally reductive for the U.S. to say that these events were entirely homegrown. Neither the U.S. nor any organizations receiving funding by the U.S. have done this, but they have sought to have it both ways or balance claiming some credit with not being seen as too involved.

CHAPTER 5

Russia

The Color Revolutions also had a substantial impact on U.S.-Russia relations. Moscow viewed these events as U.S. meddling in the region and in some cases, notably with regard to Georgia, supporting governments that were considerably more confrontational with Russia than their predecessors had been. However, to fully understand the impact of the Color Revolutions on U.S.-Russia relations, it is necessary to take a closer look at political developments throughout the region during this period.

The roughly 20-month span during which the three post-Soviet Color Revolutions occurred was part of a decade long trend at the beginning of the twenty-first century during which Russia's position and influence changed dramatically. When the decade began, Russia's ability to project its power throughout the countries of the former Soviet Union was limited by the poverty and weakness of the Russian state. This changed substantially so that by the end of the decade, Russia had reemerged as a major regional, and to a substantial extent, global power as well.

The Color Revolutions increased tensions between Russia and the U.S., but in a somewhat asymmetric way. Many in Russia, including some in the government, viewed the Color Revolutions as part of a broad U.S. plan to encircle Russia with pro-western countries. Moreover, these countries, Georgia and Ukraine in particular, are viewed by Russia as part of their backyard. The term preferred by Russia is "near abroad." In addition, the Color Revolutions increased Russian concerns about U.S. democracy assistance not only in other post-Soviet countries such as Kazakhstan, Belarus, Azerbaijan, and Armenia, but in Russia itself. Accordingly, Russia and other countries in the region passed laws that led to harassment and increased surveillance of U.S.- and European-funded democracy organizations.

Post-Color Revolution governments, particularly in Ukraine and Georgia, contributed to Russian fears by showing themselves clearly pro-U.S. in orientation. This was more acute in Georgia, where Saakashvili seemed to have a unique ability to irritate Russian president and later prime minister Vladimir Putin, both politically and personally. Since the Rose Revolution, relations between the countries have been very tense, erupting into open warfare in summer 2008.

Thus, Russia viewed the Color Revolutions as a series of U.S.-supported events that created problems on its southern, western, and, to a lesser extent, eastern borders, put Russia in danger of being encircled by pro-western countries, and expanded the U.S. reach to Central Asia, the Caucasus, and the Slavic heartland. For the U.S., the Color Revolutions were a series of important but largely overlooked foreign policy triumphs during a difficult period. During these years, the U.S. was preoccupied with the war in Iraq (which began a few months before the Rose Revolution), the war in Afghanistan, and other terror-related concerns. Events in faraway corners of the former Soviet Union barely received any attention in the U.S. media and were viewed as, at most, second tier concerns by the Bush administration and most American pundits and opinion makers.

Bulgarian scholar Ivan Krastev (2005) has described the Orange Revolution, in particular, as being like September 11 for Russia. By this Krastev means that it was a major and unexpected development that forced Russia to reassess its position in the world and was viewed as a threat by many in Russia. Krastev's analysis encapsulates the difference in how the U.S. and Russia viewed the Orange Revolution. For the U.S. not only were the Color Revolutions not even remotely comparable as paradigm changing historic events to the attacks of September 11, but it is difficult even to understand why these events had such an impact on Russia.

From the time of the Rose Revolution to the end of the Bush administration, relations between the U.S. and Russia grew significantly worse. Some of the issues central to the relations between the two countries arose directly out of the Rose Revolution. These include Georgia's renewed and ultimately unsuccessful efforts to assert sovereignty over South Ossetia and Abkhazia, but there were other sources of tension as well. The prospect of a strong independent Georgia is still not something with which Russia is entirely comfortable. The struggle for the future of Ukraine, which manifested itself in the alternation between the orange and blue forces in the years immediately following the Orange Revolution, is a direct result of the Color Revolutions. Increased concern over U.S. and European democracy assistance elsewhere in the region can also be traced back to these revolutions.

There are, however, other aspects to the U.S.-Russia relationship which have become important in recent years and on which the Color Revolutions have only peripheral bearing. These include missile defense, Russia's involvement in Iran's nuclear ambitions, access to transit routes and airspace for the war in Afghanistan, NATO expansion, cooperation on security issues, and energy. While none of these are caused by the Color Revolutions, U.S. support for these movements has had an impact on the U.S.-Russia relationship and made it more difficult to cooperate on these bigger picture challenges.

The U.S.-Russia relationship is broadly asymmetrical, and the Color Revolutions are only one of the ways this can be seen. This asymmetry is undergirded by a widespread Russian perception that the U.S. does not respect their new position as a global power and regional superpower. U.S. support for democracy and NATO membership on Russia's borders as well as ongoing desire to remain involved in Russia's domestic politics are only some of the causes of this perception. An additional cause is the reality that Russian policy makers are significantly more concerned about the U.S. than U.S. policy makers are about Russia. For the U.S., Russia is, for better or worse, a second tier issue. In Russia, the Color Revolutions have contributed to perceptions of U.S. interference.

In evaluating the overall impact of the Color Revolutions, the changing nature of the Russian-U.S. relationship must be taken into consideration, but it should be understood clearly. The Color Revolutions exacerbated a tension and asymmetry that were already there. While it is difficult to argue that if events in Ukraine, Georgia, and Kyrgyzstan had gone differently, then relations between the U.S. and Russia would be smooth, it is also clear that the Color Revolutions made the situation worse. However, this must be weighed against the potential value of allies like Georgia, and to a greater extent, Ukraine, as a way to balance a newly powerful, potentially aggressive Russia. All the same, Yanukovich's election in 2010 makes it clear that Ukraine is unlikely to move its foreign policy orientation decisively away from Russia in the near future.

The Color Revolutions, regardless of their origins or even their initial goals, have undermined Russia's ability to influence its "near abroad." Although all three countries are part of Russia's "near abroad," Russia has different interests in each of them. Its interest in Georgia, for example, not unlike the U.S. interest, is real, but seemingly out of proportion to a country so small, resource poor, and economically weak. Nonetheless, Russian governments have made it clear that they do not want an independent, NATO oriented Georgia on their southern border. Moreover, Georgia's efforts to restore its territorial integrity, and western support for those efforts, created further concern in Russia, particularly before the war of August 2008 (Makhovsky 2010). An important element of Russia's interest in Georgia can be described as symbolic or even emotional rather than purely strategic. Russia still views Georgia as home to the best beaches, wine, and food in the former empire. It had been an important playground for the Russian elite going back to Tsarist times. To lose all that to the west would be more symbolic than an actual blow to the Russian elites, who can now go anywhere they want for a beach vacation, good wine, or a good meal. Ukraine is of concrete, military, political, and economic importance as well. In addition to being a country with strong linguistic and cultural similarities to Russia and home to a sizeable Russian population, Ukraine is an agricultural, economic, industrial, and military power. Its size and economic strength make it much more critical to the balance of power between Russia and the west than, for example, Georgia.

With regard to Russia, the Orange Revolution was less decisive than the Rose Revolution. The Rose Revolution brought to power a regime that during its first few months demonstrated a strong pro-west orientation and opposition to Russia. After initially seeking and failing to improve relations with Russia, Saakashvili's government has consistently opposed Russia on issues ranging from major to trivial. The conflicts in Abkhazia and South Ossetia have helped keep this tension strong, but they are not the only sources of the tension.

While Shevardnadze's regime cannot be fairly described as having been pro-Russian, that government was much more positively oriented toward Georgia's northern neighbor than the current Georgian government has been. The Rose Revolution meant a change in Tbilisi from a weak, pliable government not overtly hostile to Russia to a stronger, more western leaning, and more overtly anti-Russian government. Moreover, unlike in Ukraine, the new government seemed to enjoy broad support, even in its foreign policy orientation. This remained true for at least the first few years after the Rose Revolution.

The Orange Revolution signified a more ambiguous change for Ukraine. Even president Yushchenko, who had beaten Russia-backed Yanukovich in the contested election of late 2004, did not take as strong a line toward Russia as Saakashvili did. Yushchenko was more cautious in making overtures to the west and handling his country's relationship with Russia. Yushchenko was also confronted with political realities about which the Rose Revolution government did not need to be concerned. While the latter swept out a wildly unpopular government with no broad support among the electorate, the Orange Revolution was built on a far more closely contested election, with the losing side remaining reasonably popular and very relevant to the politics of Ukraine. Maintaining a balance between Russia and the west was an essential part of maintaining power in the years immediately following. Yanukovich's election in 2010 demonstrated that much of the change regarding orientation toward the west, which Yushchenko had initiated, was only temporary, and that any Ukrainian president must pursue a policy of balancing Russia and the west.

The relative impact of the Tulip Revolution on Russian and American influence in Kyrgyzstan was more complex than either of the others. The post-2005 government, while still permitting the U.S. air force base at Manas, demonstrated none of the pro-western zeal of the Yushchenko or Saakashvili regime. While Kyrgyzstan certainly remained a place where Russia and the U.S. competed for influence, the Bakiev regime was not committed to a pro-western rhetoric and position.

Morever, Bakiev, Kulov, and most other Tulip Revolution leaders were less well known in western circles than either Saakashvili and Zhvania or Yushchenko and Timoschenko. Kulov had spent much of the time leading up to the Tulip Revolution in jail; neither he nor Bakiev had ever built relationships in the west even remotely comparable to those of the leaders of the Rose and Orange Revolutions. Additionally, Bakiev and Kulov were older and more Soviet style politicians. They were born in 1949 and 1948 respectively, so were well into adulthood when the Soviet Union collapsed. Saakashvili, Zhvania, and Timoschenko, by contrast, were born in the 1960s, while Yushchenko was born in 1955.

Nonetheless, immediately after Akaev resigned, the U.S. moved quickly to embrace the new Kyrgyz leadership and to celebrate the Tulip Revolution as yet another democratic breakthrough in the former Soviet Union. The U.S. increased assistance to Kyrgyzstan and quickly supported the new government. In the years between 9/11 and the Tulip Revolution, Kyrgyzstan had evolved into an important support country for U.S. efforts in Afghanistan. For this reason, it was critical to maintain strong ties with the new government.

The shift in Kyrgyzstan from the Akaev to Bakiev governments ultimately was far less significant to Russia. Kyrgyzstan for reasons of demographics, geography, and history had a much closer relationship with Russia than Georgia had, and was not strongly divided regarding the west and Russia, as Ukraine was and remains. Nonetheless, the Tulip Revolution itself, particularly because it came so quickly on the heels of the other Color Revolutions, clearly caused very real consternation in Moscow.

It was, however, Russia that eventually tired of Bakiev first and helped facilitate his overthrow in spring 2010 (Makhovsky 2010). The view of the new Kyrgyz regime toward Russia remains somewhat unclear. At the time it occurred, the Tulip Revolution had been of particular concern for Moscow because it occurred in a post-Soviet country that, by any measure, should have been completely remote for the United States. Kyrgyzstan does not share a border with any NATO country. Unlike Georgia and Ukraine, its path to modernity, and indeed nationhood, was constructed by Russia and later the Soviet Union. Central Asian countries like Kyrgyzstan remain distant physically, politically, and even psychologically from the U.S. The notion that the U.S. felt emboldened to foment revolution in such a place, and this was precisely how the Tulip Revolution was construed in Moscow, was perceived as evidence that the U.S. knew no limits and recognized no boundaries in its exercise of power.

As was the case in Georgia, increased U.S. assistance following the Tulip Revolution was also generally accompanied by willingness to view Kyrgystan's path to democracy more generously than was appropriate. Kyrgyzstan, however, differed from Georgia in several key ways that Russia was able to use to its advantage. First, there is a not insignificant ethnic Russian minority in Kyrgyzstan, 12.5 percent in 1999 but believed to be closer to 9 percent today, who valued a close relationship between Kyrgyzstan and Russia. Second, many Kyrgyz viewed, Russia, and even the Soviet Union, as at least partly a positive force in their country's development. It is very difficult, for example, to imagine the Kyrgyz government having a museum in the middle of the capital dedicated to the "Soviet Occupation" like the one in Tbilisi that opened in 2006. Third, Kyrgyzstan, while important to the U.S. primarily because of the Manas base, had little value or import to Europe and no aspirations or remote chance of EU or NATO membership.

Accordingly, after the Tulip Revolution, Russia gradually began to reassert its influence over Kyrgyzstan through the same combination of subsidized energy, financial assistance, and occasional threat that Russia used in other parts of the former Soviet Union. The largest single piece of evidence of Russian usurpation of American influence after the Tulip Revolution, of course, occurred in early 2009, when the government of Kyrgyzstan simply broke its agreement to let the U.S. use the base because Russia offered more money than did the U.S. This decision set off a bidding war for the rights to Manas between Russia and the U.S. which ultimately the U.S. won.

The U.S. Russia Relationship Since the Color Revolutions

The Color Revolutions had a major impact on the bilateral relations of Georgia, Ukraine, and Kyrgyzstan with both Russia and the U.S., but also on U.S.-Russia relations more broadly. They played a pivotal role in the evolution of relations from the immediate post-Cold War period to the more complex period in which we now find ourselves. Other U.S. policies exacerbated this tension. For example, the decision to all but ignore Russian views on a range of issues such as the independence of Kosovo and the ongoing expansion of NATO also contributed to the deterioration of the relationship.

The Color Revolutions, however, played a unique role in the development of U.S.-Russia relations during the first decade of the twenty-first century largely because they were understood so differently in the U.S. and Russia. In the U.S., and initially in Europe as well, they were viewed as unequivocal advances for democracy. The Bush administration hailed them as major victories for the new wave of democratic transitions and evidence that democracy was still advancing globally. In Russia, the events were viewed more simply, in terms of balances of power between the U.S. and Russia. Russia did not view the Color Revolutions as democratic; more important, it did not view the question of democratization as relevant to what was really significant. The Color Revolutions were viewed as transfers of influence and power from Russia to the U.S. Predictably, following this perceived defeat, Russia sought to undermine or roll back the Color Revolutions. The failure of the Saakashvili and Yushchenko governments was a foreign policy goal for Russia, just as their success was an American goal. The Kyrgyz case was somewhat different, as the Tulip Revolution was a briefer and more ambiguous advance for American influence in the region.

Georgia, in particular, during these years became something of a battleground between Russia and the U.S. The U.S. sought to help Saakashvili's Georgia by providing ample foreign assistance, adapting Tbilisi's positions on issues regarding frozen conflicts in South Ossetia and Abkhazia (see Cooley and Mitchell 2008), highlighting Georgia as a successful democratic transition, and advocating Georgia's membership in NATO. Russia, not surprisingly, played the opposite role. It sought to ensure the failure of Saakashvili's Georgia by boycotting Georgian exports such as wine and mineral water, raising tensions in South Ossetia and Abkhazia, providing resources to some Georgian opposition political figures, and allegedly running numerous espionage rings inside Georgia. Russia's nefarious behavior, while not altogether successful, created additional challenges for a government facing a difficult task from the beginning. Intense U.S. support for the Georgian government, while creating several problems for Georgia and the U.S., at least offered a balance to extensive Russian interference in Georgia.

Russia had a similar interest in seeing the Yushchenko regime and the Orange Revolution fail. Russia continued to work closely with the Party of the Regions; supported opposition to Ukraine's NATO aspirations; mobilized ethnic Russians in Ukraine, particularly the Crimea, to agitate for greater independence; used Russian media, widely watched in eastern Ukraine, to consistently attack the president; and, of course, used energy politics to, at times, damage Ukraine.

The U.S., however, did not act as a counterweight to Russian influence in Ukraine in the way it did in Georgia. For example, during elections Russian media advocated on behalf of Yanukovich and the Party of the Regions. Even after the Orange Revolution, Russian political consultants, or political technologists in the vernacular of the region, continued to advise and assist these political forces.[1] However, the U.S. did not play a similar role in supporting Timoschenko and Yushchenko in their party's campaigns. In this case, there was no balance from the west to the Russian efforts to sway political outcomes. There are, of course, no guarantees that more western political support for the Orange forces would have led to different outcomes in Ukraine, but it is clear that Yanukovich benefited from Russian involvement.

Russia was also better positioned to exert influence over both energy and NATO politics in Ukraine. Russia's ability to cut off energy and to renegotiate contracts for transporting energy through Ukraine meant that Yushchenko always had to consider Russia's views. The U.S. had no comparable tools at its disposal to support Ukraine in these struggles with Russia. It could not turn the energy supplies back on or change the geographical realities of supplies and pipelines. Similarly, while Russia could disrupt Ukraine's NATO aspirations by mobilizing opposition to NATO, supporting Crimean independence, or other means, it became clear by mid-2008 that the U.S. had few ways to counter these efforts. Through a combination of political realities and political misperceptions, most notably the tendency to see post-Orange Revolution Ukraine as a functioning two-party system, U.S. influence was not as strong as it could have been. This would not, on its face, have been a serious problem had Russian influence been weaker. However, Russian influence was strong and contributed to undermining the Orange Revolution.

Countering Russian influence in Ukraine would have required a higher level of commitment than the U.S. gave, including more assistance to ensure the success of the new government, political assistance to balance out that given by Russia to those seeking to undermine the advances of the Orange Revolution, and support to fledgling civil and political organizations seeking to weaken the one-party control exercised by the Party of the Regions in much of eastern Ukraine. This would obviously have further complicated the relationship between Russia and the U.S., but by the time the Color Revolutions had occurred, that relationship had begun to deteriorate anyway.

It is a simplification, but not an extreme one, to say that had the U.S. reversed parts of its policies, pursuing depersonalized and detached support in Georgia, while seeking to build stronger ties and provide political support to the leadership in Ukraine, the outcome would have been better in both countries. Nonetheless, the basic need to counter Russian influence and to recognize that the Color Revolutions did not signify an enduring victory for democracy applied in both countries.

NATO

After the Rose and Orange Revolutions, Georgia and Ukraine inched closer to their goal of membership in NATO. The bids of both countries were heartily endorsed by the U.S., but met with more mixed enthusiasm among European members of NATO. In Georgia, NATO membership was part of the battery of aspirations that would mean full integration into Europe. Georgia had been a member of the Council of Europe since 1999 and of the Organization for Security and Cooperation in Europe (OSCE) since 1992, but membership in NATO, and ultimately the EU, were far more ambitious goals that few thought were plausible during Shevardnadze's presidency. In the heady days immediately following the Rose Revolution, when anything seemed possible in Georgia, these goals suddenly seemed more realistic.

Ukraine had also been a member of the Council of Europe since 1995, and of the OSCE since 1992. However, due to the same political and geographical divisions central to most recent elections in Ukraine, views on NATO and the EU have always been more polarized than in Georgia. Nonetheless, the government led by Yushchenko and Timoschenko was committed, at least initially, to moving Ukraine in that direction.

At the time of the collapse of the Soviet Union the U.S. administration of George H. W. Bush agreed that NATO would not expand into the former Communist bloc, but by the time of the Rose Revolution in 2003 this promise had been broken because the Czech Republic, Hungary, and Poland had been admitted into NATO in 1999. Seven other countries—Bulgaria, Romania, Slovakia, Slovenia, Estonia, Latvia, and Lithuania—were admitted in March 2004, shortly after the Rose Revolution. Significantly, the 2004 NATO expansion brought three former Soviet Republics into NATO for the first time.

Russia, of course, was deeply opposed to either of these countries joining NATO. Russia's opposition lay in its perception that NATO, which had historically been an anti-Soviet alliance, was rapidly transforming into an anti-Russia alliance by peeling away Russia's traditional buffer states and slowly approaching Russia itself. This perception, however, drew as much on politically motivated, and created, fears, as on concrete strategic concerns. NATO membership for countries, like Slovenia or Estonia or even potentially Georgia, which were quite small with very weak militaries in no way threatened Russia. Moreover, NATO itself has very little independent power and, like most multilateral organizations, depends on its members for troops and support on a case by case basis. Nonetheless, this perception certainly informed Russian strategy.

For most of the new NATO members, joining the alliance has brought significant security guarantees, but it was a political process as well. Clear civilian control over the military, relatively strong democratic processes and institutions, and transparency in government were all prerequisites for NATO membership. Thus, NATO also held a symbolic value for the new members as evidence that they were becoming increasingly European—evidence borne out as all ten new members became members of the EU as well in 2004 or 2007.

While NATO may not have been a serious threat to Russia, its expansion was a symbol of Russia's global decline. Continuing this expansion into Ukraine, deep in the Slavic heartland, or Georgia, which if it ever becomes a NATO member would be the easternmost country in NATO, would only make this symbolism more acute. As Russia began to return as a regional power, stopping further NATO expansion became a top Russian priority.

While democratic development has been rocky in both countries, Ukraine moved ahead of Georgia in this regard by roughly 2007, making it a relatively stronger candidate for NATO membership. Membership for both countries was a strong policy goal of the Bush administration, but it was clear by the end of the administration that, outside the U.S., support for either of these countries joining NATO was very weak. The Obama administration has consistently expressed strong rhetorical support, particularly for Georgia becoming a member of NATO, but has done little and accomplished less in pursuit of this goal.[2]

One of the odd residues of Bush era NATO membership politics is the decision of the NATO summit in Bucharest in early 2008 to hold back a Membership Action Plan (MAP) from both Georgia and Ukraine while stating that membership for both was certain to happen at a later date. The MAP that usually precedes membership lays out benchmarks on a range of issues the receiving country must meet to move forward on its NATO bid. It is not, however, a guarantee of NATO membership. By eschewing this approach, which some felt would have brought Georgia and Ukraine closer to NATO, in favor of a vague guarantee, NATO managed to anger Russia without creating an incentive structure for further reform in Georgia and Ukraine.

Although discussions around NATO expansion often lump the potential candidacies of Georgia and Ukraine together, the two countries, and their candidacies, are quite different. The difference in public opinion regarding NATO is only one area where the two countries need to be distinguished. Gallup polls between April and August 2009 showed that 17 percent of Ukrainians associated NATO membership with representing protection for their country, while fully 40 percent saw it as a threat. In Georgia, 56 percent saw it as representing protection and only 10 percent as a threat (Ray and Esipova 2010).

Were Ukraine to become a member of NATO it would play a very different role in the alliance than would Georgia. Ukraine would contribute a great deal to NATO, as it would be one of the larger countries in the alliance with one of the strongest militaries, and could conceivably play a major role in NATO projects around the world.[3] Additionally, although membership would potentially create political divisions in the country, at the current time, Ukraine has no unresolved territorial disputes into which NATO would be quickly pulled should Ukraine become a member. Moreover, fear of Russia is not widespread in Ukraine: although Russia clashed continuously with the Yushchenko-led Ukrainian government after the Orange Revolution, these clashes were been restricted to the political and economic realms. The election of Yanukovich has, of course, ameliorated some of this Ukraine-Russia tension.

Nonetheless, NATO membership for Ukraine, if it ever were to happen, would raise some major concerns regarding the relationship between NATO and Russia including the questions of the Crimea and the Russian Black Sea Fleet. The Crimean peninsula in southern Ukraine is the region of Ukraine where the population are the most sympathetic to Russia. During the Soviet period, the Crimea was transferred from the Russian to the Ukrainian Soviet in 1954, near the beginning of Khrushchev's rule. The Crimea is also important because it has a large Russian population with little interest in joining NATO, and little interest, for that matter, in being part of Ukraine. This makes it a potential flashpoint for Russian efforts to destabilize Ukraine. Tensions between Ukraine and ethnic Russians living in Crimea could conceivably lead to Russian intervention in Ukraine. Accordingly, it is certainly possible that Russia will seek, or create, this tension so it can create more problems for Ukraine.

The situation in Georgia is quite different. Although membership in NATO is a more broadly held political goal for Georgia, should Georgia join NATO, it would play a different role from Ukraine. First, because of its relative size and poverty, Georgia would not be able to contribute significantly to NATO security projects.[4] Moreover, because of the disputes over South Ossetia and Abkhazia as well as the much stronger threat by Russia, NATO membership for Georgia would bring the alliance closer to conflict with Russia. It is not without irony that the major reason Georgia so desperately wants, and to some extent needs, NATO membership, will continue to be a major reason some NATO members will want to keep it out.

The Georgia-Russia War

The war between Russia and Georgia in August 2008 was ostensibly about Georgian territorial integrity and the futures of South Ossetia and Abkhazia, but it was much broader in scope and was at least equally concerned with Russia's more general views toward Georgia. It also had strong roots in political developments in Georgia since the Rose Revolution. From the time he became president in January 2004, Saakashvili's goals and style placed him almost on a collision course with Russia, and Vladimir Putin.

The war itself has been studied in some detail in a number of places, so it will not be addressed thoroughly here other than in relationship to the Rose Revolution and Color Revolutions more broadly.[5] The Rose Revolution itself did not put Georgia and Russia on an inexorable course toward conflict, although it did probably raise the likelihood of this occurring. However, the Saakashvili presidency and the nature of the U.S. support for Saakashvili after the Rose Revolution substantially increased the likelihood of conflict.

The Rose Revolution was a source of tension between the U.S. and Russia from its beginning because of the perception in Russia that the U.S. was behind it, but also because it reoriented Russian relations with Georgia. Saakashvili's agenda was spearheaded by an effort to build and strengthen the Georgian state, reestablish Georgia's territorial integrity, and bring South Ossetia, Abkhazia, and Ajara back into Georgia. Pursuing these goals made Russian rancor unavoidable. A strong state meant Georgia would begin to more forcibly chart its own foreign policy course, which meant closer ties to the west and less dependency on Russia. Efforts to accomplish this began with the return of Ajara to Tbilisi control in mid-2004 and the closing of Russian military bases shortly thereafter. Additionally, a brief unsuccessful incursion by Tbilisi into South Ossetia in mid-2004 solidified anti-Saakashvili sentiment among non-Georgians in South Ossetia.

Had Georgia pursued these goals in a geopolitical vacuum, it is possible that the conflict could have been avoided. Of course, this pursuit occurred not in a vacuum but in a geopolitical context, specifically strong, loud U.S. support for Georgia. Accordingly, for many the U.S. was seen as behind Georgia's actions. This was not a radical conclusion at which to arrive given the level of political and financial support the U.S. provided Georgia, a country increasingly becoming a U.S. client, rather than an ally, in the South Caucasus.[6]

The immediate cause of the war was the Georgian response to a Russian buildup of troops in South Ossetia and Abkhazia. Georgia's swift military action on August 7 was a long-shot effort to win back control of South Ossetia and push Russian troops out.[7] Russia's response was predictable and devastating: the Georgian military was badly defeated. The promise of restoring Georgia's territorial integrity had been a core component of the Saakashvili government's state building agenda since coming to power in 2004. Although succeeding in restoring Georgian sovereignty over the regions of South Ossetia and Abkhazia promised to be an extremely difficult task, it remained a publicly articulated goal of the government, which often understated the difficulty involved.

In the twelve months preceding the conflict between Russia and Georgia, tumultuous political events in Georgia pushed the government closer to conflict for at least two reasons. First, as the adrenaline of the Rose Revolution finally wore off beginning in 2007, it was increasingly clear that economic conditions in Georgia remained very difficult. The reforms undertaken by the Georgian government succeeded in improving the investment climate, and even in bringing in more foreign investment, but had little effect on many ordinary Georgians for whom unemployment and underemployment remained high. This basic economic problem was exacerbated by a Georgia government that, perhaps foolishly or over-optimistically, continually kept expectations high, inevitably leading to disappointment as economic troubles persisted.

The need to divert attention from lingering economic problems was buoyed by the stagnancy, and then reversal, of the democratic achievements of the Rose Revolution. This reversal began in earnest with the crackdown on peaceful demonstrators in November 2007, which further polarized the Tbilisi elite and did little to increase government popularity.

Saakashvili's government seemed to understand the need to focus the population on issues other than democracy and the economy. During the presidential campaign that followed Saakashvili's unexpected, and temporary, resignation after the crackdown, Saakashvili frequently touched on Abkhazia and South Ossetia as key campaign themes. These were obviously issues which helped the government more than talking about the economy or democracy in early 2008 in Georgia.

At a campaign event in December 2007, a few weeks before he was re-elected, Saakashvili claimed that "The [secessionist] regime in Tskhinvali is like a loose tooth ready for removal and I am sure—if the January 5 [presidential elections] are held normally—this is a matter of, if not weeks, then at the very most, months. I am absolutely sure of this. I have precise information to prove it" (Civil.ge 2007). This was good campaign rhetoric for the once and future Georgian president, but it boxed him into a position that was ultimately disastrous.

Although the Georgian military was resoundingly defeated by Russia, even in defeat, the government remained popular with the Georgian people. This rally around the Georgian flag lasted a few months, and alleviated domestic pressure on Saakashvili's government for a short time.[8]

The longer-term impact of the war on Georgia was considerably less favorable for the country or the government. South Ossetia and Abkhazia slipped farther and, in the short term probably irrevocably, from Tbilisi's grip. President Saakashvili, while still maintaining strong ties with the U.S., weakened his and his country's position in Europe through his unforgiving rhetoric and occasionally seemingly erratic behavior. Saakashvili no longer enjoys the access to Europe he once did. It was striking, and illustrative, that he was not even invited to the Munich Security Conference in February 2010. Not having an invitation did not prevent the Georgian president from attending, but he was not given a platform from which to address the audience. This is typical of the treatment the Georgian president has received in Georgia since the war.

The War, Color Revolutions, and Relations Between Russia and the U.S.

While the war between Russia and Georgia had broad consequences and, initially, a significant effect on U.S.-Russia relations, it brought to light the tensions in the U.S.-Russia relationship which had been lurking, and even increasing, since the first of the Color Revolutions in Georgia in 2003. By the last months of the Bush administration, tensions between the U.S. and Russia were higher than any time during since the collapse of the Soviet Union. These tensions peaked during August 2008 and were even greater than they might have been because Republican presidential candidate John McCain sought to demonstrate his toughness, and thus stronger qualifications to be Commander in Chief, through posturing and bluster with regard to Russia when hostilities erupted between that country and Georgia, most notably through his comment on August 12, 2008, that "Today, we are all Georgians."

To judge from this period, it is possible to presume that relations between Russia and the U.S. were consistently tense, or even hostile, during the Bush administration. However, this would be an oversimplification of the relationship between the two countries during the first decade of the twenty-first century. While relations between them were rarely good during this period, there were periods of cooperation, notably immediately following the terrorist attacks on the U.S. on September 11, 2001. More significantly, during these years it seemed as if the U.S. only gradually became aware of Russian strength and interests in the region.

The Bush administration approached Russia similarly to how the Clinton administration had, even though Russia in 2002–2008 was very different from the country it had been in the 1990s. The Georgia war changed that quickly. The anger in the U.S. and the immediate, if somewhat strange, speculation about a new Cold War that began after the war started can partly be explained by the acceleration of America's learning curve regarding Russia. While few serious people had any misconceptions about Putin as a benign or constructive force internationally, not many were aware of the measures to which Putin's and Medvedev's Russia would go to counter American influence in the region. By mid-August 2008, this was a mistake the U.S. could no longer make.

Accordingly, U.S. rhetoric toward Russia changed very quickly once the war in Georgia started. Before the war, the U.S. had charted a course that could have been described generously as nuanced and less generously as confused. While pursuing policies that pushed back against Russian interests in the former Soviet Union, the U.S. also seemed relatively unaware of the reaction this would engender in Moscow. Taking too much credit for the Color Revolutions may be the most obvious example of this, but it is far from the only one. NATO expansion into the Baltics, missile defense in Eastern Europe, and, far from least important, unilateral recognition of Kosovar independence are other critical examples of U.S. policies that inevitably increased tensions with Russia.

Paradoxically, the U.S. continued to speak about Russia as a potential partner in other areas in spite of the mounting evidence to the contrary, not least the increasingly authoritarian direction in which Putin's Russia was heading. It is possible that the U.S. actually believed Russia could be a useful partner, but it is equally likely that this notion was preserved in the hopes that somehow it could eventually become so. In any case, all that changed when war between Russia and Georgia broke out in summer 2008.

The unspoken but very real struggle between Russia and the U.S. that had come to the surface with the Color Revolutions was taken to a new level, no longer unspoken, after the Russia-Georgia war. Questions of how to limit growing Russian ambition in its near abroad, the danger Russia represented to new American allies from Latvia to Georgia, in short, a recognition that all was far from well with the twenty-first-century Moscow-Washington relationship, did not start with the Russia-Georgia war, but since that war they have been much harder to ignore.

Did Russia Win?

The Color Revolutions were all initially viewed, particularly in the United States, as being about democracy. They were neither democratic breakthroughs nor full-fledged democratic revolutions, but the prism through which they were understood remained that of democratic transition and therefore part of the ongoing narrative of democratic evolution in the former Soviet Union.

Most comparative studies of the Color Revolutions written in the years immediately following these events have been organized around the theme of democracy.[9] The war between Georgia and Russia presents further evidence that democracy was only one of several themes through which it is possible to understand the Color Revolutions. They were at least as much about reorienting U.S.-Russia power dynamics in the former Soviet Union as about democracy. The story of the Color Revolutions was initially one about democracy with the U.S. as the winning side, but may end up being about U.S.-Russia relations with the U.S. on the losing side.

Initially all three Color Revolutions appeared to shift influence in the region even more firmly into the hands of the U.S., but in all three countries that began to change. As the democratic promise of the Tulip Revolution quickly fizzled in Kyrgyzstan, the government began to look elsewhere for both support and models of governance. Russia was an easy and obvious choice. Relations between the two regimes became closer as Russia provided assistance, trade, and discounted natural resources. Within a few years, Russian advisors were working closely with Bakiev's government, helping the Kyrgyz leader ensure that his regime would stay in place without having to be concerned with elections and democracy.

The decision of the Kyrgyz parliament in early 2009 to cancel the existing agreement regarding Manas between Kyrgyzstan and the U.S. was at first evidence of Russia's increased influence in Kyrgyzstan. The reversal of this decision demonstrated that the U.S. was still relevant for the Bakiev regime, but also forced the U.S. into more strongly backing the increasingly authoritarian regime. It reflected very poorly on the U.S. when the Bakiev regime was ousted in 2010 with Russia, not the U.S., having drawn attention to the authoritarian nature of Bakiev's regime.

Even before the 2010 Ukrainian election, a case for increased Russian influence in Georgia and Ukraine since the Color Revolutions could be made for both countries. One of the issues making this assertion difficult to demonstrate is that presidents Saakashvili and Yushchenko spent, and in the case of Saakashvili continue to spend, much of their time in office consistently stating and restating their goal of orienting their country toward the West and the U.S. The issue, however, is not the intentions of the post-Color Revolution governments, but the outcomes and results. While at least the publicly stated intentions have been unambiguous for both countries (though even this changed in Ukraine after Yanukovich was elected president), the same cannot be said about developments in the years since the Color Revolution.

In Ukraine, the Orange Revolution was, of course, far from a final or total defeat for Yanukovich's pro-Russian Party of the Regions. The party was quickly able to regroup in time to become a competitive force in the 2006 parliamentary election, where it won a plurality of votes and, with 186 seats, became the largest single party in the Ukrainian parliament. Yanukovich also served as prime minister twice and remained a major figure in Ukrainian politics. Yanukovich has sought to bring Russia and Ukraine closer together and to further strengthen business ties between the two countries. His election to the presidency in 2010, of course, made these ties even closer.

Yanukovich was not the only vehicle through which Russia has gained influence in Ukraine in recent years. One of the most glaring demonstrations of how Russia was able to get what it wants in Ukraine, even during Yushchenko's presidency, is the question of NATO. Ukraine has sought NATO membership for years, but these efforts accelerated after the Orange Revolution. Initially this looked like a possibility, perhaps even an inevitability, but that has changed. Myriad factors such as skittishness about NATO expansion following the Russia-Georgia war, the stalling of democratic reforms in Ukraine that began shortly after the Orange Revolution, and growing European concerns about confronting Russia too aggressively made the prospect of Ukraine joining NATO in the near or medium range future quite bleak, even before the 2010 election.

Russia has also been successful in efforts to ensure that pro-Russian sentiment remains strong in many parts of Eastern Ukraine, including but not limited to the Crimea. This reservoir of positive feelings toward Russia, which is found in Kyrgyzstan and Ukraine but not in Georgia, is a major stumbling block for any potentially pro-western government in Kiev or Bishkek.[10] As long as those ties are strong, and feelings are warm, it will be very difficult for a national government to move Ukraine toward the west, particularly if, as will almost certainly be the case, that movement is considered hostile to Russia.

One of the many reasons Ukraine is important to Russia is that it is a key transit country for Russian energy, which must flow from Russia's far eastern regions to Europe. The pipelines built for this purpose during the Soviet period go through Ukraine, so control of Ukraine means control of a key energy corridor. This gives Ukraine some leverage over Russia. Ukraine could, at least in theory, create problems for Russia by charging more to transport gas or even refusing to transport it. Doing this would cut Russia off from one of its biggest markets, not only creating economic problems for Russia but also cutting off much of Europe from an important source of energy. This would put Ukraine in a position of strategic interdependence with both Russia and Europe on issues relating to energy. On balance, since the Orange Revolution, Russia has had the upper hand on energy issues. Ukrainian threats to raise prices for Russia to transport energy have proven short-lived and not entirely credible. Russia has been far more effective using the price it charges Ukraine for gas as a political tool.

In spite of the early years of the Orange Revolution and Yushchenko's presidency, Russia's overall influence in Ukraine has remained strong while key Russian policy goals have largely been met. Russian gas has continued to flow, the Black Sea Fleet has remained in Sebastopol, the Crimea remains something of a potential political time bomb for Kiev, and NATO membership for Ukraine seems very unlikely for the foreseeable future. However, not everything has gone Russia's way in Ukraine. Ukraine's nascent democratic institutions, while not consolidating as quickly as some might like, have not collapsed. Western influence remains strong particularly in western Ukraine, but when the tally sheet is taken in its entirety, it does not look bad for Russia, particularly given Yanukovich's victory in 2010.

Russia continues to have leverage over Ukraine due to the large ethnic Russian population in the Crimea. This region became particularly sensitive after the Russia-Georgia war in 2008. While Russia has taken few direct steps to destabilize Ukraine through the Crimea, it has several potential means to do this. Russia could distribute Russian passports to ethnic Russians living in Crimea, as it did for people in South Ossetia and Abkhazia. This would lay the foundation for pretenses for future intervention should Russia, at any time, feel that Ukraine was threatening the ethnic Russian population. Russia could also use its powerful media presence in the Crimea to create tension between the Crimea and the rest of Ukraine.

Last, Russia has succeeded in pushing NATO membership for Ukraine into the relatively distant future. This is a clear victory for Russia, one where Russian interests and American goals are in direct conflict. Although the Orange Revolution initially brought a more pro-American government into power in Ukraine, that government has failed to bring Ukraine into NATO or to move it markedly closer to that goal.

Describing the view that the Rose Revolution has been a victory for Russia as counterintuitive would be a major understatement. No other post-Rose Revolutionary leader, and few leaders in the world, charted a course as relentlessly pro-American as that of President Saakashvili in 2004–2008. During a period where U.S. global popularity was declining rapidly, Saakashvilli brought his country as close to the U.S. as possible. His countrymen were, for the most part, more than happy to be part of this close relationship between Georgia and the world's only remaining superpower. However, again examining outcomes rather than rhetoric leads to a different picture, one that does not look so bad for Russia.

In addition to reasserting Georgia's goal of joining NATO, the Rose Revolution government radically liberalized the country's economy, dramatically cutting taxes and regulation. It also enthusiastically supported the Bush administration's Global War on Terror and was one of the few countries to continue to support the U.S. war effort in Iraq. By the time Bush left office in January 2009, Georgia had the third largest number of troops of any foreign country in Iraq, trailing only the U.S. and UK. Few non-American leaders were more rhetorically pro-America than Saakashvili during his first four years in power.

Georgia's affinity for the U.S. went beyond policy direction and took the form of a relationship between the two presidents that bordered on sycophantic on the part of Saakashvili. The highway from the Tbilisi airport to downtown Tbilisi, after it was cleaned and fixed, was renamed after President Bush. Bush's trip to Georgia in 2005, the first ever by an American president, was almost a national holiday as the president was feted with dancing and banquets. This is not unusual; more so was the large and genuine show of support at a public rally with the two presidents, as well as the decision of the Tbilisi government to repaint almost all the buildings in downtown Tbilisi so the city would look its best for Bush's visit.

After the Rose Revolution, Georgia, which under Shevardnadze had already received more than its share of U.S. advisors and foreign assistance, received even more material and technical assistance. In addition to millions of dollars, the U.S. increased the number of military as well as civilian advisors. Virtually every important Georgian ministry, including the office of the prime minister, had at least one prominent American advisor. The relationship between the two countries was extremely close as the U.S. became increasingly vested in the success of the Rose Revolution project.

The results, however, tell a substantially different story, one of decreased American influence or more specifically of Russia achieving its goals, particularly after the 2008 war between Russia and Georgia. Georgia's bid to join NATO, a goal of the Shevardnadze regime that took on far greater importance under Saakashvili, has been set back perhaps indefinitely. Georgia has the bad luck of having its NATO and EU hopes damaged by expansion fatigue as well as the global economic downturn that has forced most NATO member states to explore less ambitious foreign policies, but the war with Russia has also severely injured Georgia's NATO aspirations. While some supporters of Georgia have argued, that had Georgia been in NATO, Russia would not have so cavalierly invaded in August 2008 (Asmus 2010; Cornell 2009), there has been greater concern that if the war had happened and Georgia had been in NATO, Russia and NATO would have been drawn into conflict with each other. Accordingly, the war has clearly dampened enthusiasm for bringing Georgia into NATO among key American allies in Europe. If Georgia's membership is an inevitable eventuality, it is now a distant one. In November 2008, German chancellor Angela Merkel described Georgia and Ukraine as not ready for NATO membership "in the foreseeable future." This continues to be a good reflection of attitudes in much of Western Europe (Morgan (2008).

Russia has also succeeded in destroying any chance of Georgia bringing South Ossetia and Abkhazia back under Georgian sovereignty. These regions have not been governed by Tbilisi since the early 1990s, but while these conflicts were frozen the possibility of solving the problem to Tbilisi's advantage could be explored, or at least pursued as an abstract political goal. The war changed this. Russia unilaterally declared both regions independent countries. Russia received very little support internationally as only Nauru, Venezuela, Nicaragua, Hamas, and Hezbollah have joined in recognizing Abkhaz and South Ossetian independence. Nonetheless, the context has changed. The war did not make South Ossetia and Abkhazia independent countries; it made them part of Russia. Russia got away with an annexation, or land grab, with regard to these regions. While this was certainly outside the framework of international law, it was, at least in the short and medium term, a successful attempt to ensure that Georgia would not be united for many years.

Georgia's relationship with the U.S. has remained very strong throughout the years since the Rose Revolution. The U.S. continues to be Georgia's strongest political and financial backer, publicly committed to bringing Georgia into NATO and its strongest defender. That relationship is evolving and may change, but so far, in the face of war, internal turmoil in Georgia, and changes in the American administration, it has not. The same cannot be so unambiguously said about Georgia's relationship with Europe.

As evidenced by the opposition toward NATO expansion, many powerful European countries seeking to balance Georgia and Russia have tilted away from Georgia. Many leaders in Europe ceased viewing Georgia as a special democratic case after the crackdown in Georgia in November 2007 and have had a much more critical view than the U.S. of Georgia's role in the war with Russia as well as with democratic development in Georgia since that time. Many formerly Communist states in Eastern Europe are more sympathetic to Georgia, but they have little ability to influence overall European policy.

Russia's contempt for Saakashvili is at times palpable. Among the more colorful things the Russian leadership has said is that he is a "political corpse"[11] and that Putin would like to "hang Saakashvili by his balls."[12] One of Russia's publicly stated goals toward Georgia has been to destabilize the country and get Saakashvili out of office. It certainly has not succeeded in the latter, but the question of Georgia's stability is less clear.

Beginning in late November 2007, Georgia has lost a war, seen peaceful demonstrations violently dispersed, seen other peaceful demonstrations drag on for months amid a low level of government harassment, had two national elections which, while not terrible, fell short of being free and fair, changed its constitution, lived under constant threat of further attack from Russia, and seen numerous high ranking politicians including the speaker of parliament and the ambassador to the UN leave the government and call for the president's resignation. This is not the profile of a country rich in political stability.

The constant, though often low level domestic instability in Georgia that began in late 2007 is not all caused by Russia, but Russia has contributed to it. The 2008 war and the constant pressure applied by Russia both before and after that war have contributed to this instability. However, the Georgian government has contributed as well by using unnecessary violence to crack down on demonstrators in November 2007 and relying too heavily on administrative resources and other unsavory tactics both to reelect President Saakashvili in January 2008, and, more significantly, ensure a parliament with a strong NM majority in the parliamentary elections of May 2008. This erratic behavior continued into 2009 and 2010 as Georgia sought to send several hundred uninvited election observers to Ukraine to intimidate voters in the east, which was Yanukovich's base, and airing a program that featured a fake invasion of Georgia by Russia on a government-run television station. Regardless of the causality, domestic instability in Georgia is yet another way Russia appears to be achieving its goals in Georgia.

Color Revolutions, Russia, and the former Soviet Union

The Color Revolutions occurred just as Russia had reasserted itself as an important actor in the countries of the former Soviet Union. Although it is difficult to argue that there is a strong correlation between the events, they are deeply related. Had the Color Revolutions occurred a few years earlier, it is likely that the path to democracy, and for Georgia, where the desire was unambiguous, to NATO and the west, would have been much smoother. Georgia's NATO prospects have certainly suffered due to the war with Russia and Georgia's own democratic shortcomings, but Georgia is right in arguing that countries with weaker democratic credentials have gotten into NATO. However, this occurred before Russia returned as a force to be reckoned with in the region. Similarly, Russian efforts to sabotage the gains of the Orange and Tulip Revolutions would not have been possible had these events occurred only a few years earlier.

The Color Revolutions catalyzed the need to revisit Russian-American relations and craft a policy based on understanding the interests and abilities of Russia, particularly in the former Soviet Union. This simply had not been necessary for the first 10–14 years following the collapse of the Soviet Union. Russia, while far from a benign force, has since 2003–2005 been able to pursue more effectively its interests in the region. U.S. policy has suffered from not fully recognizing that Russia has interests in the region that may clash with those of the U.S. This has led the U.S. not to be prepared for an active, aggressive Russian foreign policy and adjust policies accordingly.

As the Color Revolutions evolve to look more like parts of the ongoing story of political development in Georgia, Ukraine, and Kyrygzstan, rather than major turning points toward democracy, the need to put these countries in a broader context of Russian-U.S. relations becomes unavoidable. Viewed this way, it looks as if Russia and the U.S. have been involved in a tug of war for influence in the former Soviet Union since the collapse of the USSR in the early 1990s. The Color Revolutions are part of this longer-term development rather than unique stand-alone events.

The Color Revolutions represented peaks of U.S. influence in the region, but these could never have been very durable. Russian efforts to push back against the Color Revolutions and to preempt their spread were in firm position by late 2005 when parliamentary elections occurred in Azerbaijan. The more relevant question is not so much the origins of this pushback, but why it took so long to get started.

CHAPTER 6

Democracy After the Color Revolutions

In November 2007, the Georgian government violently cracked down on peaceful demonstrators, using water cannons and sonic devices to send demonstrators fleeing. Less than two years later, in Kyrgyzstan President Bakiev was reelected by a landslide in an election that would not have looked out of place in Azerbaijan, Uzbekistan, or Russia. In January 2010, the man whose efforts to steal the 2004 election precipitated the Orange Revolution was sworn in as president of Ukraine. These are very strange legacies for a movement that seemed so deeply tied to the advance of democracy.

Assessing the extent of democratic development since the Color Revolutions is important because for most observers the Color Revolutions are still part of the story of democratic development. While enthusiasm for Color Revolutions as a path to democracy has been tempered, there is still a belief that electoral breakthroughs can bring down nondemocratic leaders. Bunce (2010) cites the Color Revolutions as evidence that "from 1996 to 2005 there was a wave of elections in the post-communist region in particular that ended the rule of authoritarians and brought democratic oppositions to power" (44). This is illustrative of a common approach to studying Color Revolutions and their role in ending authoritarian regimes. In Georgia and Ukraine, and arguably Kyrgyzstan as well, however, the regimes ousted by the Color Revolutions were not authoritarian. Moreover Color Revolutions have failed in countries with more authoritarian regimes like Azerbaijan and Belarus as well as several countries outside the post-Soviet region.[1] In general, the lessons the Color Revolutions offer for other countries seeking to become more democratic must be significantly muted if the evidence shows that these three countries themselves have not moved in this direction.

In Georgia, Ukraine, and Kyrgyzstan the democratic promise of the Color Revolutions dissipated, or at the very least stagnated, relatively quickly following the initial democratic breakthrough. Although democracy went off course in all three countries, the way it went off course was different in each case. In Kyrgyzstan, newly elected president Bakiev quickly transformed his country into a kleptocracy similar to the one he had overthrown, before being ousted himself after less than five years in power. In Georgia, the Saakashvili regime oversaw the consolidation of power in one party and to a great extent the president, and restricted freedom of speech and assembly. In Ukraine, weak institutions and enduring political corruption contributed to undermining the initial democratic breakthrough of 2004–2005.

Whereas patterns can be identified during the Color Revolutions themselves, the subsequent democratic developments in these countries are all quite different. Although it is possible and can be useful to outline a vague hierarchy that shows Ukraine has made the most steps toward democracy, Kyrgyzstan the least, with Georgia in the middle, the differences in democratic development have been as much of kind as of degree. Nonetheless, some data present a good outline of the development of democracy before and after the Color Revolutions.

Table 3 shows the Freedom House scores for the three countries beginning in 2004, which draw on data from 2003. The scores are divided into two categories, political rights and civil liberties. According to Freedom House, political rights primarily measure "electoral process," "political pluralism and participation," and "functioning of government,"while civil liberties measure "freedom of expression and belief," "associational and organizational rights," "rule of law," and "personal autonomy and individual rights." Scores range from 1 to 7 with lower scores indicating higher levels of democracy. The year 2004 represents the last of the Shevardnadze regime in Georgia while 2005 represents the last years of the Kuchma and Akaev regimes in Urkaine and Kyrgyzstan.

Table 3. Freedom House Scores

	2004 Pol/Civ	2005 Pol/Civ	2006 Pol/Civ	2007 Pol/Civ	2008 Pol/Civ	2009 Pol/Civ	2010 Pol/Civ
Georgia	4/4	3/4	3/3	3/3	4/4	4/4	4/4
Ukraine	4/4	4/3	3/2	3/2	3/2	3/2	3/2
Kyrgyzstan	6/5	6/5	5/4	5/4	5/4	5/4	6/5

Data from Freedom House www.freedomhouse.org. Pol = political liberties; Civ = civil liberties.

Akaev's regime was considerably more repressive than Shevardnadze's or Kuchma's, so the combined score of 11 during the last two years of Akaev's time in power is higher than Georgia's or Ukraine's during the pre-Color Revolutionary years. Kyrgyzstan's score changed slightly following the Tulip Revolution, but by the 2010 rating, based on data from 2009, Kyrgyzstan had become as unfree as it had been under Akaev. This suggests that whatever democratic advances occurred after the Tulip Revolution happened early and then were more or less frozen and reversed. It also suggests that Bakiev's Kyrgyzstan was less democratic than either Ukraine or Georgia had been during the last days of the pre-Color Revolution regimes in those countries. These data are consistent with other evidence from election and other reports from Kyrgyzstan since 2005.

The Freedom House data on Ukraine are the most encouraging. The overall score of five which Ukraine maintained from 2006 to 2010 indicates that Ukraine has stabilized on the high end of the partly free category. Thus, while the Orange Revolution cannot be said to have made Ukraine a democracy, it can, according to these data, be said to have moved Ukraine closer to democracy and brought about enduring improvement. It is possible, however, that this will begin to change during Yanukovich's presidency.

The data also suggest that some of this advancement had begun to occur during the last days of the Kuchma regime. The events of the Orange Revolution, after all, required a fair amount of freedom and democratic space, and like those in Georgia in 2003 would not have occurred in a stronger, more authoritarian state. In Georgia, as in Kyrgyzstan, the democratic trends have reversed themselves during the years following the Color Revolution. According to Freedom House, by 2008 Georgia was no more democratic than it had been in 2003 when Shevardnadze was president and trying to get away with stealing one last election. In the years initially following the Rose Revolution, Georgia made some meaningful democratic gains, but this began to reverse itself in 2007, as reflected in data from 2008–2010. In 2007, Saakashvili's government violently broke up peaceful anti-government demonstrations in downtown Tbilisi. That led to, or was evidence of, democratic backsliding by Georgia that has not yet reversed itself.

The data here also show that even in the early days of the Rose Revolution, when the government was aggressively pursuing reform across several sectors and the new Georgian regime was held up by the U.S. as a symbol of the success of U.S. democracy assistance policies, Ukraine was already the most successful case of democratization. In all three cases, the Freedom House data are only a general overview of the trends regarding democratization. Looking more closely at the three countries and drawing on additional evidence will help fill out the pictures.

Ukraine

Of the three countries, Ukraine had the strongest post-Color Revolution democratic development, but, by any measure, still cannot be called a consolidated democracy. Ironically, perhaps, the failure of the Orange Revolution to completely eliminate the previous administration and political regime was both a facilitator and limiting factor for Ukraine's democratic development beginning in 2005. Unlike in Kyrgyzstan and Georgia, the defeated candidate did not fade to political obscurity or to Moscow when his efforts to steal the election were thwarted. Instead, Viktor Yanukovich remained an important political leader in Ukraine during 2005–2009 before being elected president in 2010.

The presence of Yanukovich and the Party of the Regions in Ukrainian political life injected accountability into the political system that did not exist in Georgia or Kyrgyzstan. People who were unhappy with the new government in Ukraine had other political options. Moreover, one option, Yanukovich's Party of the Regions, was clearly identified with the previous regime. In this sense, Ukraine developed a party system that, especially to outsiders, looked recognizably like a two-party system. The strength of the Party of the Regions also made it impossible for Ukraine to develop the one-party, or strongman, systems that emerged in Georgia and Kyrgyzstan beginning in 2004–2005. Because the Party of the Regions remained politically relevant and, in the eastern part of Ukraine, even dominant, neither party of the Orange Revolution, Timoschenko's Block Yulia Timoschenko (BYT) or Yushchenko's Our Ukraine, could emerge as the locus of political power.

While the persistent relevance of the previous regime differentiates the Orange from the Rose or Tulip Revolution it would be inaccurate to view the Party of the Regions as primarily a constructive force for Ukrainian democracy. Although there have been two and at times three or more parties sharing power in Ukraine for most of the time since the Orange Revolution, there has not been a true competitive national multiparty system. Party politics in Ukraine since 2004 have been characterized by a dual system. In the western parts of the country, where Yushchenko ran strongly in 2004 and which provided most of the support for the Orange Revolution, two parties, Our Ukraine and BYT, have competed for power for most of this period. In recent years, there has been less competition; BYT has clearly emerged as the dominant party in western Ukraine. Eastern Ukraine, on the other hand, continues to be dominated by the Party of the Regions.

The partisan division in Ukraine is not, however, a simple regional split based on party allegiances. In Eastern Ukraine, which includes the industrial base of the country, the Party of Regions has put a strong patronage system in place, one with some echoes of the old Soviet regime. The party has relied on close ties between local government, industry, and the Party of the Regions to ensure that, for instance, the party is involved in distribution of jobs and economic opportunities. This, not surprisingly, also includes occasionally intimidating supporters of other parties, threatening them with loss of livelihood and similar lower level forms of harassment. During elections, fraud is still more common in the east than in the west.

While the Party of the Regions clearly has used undemocratic means to bolster its popularity in the eastern and southern parts of the country, it enjoys a legitimate base of support as well. It is more open to working with Russia and bringing Russia and Ukraine closer together than either of the major parties. This position reflects the views in the east, where warm feelings toward Russia are strong and many ethnic Russians live. The corresponding coolness of the Party of the Regions toward strong nationalism also resonates well with voters in eastern Ukraine. Additionally, for several years immediately following the Orange Revolution, the Party of the Regions was able to point to solid economic growth in the east. This changed substantially with the global economic downturn in late 2008.

Another reason the Party of the Regions remained strong in eastern Ukraine throughout this period is that, in many respects, BYT, Our Ukraine, and some of the other parties in western Ukraine did not try sufficiently hard to appeal to voters in the east. This is due partly due to the strength of the Party of the Regions, but also to a feeling by many western Ukrainian political leaders that voters in the east are somehow not as progressive or western oriented as those in the west and therefore not really worth trying to reach.

Since the Orange Revolution, the political stalemate involving the three main parties has been the most consistent story in Ukraine. Ukraine has the same election every twelve to twenty-four months with the expectation each time that things will work out differently and a clear winner will emerge. This has not yet occurred, as BYT, the Party of the Regions, and Our Ukraine have run against one another, formed various small or grand coalitions, and fought while the stalemate has remained. Even the 2010 election that resulted in Yanukovich finally winning the presidency was close, with Yanukovich defeating Timoschenko in the runoff by a margin of only 48.95 to 45.47 percent.

The political stalemate is exacerbated by a constitution that requires the president and prime minister to share power relatively evenly. The president is elected directly while the prime minister is chosen by parliament and forms a government. While Yushchenko remained president through the first five years following the Orange Revolution, the country had three prime ministers, including one, Yulia Timoschenko, who served on two separate occasions. However, the number of prime ministerial transitions overstates the stability of the office. Because transitions have been so common, speculations about changes in the office, which can be brought about by shifting allegiances in the legislature or through new elections, are almost constant.

The unusual structure of the Ukrainian parliament contributes to this lack of stability in the government. The parliament consists of 450 people all elected from a single unified national list. While such list systems are not unusual, they are rare in countries the size of Ukraine. Most are found in smaller countries and, significantly, form a smaller legislature. Israel's 120-member Knesset is a more common size for a legislature drawn from a single national list.

The structure of the Ukrainian parliament has been a not insignificant obstacle to political reform in Ukraine. Party list systems tend to concentrate power in political parties, specifically in the leaders of those parties. To get elected to parliament, a candidate does not so much have to go directly to voters, but has to appeal to a much narrower group of people, specifically those appointing positions on the party lists. This often creates a system where close relationships with leaders and the ability to provide resources to the party are more decisive in determining who gets on the list than ability or connections with the people. MPs, therefore, essentially represent the leaders of their parties rather than the people who elected them. During the election, only the top few people on each list are visible to the media, actively campaigning, participating in elections, and the like. Once elected, many MPs owe their loyalty not directly to any constituency or group of voters, but to the party leaders who put them on the list.

This practice contributes to strong parties, but frequently, as in Ukraine, to strong parties organized around a single leader. In parliament, the major decision making, priority setting priorities, and legislation drafting is located among a few leaders from each party, while the remainder of those elected on the lists, particularly from the larger parties, are relegated to the back bench. Back benchers are found in any legislative system, but they are more numerous than usual in Ukraine, due in part to the electoral system. They contribute to instability because they have shown themselves relatively easily cajoled, intimidated, or bribed into switching parties, upsetting the balance of partisan power, and leading to new governing coalitions with some frequency during the years following the Orange Revolution. Because these back benchers tend to be the least serious about the real work of parliament and most motivated by economic gain of a very direct kind, they are very susceptible to this dynamic. Therefore, the stability of any government can be disrupted by a dozen or so back benchers looking to make some quick money.

The stalemate itself is not a sign of the failure of democracy in Ukraine. Political stalemates have lasted for years in many more consolidated democracies. In some cases they seem to be almost the norm. However, in Ukraine the stalemate has at best significantly slowed democratic advance and reform more generally because of constant government turnovers and corresponding difficulty passing laws and implementing new policies. A more critical read would say it has allowed the Party of the Regions to maintain its undemocratic hold on economic and political power through the eastern part of the country.

Ukraine's post-Color Revolution party system is substantially different from that of Georgia or Kyrgyzstan and has had a mixed effect on political development since the Orange Revolution. It also demonstrates that while the country has not split apart during or after the Orange Revolution, the geographical cleavage remains very sharp with the Party of the Regions retaining its base in the east and BYT and Our Ukraine remaining strong in the west. In the legislative elections of 2006 and 2007, all the oblasts in which the Party of the Regions won an outright majority or combined with the Communist Party to win an outright majority were in either eastern or southern Ukraine. Not surprisingly, all the oblasts in which BYT and Our Ukraine combined for at least 50 percent of the vote, were in the west and the north.

The outcomes of the 2006 and 2007 elections had implications for the consolidation of Ukrainian democracy, but the elections themselves came closer to meeting international election standards than similar elections under Kuchma had. The OSCE/ODIHR reports from 2006 and to a lesser extent 2007 made this clear:

> The 26 March parliamentary elections were conducted largely in line with OSCE Commitments, Council of Europe commitments and

other international standards for democratic elections. Overall, civil and political rights were respected, including the fundamental freedoms of expression, association and assembly. An inclusive candidateregistration process and a vibrant media environment provided for genuine competition. This enabled voters to make informed choices between distinct political alternatives. Progress in the electoral process, already evident during the 26 December 2004 repeat second round of the Presidential election, was further consolidated.[2]

The elections were conducted mostly in line with OSCE and Council of Europe commitments and other international standards for democratic elections, and confirmed an open and competitive environment for the conduct of elections. However, the IEOM also noted some areas of concern, including some recent amendments to the election law, the inadequate quality of voter lists (VLs), and possible disenfranchisement of voters who crossed the state border after 1 August 2007.[3]

Democratic development is concerned with more than just elections. In this regard, the developments since the Orange Revolution are mixed, but generally positive. Ukraine is, by most measures, more free since the Orange Revolution. This is reflected in Freedom House scores for civil liberties, which improved from 4 to 3 before settling at 2 beginning in 2006. The democratic momentum of the Orange Revolution, considerably stronger in the western part of the country, has contributed to a freer Ukraine than had existed under the previous regime (see Aslund (2009).

There are some signs that Yanukovich is beginning to restrict some of these freedoms, particularly with regard to media. Kuzio writing in 2011 warns that "The Yanukovych administration has moved farther down the path of authoritarianism in only one year in office than Kuchma did in a decade," adding "Media censorship took place under Kuchma, but the situation is worse today" (Kuzio 2011). Karatnycky, however, asserts that "In the media and public information sphere, there was less of an erosion than partisans might think" (Karatnycky 2011).

Kyrgyzstan

In Kyrgyzstan the path of democratic development since the Tulip Revolution has been different from that of post-Orange Revolution Ukraine.

Elections during Bakiev's presidency remained fraught with fraud and intimidation. The country continued to be dominated by one powerful group of politicians until the events of April 2010. There was little political competition, ample government harassment of political opposition, and weak civil society during those years.

While the competitive, if not always democratic political party system has contributed, both positively and negatively, to democracy in Ukraine, in Kyrgyzstan party politics remained dominated by one poorly organized political force. The Orange Revolution was characterized by an important, even dramatic shift in power from one political force to another, but the defeated political force emerged to provide a political counterweight. In Kyrgyztstan, the Tulip Revolution largely replaced one strongman regime with another. During the Tulip Revolution period there were two presidential elections in Kyrgyzstan. The first saw Bakiev consolidate power effectively, and in an election that was virtually uncontested, win 88.9 percent of the vote. Four years later, he was reelected with 76 percent of the vote. No political opposition emerged, or was allowed to emerge, that could compete with the president for political power.

Uncompetitive elections are not, on their own, proof of the weakness of democracy, but in Kyrgyzstan they are symptomatic of more basic problems. The contrast between the 2005 election, which saw Bakiev elected on the heels of Akaev's resignation, and 2009 election in which he was reelected, is stark, making it clear that the direction of Kyrgyz democracy in the intervening four years, at least regarding elections, was not good.

In 2005, the ODIHR report began by claiming:

> The 10 July 2005 early presidential election marked tangible progress by the Kyrgyz Republic toward meeting OSCE commitments, as well as other international standards for democratic elections. This was the case in particular during the pre-election period and the conduct of voting, although the quality of the Election Day process deteriorated somewhat during the counting of votes. Fundamental civil and political rights, such as freedom of expression and freedom of assembly, were generally respected throughout the election process.[4]

Four years later the ODIHR report began with a different tone:

> Notwithstanding some positive elements, including distinct choices of presidential candidates and the continuing engagement of civil

society, the 23 July presidential election failed to meet key OSCE commitments for democratic elections, including the commitment to maintain a clear separation between party and state. Election day was marred by many problems and irregularities, including evidence of ballot box stuffing, inaccuracies in the voter lists and some evidence of multiple voting. The process further deteriorated during the counting and tabulation. While contestants were generally able to campaign openly around the country, the campaign was unengaging and low-key until the week before election day. The limited and unbalanced coverage of election contestants in the broadcast media, especially the bias displayed by the state media for the incumbent, did not provide voters with sufficient and diverse information from which to make an informed choice. This bias together with the misuse of administrative resources in support of the incumbent's campaign granted him an unfair advantage.[5]

The Tulip Revolution was, from the beginning, a poor imitation of the Rose and Orange Revolutions, particularly with regard to democracy. It was characterized by greater violence and less democratic impulse than the others. In some respects, it was never clear that it even had the potential to be a democratic breakthrough. Initial perceptions were perhaps more positive than they should have been because of the temporal and political proximity to events in Georgia and Ukraine. Olcott, writing in March 2005, almost immediately after Akaev left office, made a strong connection between the events in Kyrgyzstan and events in Georgia and Ukraine. "For the third time in eighteen months seriously flawed elections have brought down the government in a CIS (Commonwealth of Independent States) state, and for the first time this has occurred east of the Urals. The 'tulip revolution' could prove to be the most remarkable of all, causing positive reverberations throughout a region that many had written off as lost from the point of view of building democratic societies" (Olcott 2005). Olcott also included a warning those celebrating Kyrgyzstan's democratic breakthrough might have benefited by heeding: "The current danger in Kyrgyzstan comes not from its masses. It comes from a fractious and potentially greedy elite."

While the Bakiev government was certainly less democratic than the post-Color Revolutionary regimes in Ukraine or Georgia, it is also apparent that the regime was considerably less concerned about democracy, particularly about showing the west its democratic credentials, than were the governments of Yushchenko or Saakashvili during this period. This is largely due to Kyrgyzstan's relationship with the west, particularly the U.S. For Ukraine, and particularly Georgia, democracy is a lynchpin to greater integration with the west, and integration with the west is central to the economic health and national security of both countries. Kyrgyzstan, is an Asian country for which integration with the west is a distant, less plausible goal.

Kyrgyzstan's very different relationship with Russia also makes impressing the west with democratic credentials less important. While there is close to an anti-Russian consensus in Georgia and strong anti-Russian feeling in western Ukraine, the opposite dynamic is at work in Kyrgyzstan. There is little strong anti-Russian sentiment; and many Kyrgyz see Russia as central to the country's future. According to a July 2008 Gallup poll, 63 percent of respondents agreed it was "more important to have a good relationship with Russia, even if it might hurt relationships with the U.S.A," while only 3 percent believed the reverse (Ray 2010). Moreover, the large Russian minority in Kyrgyzstan live free of harassment or significant prejudice. Russian remains a lingua franca in a way that is less true in much of Ukraine and not at all in Georgia.

The Russian political and economic presence through business and government ties is strong. Russia provides energy at discounted prices to Kyrgyzstan, as it does to other countries nearby who remain sympathetic to Russia. Hundreds of thousands of Kyrgyz work in Russia and send remittances home. Russian political consultants also provided occasional advice to the Bakiev regime and will almost certainly play a similar role in the new Kyrgyz government. Until 2010, when it met its short-term needs, Russia had shown no concern for democratic development in Kyrgyzstan. This has provided the Bakiev regime with an alternative to western support, and western pressure, which Saakashvili and Yushchenko never had.

Russia is only one of the powerful nondemocratic regimes in the region. Chinese ties to Kyrgyzstan increased during Bakiev's presidency as well. The assistance and investment China has provided in Kyrgyzstan also do not require any commitment to democratic reform in return. Thus, the U.S. and the west are unable to put pressure on Kyrgyzstan as they can in Ukraine and Georgia because Kyrgyzstan has more options. In addition to having had other potential powerful allies and patrons in Moscow and Beijing, Kyrgyzstan was in a different strategic position with respect to the U.S than Ukraine or Georgia. While Georgia and Ukraine are both important to the U.S. for geopolitical reasons, jockeying for influence in Eurasia, and energy politics, these are difficult to measure, even abstract ideas. Kyrgyzstan's strategic value to the U.S is much more concrete and easy to understand. The air force base at Manas is a very easy issue around which to negotiate, or as appeared to be the preference of the Bakiev government, to sell to the highest bidder.

The value of the Manas base gives Bishkek leverage over Washington that does not exist in Tbilisi. Moreover, turning to Moscow or Beijing for support would not have been a plausible threat by Saakasvili or Yushchenko, but from Bakiev it was, and from Kyrgyzstan it still is. Bakiev used his leverage over the U.S. and his cozy relationships with authoritarian regimes in Moscow and Beijing to create a regime in Kyrgyzstan that rapidly moved away from any democratic potential the Tulip Revolution once had. While the governments in post-Color Revolution Ukraine and Georgia can certainly be criticized on the grounds that they have also moved away from the initial democratic promise, they nonetheless represented significant changes from their predecessors. Although one can argue that the Rose Revolution did not bring Georgia significantly closer to democracy, one cannot seriously argue that Saakashvili's Georgia resembles Shevardnadze's but with different individuals in power. That argument could have been made with regard to Bakiev's Kyrgyzstan.

By the end of his time in office, Akaev governed over a strongman regime with weak political institutions. Akaev did not have a dominant political party he used to stay in power and to structure the state. Nor did he have a strong state that asserted its strength over the country. Instead, his regime was a kleptocracy in which a few families took what they could with little regard for the development of the state.

Bakiev's regime developed similar characteristics. Bakiev's large family was involved in governance, power, and the economy at the highest levels. The government was based heavily on corruption and patronage, both of which originated with several families, including Bakiev's. Once a business grew past having a few employees, it was faced with the choice of paying off the government or being harassed out of business. Several major businesses and resources were owned by members of Bakiev's family or others close to the government.[6]

Bakiev was considerably less interested in institutionalizing his regime through creating structures that might have allowed it to endure for more than a few years, or in building a Kyrgyz state that could have governed and asserted sovereignty over all Kyrgyzstan. It is not at all strange to find corrupt leaders who are not interested in creating a meaningful state for their people, but the lack of interest the Kyrgyz regime shows in building structures to keep themselves in power is unusual. Instead, the regime relied on intimidation, threats, violence, and bribery, all of which are costly, unreliable, and ultimately unsuccessful strategies for staying in power.

In the years leading up to the Tulip Revolution, democracy in Kyrgyzstan was weaker than in either Georgia or Ukraine on the eve of the Rose or Orange Revolution. It should not be surprising that a few years after the Color Revolutions, democracy in Kyrgyzstan was still the weakest. This demonstrates the limited transformative power of the Color Revolutions and the ongoing relevance of the existing political structures at the time in all three countries. For example, the absence in Kyrgyzstan of a national legislature that was as sophisticated and embedded in the country's political development as was the case in Georgia or even Ukraine, made it more difficult to develop a functioning legislature after the Tulip Revolution. Similarly, while Kyrgyzstan during Akaev's presidency may have had the strongest and most independent civil society in Central Asia, civil society in Kyrgyzstan was not as strong as in pre-Color Revolution Georgia or Ukraine. These contexts and baselines remained relevant even after the Tulip Revolution. Kyrgyzstan was also similar to Georgia in that after the revolution the old regime disappeared from political life. There was no party of Akaev loyalists with a base of support that could have kept Bakiev accountable.

The absence of a foundation on which to build these institutions after the Tulip Revolution meant there were fewer checks on the president than even in Georgia. Like Saakashvili, Bakiev had initially been elected with an overwhelming majority of the vote. However, Bakiev was not the heroic figure Saakashvili had been in Georgia, nor had he played such a central and extraordinary role in the revolution itself. The decision for Bakiev to be president was made by the political leadership that had pushed Akaev out, based on compromise and political considerations more than popularity, democracy, or substance. Saakashvili had essentially won the election that precipitated Shevardnadze's downfall. Bakiev had no such claim on revolutionary legitimacy.

Georgia

The initial hope for democracy surrounding the Rose Revolution was greater than in either Kyrgyzstan or Ukraine. It was the first of the Color Revolutions, and also the first significant step forward of any kind for democracy in a number of years in the region. The leaders of the Rose Revolution, most prominently Zurab Zhavnia and Mikheil Saakashvili, were well known in the west, especially the U.S., and viewed as representing the best chance for democracy in Georgia. This sense of hope and corresponding expectations were increased by the eloquent, unambiguous, and frequent government pledges that it sought to build democracy in Georgia.

The peaceful nature of the Rose Revolution and the election of President Saakashvili in January 2004 also contributed to this hope. The 2004 election was the freest and fairest in the history of independent Georgia, though not the most competitive. This gave strong democratic legitimacy to the actions of November 2003 which could otherwise have cynically been interpreted as an ouster of a democratic president by mobs on the street.

The hope around democracy in Georgia may have been greater than in either of the other two Color Revolutionary countries, but the outcome has been frustratingly and confoundingly mixed. One useful way to understand the democratic trajectory of post-Rose Revolutionary Georgia is to break it into two periods. The first period, roughly three and a half years, ran from January 2004 through mid-2007; the second began in late 2007.

During the first period, there were clear problems with Georgian democracy. The concentration of political power in one party and in the office of the presidency, the restricted media environment, and efforts by the government to ensure that opposition efforts remained weak all represented clear problems with Georgian democracy. Similarly, the failure of an independent judiciary to emerge also raised concerns from many about the direction of democracy in Georgia.

Although this first period was characterized by many questions about democracy, strong and obvious positives also existed that could be identified as triumphs of Georgian democracy. The two elections in 2004, that elected Saakashvili to the presidency and saw a new parliament elected, were both extremely good by the standards of Georgia or the broader region. Similarly, the Georgian government's peaceful victory over Aslan Abashidze, the warlord who governed the region of Ajara, meant that people in that region gained political rights and freedom for the first time.

Saakashvili's government also made major strides in combating the petty corruption that had been extremely widespread during the previous administration. Through eliminating most of the corruption, bribes, and shakedowns which were part of most exchanges between ordinary citizens and representatives of the government during Shevardnadze's years as president, the new government made it possible for Georgian people to interact with their government in a more effective way and to lay the groundwork for the sense of ownership citizens of democracy must feel toward their government.

During this first period, democratic development was far from perfect. It was perhaps, on balance, more negative than positive, but the challenges facing the Georgian government were enormous, and democracy was only a mid-level priority at best. Nonetheless, the notion that the Georgian government, while flawed, was at heart democratic was still plausible. This position was buoyed by the ongoing popularity of Saakashvili and his party. The government enjoyed broad support from the Georgian people as it pursued its agenda of state building, economic and political reform, and commitment to restoring Georgia's territorial integrity. During this time, Georgia was essentially a semidemocracy, with some elements of democracy but many remnants of previous undemocratic regimes.

While Saakashvili's United National Movement (UNM) dominated politics and won all the elections with huge majorities, there was a nascent competitive party system in Georgia. Parties such as New Rights and Labor, which had initially opposed the Rose Revolution, existed. The New Rights Party was part of an opposition block in parliament. Others, such as the Conservatives and Republicans, broke from the UNM to form a pro-Rose Revolution opposition.

The second period presented a very different face of Georgian democracy and politics. Beginning in late 2007, Georgia entered a period of low level political crisis that became a constant part of political life. This crisis was brought on and characterized by Georgia moving away from any real democratic reform. The beginning of the period can be traced to a comment by Irakli Okruashvili, a long-time Saakashvili confidant who had served as interior minister and defense minister in Saakashvili's government. Okruasvhili left Saakashvili's government in November 2006 and in September 2007 accused his former boss of corruption and being complicit in the death of prime minister Zurab Zhvania.[7] Okruashvili's comments led to a renewed barrage of criticisms aimed at Saakashvili's government from citizens and politicians frustrated with unmet economic promises, government arrogance, and stalled democratic reform.

This set the stage for large demonstrations in November 2007, which, though bigger than the ones that had brought down Shevardnadze in 2003, a point not lost on Saakashvili's government, were nonviolent. The Georgian government tolerated the opposition for a few days before violently dispersing demonstrators with tear gas, water hoses, sound booms, and beatings. These actions followed by Saakashvili's decision to resign and seek immediate reelection. In those few days, Georgian democracy seemed to veer off course, where it has remained through the present.

In addition to violently suppressing the demonstrations, the Georgian government shut down and destroyed the office of the television station Imedi. Imedi was the only major television station that had a national reach and was not pro-government in slant. It was owned by the controversial Georgian billionaire Badri Patarkatsishvili, who after initially being a supporter of the Rose Revolution had taken an increasingly hard line against Saakashvili's government. Patarkatsishvili had been a generous source of funding for the anti-Saakashvili movement, and had questionable ties to the Kremlin. A Georgian Jew born in Tbilisi, he made his fortune in Russia during the first few years after the collapse of the Soviet Union, but returned to Georgia in 2000 because he was wanted by Russian authorities for alleged criminal activities. By 2006, the Russian government stopped asking the Georgian government to extradite Patarkatsishvili to Russia because he had found his way back into Moscow's favor (Socor 2007).

Saakashvili's resignation initiated a period not only of democratic backsliding, but of significant tumult in Georgian politics. In the thirty months following the dispersal of the demonstrations and Saakashvili's resignation, Georgia experienced two elections of questionable quality; numerous top government officials such as speaker of parliament Nino Burjanadze and ambassador to the UN Irakli Alasania breaking with the government and joining the opposition; defeat in the 2008 Russia-Georgia war; demonstrations and vigils from April to July 2009 calling for the resignation of Saakashvili; numerous allegations by the government of mutinies and Russian plots; the decision by the government to send uninvited and untrained election observers to eastern Ukraine for that country's election in 2010; the Imedi television hoax that featured a fake Russian invasion; and constitutional reforms in the second half of 2010 that raised speculation Saakashvili would remain in office after finishing his two terms as president.

The second period differed from the first in Georgia in several ways. Elections were conducted less fairly. Media freedom and judicial independence became weaker. The constant political crises contributed to making Saakashvili's government increasingly embattled, causing them to rely on accusing the opposition of ties to Russia, harassment of demonstrators, and appeals to Georgian nationalism to remain in power.

The January 2008 presidential election was a snap election called after Saakashvili's surprise resignation. Saakashvili was, of course, reelected. He won 53.47 percent of the vote in the first round, thus narrowly avoiding a runoff, which he probably would have won. Due to the close margin by which he avoided a runoff, as well as reports of election fraud, many in Georgia believed the latter was the cause of the former.

The election itself presented an interesting question for Georgia's democratic credentials because even though, according to the OSCE/ODIHR the election was mixed,

> Although this election represented the first genuinely competitive post-independence presidential election, shortcomings were noted. The campaign was overshadowed by widespread allegations of intimidation and pressure, among others on public-sector employees and opposition activists, some of which were verified by the OSCE/ODIHR EOM. The distinction between State activities and the campaign of the ruling United National Movement (UNM) party candidate, Mr. Mikheil Saakashvili, was blurred. In addition, as referenced in a Post-Election Interim Report issued by the OSCE/ODIHR on 18 January, other aspects of the election process, notably vote count and tabulation procedures, as well as the post-election complaints and appeals process, further presented serious challenges to the fulfillment of some OSCE commitments.[8]

The candidate who won was clearly the preferred candidate of most voters in Georgia.

The parliamentary election in May 2008 was an opportunity for opposition voices to win more representation in parliament. As with the presidential election in 2008, the parliamentary election was imperfect but not terrible. The OSCE/ODIHR identified some flaws with the election:

> While overall, all parties were able to campaign, there were credible reports of obstruction of opposition campaign events. The campaigning of some opposition parties was negative in tone, highlighting mistrust in the state authorities and the election administration, and focusing on alleged violations and plans by the authorities to manipulate the elections. This expression of mistrust was compounded by reports of widespread intimidation of opposition candidates, party activists and state employees in many regions. Of the numerous specific allegations examined by the OSCE/ODIHR EOM, several were clearly found to be credible, including a number of verified cases of pressure exerted by local officials on opposition supporters, including in particular teachers, to desist from

campaigning.... The distinction between state and party was frequently blurred. There were cases of state officials conducting official duties in combination with campaign events of UNM majoritarian candidates, or government social programmes being combined with UNM campaign activities. Opposition parties also alleged that the UNM had privileged access to administrative resources, and that regional governors engaged in campaigning for the UNM, in contravention of the law.[9]

However, their report was not altogether negative:

Generally, the media provided voters with a diverse range of political views, allowing them to make a more informed choice.... Election Day was generally calm, and according to CEC data, 53 per cent of voters turned out to vote. Overall, voting was assessed positively by a large majority of IEOM observers.[10]

The UNM won the election handily to retain firm control of parliament, but three of the four opposition parties that had won seats in parliament decided to boycott parliament and not take their seats because of their belief the election was not conducted fairly. This rather foolish decision allowed the UNM to remain the dominant, and at times, almost the only, voice in the legislature.

The second period was also characterized by a more restrictive media climate and a less independent judiciary than in the years immediately following the Rose Revolution, while elections changed from being essentially free, fair, and uncompetitive during the first period to being partly free, partly fair, and a little more competitive during the second period.

Since the early days of the Rose Revolution, media freedom had been a problem in Georgia. The media had been reasonably free during Shevardnadze's presidency, although poverty and energy shortages were an effective censor to many. During Saakashvili's tenure as president, the media were more influenced by the government, but the closing of Imedi accelerated this. Imedi never reappeared as a major independent network, and quickly became a staunchly pro-Saakashvili station. Beginning in 2008, the only nongovernment-controlled television stations were local with little reach outside Tbilisi. These included Kavkasia and Maestro.

Similarly, the lack of judicial independence, always a problem in Saakashvili's Georgia, became worse. Human Rights Centre, a Georgian NGO primarily funded by European donors, observed in 2009 that

It is a problem that judges fail to be impartial in their verdicts. The monitoring carried out by the Human Rights Centre demonstrated that judges mostly render independent verdicts in civil cases but they subordinate to the pressure from the executive branch of government and the prosecutor's office when it comes to administrative and criminal cases. Independent court decisions in criminal cases are an exception rather than a rule. This allegation can be proven by the very small number of acquittals and the verdicts that mostly match the request of a prosecutor. Application of plea bargain procedure remains problematic. (Human Rights Centre 2009: 3)

During the second period, the political climate in Georgia changed as well. In the early years of the Rose Revolution the government was able to use its popularity, which remained high, to deflect criticism and explain away any democratic shortcomings. By late 2007, this was no longer possible. Instead, the government took on the opposition more directly, hinting that much of the opposition was linked to Russia and occasionally circulating videos of questionable parentage seeking to prove this. The response by the opposition was to step up criticism of Saakashvili and more loudly call for his resignation. This contributed to the tense political climate which existed throughout this time.

Saakashvili's government had never been tolerant of political opposition. During the first years this might have been attributed to impatience and excessive self-confidence on the part of the government. However, during this first period, the nascent opposition was, in fact, quite weak. The government certainly created problems for the opposition during these early years through changing the electoral rules, failing to build real barriers between the ruling party and the state, and the like.

Beginning in November 2007, the opposition was no longer as weak as in the early days after the Rose Revolution, but government intolerance became considerably stronger and uglier. The government played on the legitimate concerns throughout society regarding Russian influence and efforts to weaken and destabilize in order to raise suspicions about all political opposition. Beginning with the large demonstrations in November 2007, the government alleged that Russian money was funding the opposition and that opposition leaders were in close contact with, and getting direction from, Russia. The government viewed, or at least presented, itself as uniquely able to defend Georgia against Russia. This led easily to painting any anti-government voice and action as Russian.

The government strategy was effective because their claims had some basis in reality. Even before the August 2008 war, Russian anger at the Georgian government and efforts to weaken and destabilize Georgia were real. Moreover, it is certainly likely that some, though far from all, opposition leaders and parties had ties with Russia. Over time this line of attack became less plausible as some opposition leaders the government suggested were somehow working with Russia had been high ranking government officials such as Alasania, former Georgian ambassador to the U.N., and former foreign minister Salome Zurabishvili.

Trying to link opposition figures to Russia was only one way the government sought to move against opposition political forces. During this period it applied stronger pressure on wealthy Georgians who were interested in supporting the opposition, making it clear that their businesses would suffer if they contributed to opposition political parties.[11] It was widely believed that the government listened in on meetings and phone calls conducted by the opposition. When recording equipment was found in the office of the Conservative Party, the government responded that the devices in question could have been purchased anywhere. This may have been true, but was of limited relevance (Civil.ge 2009c).

During the spring and summer of 2009 there were constant demonstrations and vigils in the streets of Tbilisi. The government handled these demonstrations better than they did in November 2007, but this is something of a low bar by which to evaluate the government. Although the demonstrations were allowed to persist with no violent dispersals on the part of the government, there were numerous reports of police officers out of uniform beating and arresting protesters as well as arrests of opposition activists throughout the country, mostly on drug and weapons charges. Human Rights Watch reported that

> during the protests, human rights groups documented a suspicious pattern of attacks on opposition activists by unidentified assailants, and police used excessive force against and detained protestors, and attacked journalists . . . unidentified men in civilian clothes, often armed with rubber truncheons and wearing masks, beat and threatened a number of individual demonstrators leaving protests at night; civil society groups and the ombudsman reported dozens of similar incidents. The authorities opened over 50 individual cases, but failed to meaningfully investigate—suggesting acquiescence or support for such attacks. (Human Rights Watch 2010)

May 2011 protests were also met by violent reactions by government forces.

Throughout this period, Georgia's pro-western and pro-democracy rhetoric remained unchanged with the government periodically announcing imminent reforms. These included at different times promises of a "second Rose Revolution" (Civil.ge 2008b) and the appointment for a brief period of a special minister to focus on democratic reform. The latter was something of a tragicomic gesture because Dmitri Shashkin, the minister responsible for democratic reform, was also, at that time, minister of penitentiary and probations, making Shashkin the world's only minister for prisons and democracy.[12]

During summer 2009, the government pointed to the demonstrations as evidence of their country's democratic strength. A government publication in April reported that, "Meanwhile, the Government won praise from international observers for the professionalism and transparency with which the police have handled the peaceful demonstrations" (Georgia Update 2009: 1). There was, of course, some truth to this sentiment, as demonstrations like that would not be allowed in an authoritarian country; and Saakashvili's Georgia was not an authoritarian country. The use of listening devices, evening beatings, and harassment of demonstrators, on the other hand, do not qualify as a particularly open or democratic response to demonstrations either.

Throughout the post-Rose Revolution period, Georgia was neither democratic nor authoritarian but somewhere in between. During the first period of Saakashvili's presidency, the regime was an unconsolidated democracy. The gains of the Rose Revolution were real and clear. Although democracy in Georgia was far from perfect, progress was being made. The country was moving toward democracy, but it was proving difficult to change institutions. Additionally, the government developed the bad habit of cutting corners with regard to process and democracy to more quickly push through their reform agenda. These are the characteristics of a semidemocracy.

During the second period, this changed. The government was no longer moving toward democracy, but was using components of democracy, such as semi-fair elections and democratic rhetoric, to keep an increasingly undemocratic government in power. The parliamentary elections of 2008, for example, saw the government use administrative resources to consolidate its power, while seeking to present the election internationally as evidence of democratic credentials. Similarly, a few opposition television stations were allowed to have strongly anti-government programs, but these stations reached almost nobody outside the capital.

If the Rose Revolution is placed in the larger context of political development in post-Soviet Georgia, it can be understood as a clear move from the anarchy and lawlessness of the Shevardnadze years toward more order and a stronger state all in the gray area between democracy and authoritarianism because independent Georgia has never truly had either.

Democratic Trends in Georgia, Ukraine, and Kyrgyzstan

In the first few years following the Color Revolutions, Georgia and Ukraine have followed broadly similar, but not identical courses of democratic reform overlaid with sometimes paralyzing domestic political stalemates and increasingly unpopular presidents, while Kyrgyzstan followed a different course of replacing one kleptocratic regime with another that may or may not be more democratic than its predecessor.

Another approach would be to see Ukraine as the outlier as it is the only country to make, and maintain, meaningful democratic advances, even experiencing a peaceful transition of power—something that has not occurred in Georgia or Kyrgyzstan. In this taxonomy, the similarities between Kyrgyzstan and Georgia should be understood but not overstated. For the last decade, Georgia has been more democratic than Kyrgyzstan, and that remains true today. However, in both countries the post-Color Revolution regime initially consolidated power; in Georgia it developed a stronger state, particularly with regard to security forces, while making democracy a considerably lower priority. This failure to engage in serious state building undoubtedly contributed to the collapse of the Bakiev regime, while in Georgia the state has grown strong enough to remain in power despite various challenges and crises.

There were some differences between democracy in Georgia and Kyrgyzstan as well. Although civil liberties and free media are not as strong in Georgia as they were in the last years of the Shevardnadze period, they are still considerably stronger in Saakashvili's Georgia than they were in Bakiev's Kyrgyzstan. The Georgian parliament today does not play the key role in democratic development that it did in the Shevardnadze period, and has become something of a rubber stamp for Saakashvili,[13] but it is a much more open and serious legislative body than the Kyrgyz legislature was under Bakiev. However, Georgia had been more democratic than Kyrgyzstan for years before the Color Revolutions as well.

The question this raises is whether these are differences of degree, Georgia being similar to Bakiev's Kyrgyzstan, but more liberal, or of kind, with Georgia and Kyrgyzstan having different kinds of regimes during this period. For the first period following Georgia's Rose Revolution, it was clear that this was a difference in kind. Georgia during those years seemed to be moving, albeit with difficulty, occasionally serious difficulty, toward democracy. Saakashvili's mostly successful attempts to root out the petty corruption that had been almost ubiquitous in Shevardnadze's Georgia, the improvements made in the conduct of elections and the economic reform of these years were unlike anything seen in Kyrgyzstan since the Tulip Revolution. During these years, while democracy could not be said to have been a top priority of the Georgian government, the regime was still in transition.

The Georgian regime since late 2007 has still been more liberal than Bakiev's Kyrgyzstan, but both countries were semi-authoritarian regimes. In both cases, for example, administrative resources were used to ensure electoral outcomes favorable to the government, while opposition politicians were not allowed to operate free of harassment.

The major difference in the two regimes was not about democracy but about the broader goals of the regime. In Georgia, state building continued to be the primary goal of the regime throughout both the post-Rose Revolution periods.[14] In Kyrgyzstan the state concerned itself less with building a functioning Kyrgyz state and more with rent-seeking, enriching the leadership and regime survival.

The Akaev regime was the least democratic of the three pre-Color Revolutionary governments; and the Tulip Revolution strayed from the peaceful mass protest model of the Rose, Orange, and even Bulldozer revolutions. For this reason, it should not be at all surprising that Kyrgyzstan remained the least democratic during Bakiev's rule. The difference in this regard between Ukraine and Georgia is intriguing.

The relative success of Ukraine in comparison to Georgia provides some insights into democracy that may seem unexpected. A major difference between the Orange and Rose Revolutions is that while the former led to a divided country, the latter led to one unified, at least at first, behind a president and a party committed, at least publicly, to democracy. The success of Ukraine suggests that enduring political cleavages are important for consolidating democracy. Unity of the kind found in Georgia seems like a valuable political good, but it turned out to have hindered Georgia's democratization.

The enormous popularity enjoyed by Saakashvili and the lack of any opposition based on vision, platform, or ideology empowered him to frequently ignore process in his rush to do what the people wanted him to do. This unity also meant that from the beginning of the Rose Revolution, there were no external checks on Saakashvili's government. Unity, which in all three Color Revolutions was an essential, if occasionally brief or late, component of the initial democratic breakthrough, is less of an unambiguous asset in doing the more difficult work of democratic consolidation. Ironically, the pre-Color Revolution unity was weaker in Georgia than in the other two countries. The rivalry between Saakashvili and the other two principal leaders of the Rose Revolution, Zurab Zhvania and Nino Burjanadze, was intense and did not recede until shortly before Shevardnadze's resignation. The decision by these three to form one party and run together in the 2004 parliamentary election, which was to make up for the fraudulent one of 2003, turned out to be a major mistake because it institutionalized a new one party dominant system. Had that election instead pitted a Saakashvili party against a Zhvania-Burjanadze party, it would have institutionalized a system of two competing pro-Rose Revolution parties.

In Ukraine Timoschenko and Yushchenko, although frequent coalition partners in government, retained separate parties and often competed against each other both in elections and in government. Ukraine's democratic development benefited from party competition among supporters of the Color Revolution in a way that did not exist in Georgia, thus instituting more political pluralism in the former country.

Unity, of course, did not last very long in Georgia. By 2009, the Georgian political debate, with a few exceptions, pitted Rose Revolutionaries such as Saakashvili and those around him against former Rose Revolutionaries including Saakashvili's former speaker of parliament, UN ambassador, foreign minister, and numerous former NGO allies. However, while unity no longer existed with regard to political alliances, few differences remained between these two groups regarding major policy directions. Instead, the major difference revolved around the performance of the government and on views of Saakashvili himself.

Second, the temptation to link democracy and reform is strong, but while there is certainly overlap between these two concepts, this overlap is limited. The Georgian government's fight against corruption, along with efforts to reform the tax code, make it easier to invest and do business in Georgia and made a great impression on many in the west. The government managed to push these reforms through with impressive speed, but they were able to do it because of their increasing disregard for democratic processes. Few of these reforms were debated or discussed by the legislature; and the views of the public were sought for even fewer. Representative Howard Berman (D-Cal.), writing in the *Washington Post*, was one of the first American officials to understand this nuance: "an amended tax code and streamlined bureaucracy, while important, do not by themselves constitute true democracy" (Berman (2009). Reforms that sought to modernize and westernize the government and business policies of Georgia overshadowed the lack of any forward movement regarding democracy.

In Ukraine the reverse was true. The reform process was much slower than in Georgia. The various political factions and parties fought over the direction of the reform and no real consensus existed on many major issues. While this was frustrating for both Ukrainian reformers and western allies, it also was evidence of some real democratic development. Although political institutions in Ukraine remained deeply flawed, with corruption rampant in the legislature and administrative resources still widely used at election time, political institutions, notably the parliament, began to emerge as fora where issues could be discussed and substantive disagreements could be presented. In Ukraine, the slow pace of reform and the constant fighting between political parties obscured a strengthening of democracy.

In all three countries, the difficult post-Color Revolutionary paths toward, and sometimes away from, democracy, underscore the difficulty of democratic consolidation. The electoral breakthroughs themselves turned out to have been the easy part. The regimes of Shevardnadze, Kuchma and Akaev were sufficiently weak and either unwilling or unable to push back against the protests, so ousting these regimes was, for the most part, pushing an open door. The ease with which this was done raised expectations both domestically and internationally.

Overthrowing dictators had been viewed as the difficult part of bringing about democracy. This may, in fact, be true, but it is not relevant to the Color Revolutions because none of the leaders who were overthrown had been dictators. Overthrowing tired post-Communist semidemocratic kleptocrats proved considerably easier than getting rid of dictators, but also less central to democratic progress. Destroying authoritarian regimes such as the one in the Soviet Union, Franco's Spain, or right wing authoritarian regimes in Latin America is an integral first step toward democratization. Destroying semidemocratic regimes is a far more ambiguous step in this direction. The former clearly represent forward steps for democracy, but the latter are frequently only sideways steps. This appears to be most true in Georgia and Kyrgyzstan where the new regimes are different types of semidemocracies (Georgia before 2008) or semi-authoritarian regimes (Kyrgyzstan and to some extent Georgia from 2008 on), but they have not moved significantly closer to becoming full democracies. Ukraine may be an exception, but recent developments indicate that the early momentum of the Orange Revolution has stopped and democracy has stalled at what Freedom House would define as the high end of the partly free category.

The impact of the Color Revolutions on the democratic development of all three of these countries has proven to be slight. While it is impossible to know what would have happened in each of these countries had the Shevardnadze, Kuchma/Yanokovich, or Akaev regimes remained in power and the Color Revolutions not occurred, it is useful to view these transitions as being as much about continuity as about change. All three post-Color Revolution leaders had been at one time close associates of the outgoing president. In the cases of Yushchenko and Saakashvili they were viewed as being part of the liberalizing or reform faction in the president's party. Bakiev was a little different in this regard, but had, at one time been close to Akaev.

There are important elements of continuity in all these cases, which are less ambiguous than any democratizing trends. Yushchenko's Ukraine, like that of his predecessor, remained divided on regional lines and dominated by the Party of the Regions in the east. The country was certainly more liberal and less pro-Russia, but the strong ties between industry and government and widespread influence of money in politics remained. Bakiev, like his predecessor, ran Kyrgyzstan like a family fiefdom as members of the president's family and close associates divided the political and economic spoils. Saakashvili's Georgia, while, at least at first, stronger than that of his predecessor, was still dominated by a single party with power highly concentrated in the presidency.

These elements of continuity are significant, but this continuity came at a cost because of the expectations for the Color Revolutions. Uneventful transitions to a new leadership in each of these countries may well have resulted in similar overall advancement for democracy, but the cost would have been less. The disappointment with the slow pace of democratic reform will make future democratic movement in these countries considerably more difficult.

CHAPTER 7

Exporting Color Revolutions

AFTER THE SUCCESS of the Rose Revolution in Georgia, democracy activists in the former Soviet Union and in the West—especially the United States—believed the Georgian model could be replicated in other countries in the region. The Orange Revolution, only a year later, and the Tulip Revolution a few months after that, only increased this belief. However, the Color Revolutions proved to be an extremely short-lived phenomenon.

To some extent, the failure of Color Revolutions to occur anywhere after the Tulip Revolution in spring 2005 can be attributed partly to backlash from authoritarian and semi-authoritarian governments in the remaining countries of the former Soviet Union, where the other states did not want to see Color Revolutions, but also to the changing global context, particularly the U.S. involvement in Iraq.

In the west there was anger and frustration with the increasingly dubious policies of the Bush administration's new emphasis on democracy assistance. Democracy assistance evolved from a perceived bipartisan policy to one closely associated with the neoconservatives around Bush. By 2006–2008, suspicion about the value and morality of democracy assistance had become part of the standard antiwar and anti-Bush worldview. Ironically, Bush's enthusiasm ended up helping erode support for that policy.[1]

During these years, activists throughout the former Soviet Union sought to imitate the Color Revolutions, but many, like numerous western policy makers, lacked a clear understanding of what had occurred in Georgia, Ukraine, and Kyrgyzstan. The use of the term Color Revolutions made it possible to lump all these events together, and even include the deposal of Milosevic in Serbia in 2000. Once a term had been created, a tendency to stress their similarities led to the notion that a Color Revolution formula existed and could be applied more broadly.

This book has sought to demonstrate that while there are important similarities which characterize the Color Revolutions, the differences and individual contexts are at least as important. For example, the Ukrainian and Serbian cases occurred around presidential elections, while the Rose and Tulip revolutions occurred around parliamentary elections. Large demonstrations played a much bigger role in Ukraine and Serbia than in Georgia and Kyrgyzstan where the demonstrations were, generally, much smaller. The Rose and Orange Revolutions benefited from gifted and charismatic leaders such as Saakashvili, Timoschenko, Zhvania, Yushchenko, and Burjanadze. The leaders of the Tulip and Bulldozer Revolutions did not enjoy the same popularity or charisma. Opposition unity was essential in Ukraine and Serbia, essential but late in Georgia, and less relevant in Kyrgyzstan.

Moreover, even some of the similarities were not quite understood. Pre-Color Revolution regimes in Ukraine, Kyrgyzstan, and particularly Georgia were weak; civil society was relatively free, and political institutions such as legislatures and elections were, by post-Soviet standards, relatively functional. These were the conditions that made Color Revolutions possible.

The challenge for those seeking to replicate Color Revolutions in other countries, then, was not so much providing would-be Color Revolutionaries with the skills and resources to challenge unfair elections and take to the streets, but rather finding countries where the relative strength of the state, civil society, and political institutions was conducive to a Color Revolution scenario.

Almost immediately after the Rose Revolution, activists from Georgia began to get in contact with leaders of the political and civic opposition in Ukraine, much as the Serbs who had helped overthrow Milosevic had worked with the Georgian opposition the year before. After the Orange Revolution, Ukrainian activists began to do the same thing. While there was no official U.S. policy of seeking to spread Color Revolutions throughout the former Soviet Union, this cross-fertilization was sporadically encouraged by both the U.S. government and various NGOs close to it. Often, for example, travel funding came from the NED, OSI, or other U.S. based funders.

Beissinger (2007) uses the term "modular" to describe the spread of Color Revolutions from Georgia to Ukraine to Kyrgyzstan. While acknowledging the differences in events, Beissiner argues that "elite defection" and "elite learning" were modular in nature, as events in, for example, Georgia informed decision making and actions in Ukraine: "each successful democratic revolution has produced an experience that has been consciously borrowed by others, spread by NGOs, and emulated by local social movements, forming the contours of a model. With each iteration the model has altered somewhat as it confronts the reality of local circumstances" (261).

Mobilizing Against Color Revolutions

While civic and political activists from Georgia and Ukraine sought to share what they had learned about how to leverage stolen elections into regime change or democratic breakthroughs, leaders around the region learned a different set of lessons from the Color Revolutions. Regimes like Alexander Lukashenko's in Belarus, Ilham Aliev's in Azerbaijan, and Nursultan Nazerbayev's in Kazakhstan began to pass laws and establish policies of their own, based on these lessons, which sought to make Color Revolutions impossible in their countries. The most powerful country which embraced this effort was Russia, where the Putin regime not only implemented these policies at home but offered support and assistance to other leaders in the region seeking to avoid the fate of Shevardnadze or Akaev.

The Color Revolutions were believed by these authoritarian and semi-authoritarian leaders to be strong evidence of the risks of allowing too much freedom. Akaev and Shevardnadze particularly had long been lauded by Americans and Europeans for the relatively open nature of their countries and media as well as other freedoms enjoyed by citizens of Kyrgyzstan and Georgia. From the perspective of Baku, Moscow, Minsk, and other capitals in the region, it was apparent that these freedoms, which allowed for a constant drumbeat of media criticism of the government and made it possible for opposition parties and other groups to organize and mobilize, also contributed directly to the downfall of Shevardnadze, Akaev, and even Kuchma.

Ambrosio (2009) argues that opposition to democratization, or more precisely democracy promotion, is an essential component of democratic development. Accordingly he asserts that, in addition to studying external forces working to strengthen democracy, resistance to these forces should be studied as well. Ambrosio identifies five main strategies of "authoritarian resistance" used by Russia and other regimes in the region. The first is "*insulating* their country from external democratic pressures." The second is to "*redefine* the problem of external democracy promotion to their advantage." Third is to "*bolster* or support fellow autocrats," so that democracy does not attain an air of inevitability as it did in Eastern Europe in 1989. Fourth is to "subvert or sabotage democratic states through a mix of diplomatic, political and military pressures." Obviously, not all authoritarian states are strong enough to do this, but this certainly is relevant to Russia's relations with Georgia and Ukraine. Last is "establishing and supporting international organizations to protect their own and like-minded governments from the possibility of regime change" (Ambrosio (2009: 19–25).

Beissinger, like Ambrosio, points out that modularity is not restricted to Color Revolutionaries but applies to those opposed to Color Revolutions as well as

> growing restrictions on civil society organizations in Russia, Belarus, Uzbekistan, Azerbaijan, and Kazakhstan. In the wake of the Orange and Tulip Revolutions authoritarian regimes have cracked down on opponents, closed down or monitored more closely relations with democracy-promoting NGOs, and established closer relations with Russia as a way of providing international support against the threat of transnational revolution. Some have established their own pro-regime youth movements to counteract the influence of transnational youth movements. (Beissinger 2007: 270)

As Beissinger and Ambrosio indicate, leaders in Moscow and elsewhere arrived at the conclusion that NGOs, particularly American NGOs, seeking to build democracy, strengthen civil society, create open societies, or generally support greater freedom represented a real threat. Democracy-related organizations such as NDI, IRI, and others had operated in many of these countries, and much of the region for several years before the Color Revolutions. In some countries, and at some times, they had confronted low level harassment and surveillance and frequently did not have great access to the government, but they had been allowed to operate more or less as they pleased.

Organizations seeking to build democracy often annoyed or puzzled nondemocratic leaders who could not quite figure out what these organizations really were. Furthermore, these governments were never convinced that organizations like NDI and IRI were genuinely independent of the U.S. government.[2] However, until the Color Revolutions, they were not viewed as a serious threat to any regime. Beginning with the Rose Revolution, this perception changed. Democracy assistance organizations, most notably NDI as well as OSI, a private American foundation, were viewed as having played a significant role in the Rose Revolution. This view became even stronger after the Orange Revolution.[3]

These concerns about allowing too much media freedom and independent civic life as well as more specific concerns about the work of U.S.-based democracy assistance organizations led many countries in the region to crack down on both. Having seen the import of media that were not controlled by the government, particularly Rustavi-2, the independent television station that had been so central to the Rose Revolution, governments from Astana to Minsk made it more difficult to get television licenses and sought to strengthen their control over television stations through passing laws on media, threatening stations critical of the government, and harassing independent and investigative journalists.

Laws were also passed that made it harder for NGOs to operate. For many domestic NGOs, registering became more difficult and visits from the tax auditor and other forms of petty harassment became more common. Domestic NGOs that received foreign assistance were particularly vulnerable as Russia, for example, passed laws limiting the money these NGOs could receive and creating difficult and time-consuming regulations for financial reporting.[4]

It was not just domestic NGOs that were confronted with new laws and increased harassment following the Color Revolutions. International organizations found themselves frequently working in a more difficult environment as well. Governments created new barriers for them. Registering became very difficult. Access to the government was very limited as democracy organizations were increasingly marginalized politically. Occasionally Americans or other foreigners working for these organizations were not given visas or even kicked out of the country. The government of Uzbekistan, for example shut down the local offices of George Soros's Open Society Institute in 2005. During this time it was not unusual to see U.S. democracy organizations accused of seeking to overthrow governments. This was particularly true in Belarus and Azerbaijan. In the former, at least, these accusations had some merit.[5]

In addition to restricting freedoms generally and creating more specific obstacles for civil society organizations, governments seeking to avoid Color Revolutions in their own country pursued other policies, based on other lessons. In Georgia, Ukraine, and even Kyrgyzstan, one of the hallmarks of the Color Revolutions was the lack of violence on both sides. The opposition, particularly in Georgia and Ukraine, acted nonviolently, but equally significantly, the government did not respond to the protests and demonstrations by using violence either. In the Tulip Revolution there was more looting and violence of that sort, but the government did not violently crack down on the demonstrators.

It was not only the absence of violence that made the Color Revolutions possible, but the absence of the threat of violence. Demonstrators on the Maidan in Kiev or on Rustaveli Avenue in Tbilisi, as well as the leaders in both cases, were confident that government authorities would not turn to violence to quash them and that a Tiananmen Square style repression was not a possibility. This confidence was extremely empowering to the demonstrators as well as to ordinary citizens who joined in these demonstrations as they built to their climax.

In order to combat Color Revolutions in their own countries, leaders in Baku or Astana did not necessarily need to initiate violent crackdowns against demonstrators. Rather, they needed to make a credible threat of violence strong enough to preclude the demonstrations altogether. The most effective way to do this was through pre-election violence initiated by the government, supported by threats and strong language indicating that the government would not tolerate any post-election scenarios involving large demonstrations or demands for resignations. Successfully instilling this fear throughout the region after Ukraine, and particularly after Kyrgyzstan, was one of the main ways the wave of Color Revolutions was stopped so abruptly after June 2005.

Other more technical approaches were used by governments to reduce the chance of Color Revolutions in their own countries. Apparent minor changes to election laws were one of the ways they sought to do this. While elections are natural flashpoints for political change, not all elections are the same; and not all elections have the same potential to catalyze this type of change. The elections with the greatest ability to generate the attention and focus necessary for a Color Revolution type breakthrough must be national in scope, but not even all national elections, structurally, are the same.

When a country is electing a president, the election has a strong national focus, as candidates for that office must speak about national issues. These candidates also must campaign throughout the country, giving opposition figures the opportunity to spread their message and mobilize supporters across the country. If the opposition is able to unify around a single opponent, such as Yushchenko in Ukraine or Vojislav Kostunica in Serbia, that candidate becomes a symbol for the opposition and for change itself.

Few of the countries of the former Soviet Union had national list systems like Georgia's, which made it possible for parliamentary elections to be truly national. A number of other post-Soviet countries such as Azerbaijan and Kyrgyzstan had moved toward parliaments consisting of single mandate seats in the late 1990s and early twenty-first century. Single mandate seats made it harder for national figures such as Saakashvili to emerge and become stronger during parliamentary elections. This helped semi-authoritarian leaders consolidate power even before the Color Revolutions.

Large street demonstrations, refusing to accept fraudulent electoral outcomes, foreign election monitors, and technical support for political forces provided by donors were among the tactics and characteristics of the Color Revolutions which Russia and other governments seeking to resist Color Revolutions employed after, and in some cases before, 2005. By using these tactics, which had been associated with democracy and used by citizens advocating for greater liberalization and freedom, countries seeking to prevent the spread of, or roll back, Color Revolutions successfully muddied the strategic waters of democracy.

One example is the CIS Election Monitoring Organization (CIS-EMO), which was founded in late 2002 but became more active beginning with the Ukrainian presidential election in 2004. Ambrosio (2009: 56) describes this organization as "another tool to undermine the legitimacy of the European observers." Since that time, the CIS has consistently labeled elections, including the Kyrgyz election of spring 2005 which led to the Orange Revolution, as well as elections since then in Uzbekistan and Tajikistan, as free and fair. Generally, the CIS-EMO can be relied on to report findings diametrically opposite to those of the western election monitoring missions such as the OSCE/ODIHR.

The CIS-EMO has not emerged as a real rival to the OSCE/ODIHR or other western supported international election monitoring organizations, but it has complicated the west's election monitoring strategy. Most of the elections monitored by the OSCE/ODIHR exist in an enormous gray area between completely fraudulent and completely fair. For this reason, the perception that geopolitics motivates some of the work the OSCE/ODIHR does cannot be avoided. By offering a different interpretation of the same events, from a different geopolitical angle, CIS election monitors have been able to muddy the waters. Their argument is based on the reality that flaws can be found in any election in the region, so it is easy to view election assessments as largely subjective.

The CIS-EMO is influential because most of the countries from which these monitors come, and whose elections they observe, have relatively unfree media. For example, the Russian media will cover, largely uncritically the CIS-EMO evaluation of an election in a neighboring country like Uzbekistan or Armenia. This is not dissimilar to how western media outlets are largely uncritical, and unquestioning, toward western election monitoring organizations.

In addition to election monitoring, Russia and other countries in the region have supported, and largely created, pro-government youth groups that agitate in support of leaders such as Putin and Lukashenko. These groups include organizations such as Nashi in Russia. Following the November 2007 election, Nashi occupied the streets of Moscow to preempt any chance of anti-government demonstrators using the election as a catalyst for a Color Revolution.[6] The Belarusian Patriotic Youth movement plays a similar role in Belarus.

Russia's involvement in Kyrgyzstan in the waning days of the Bakiev regime was the most successful example of Russia using techniques associated with democracy assistance to achieve its aims. Although the extent to which Russia was involved in those events is still unclear, Russia certainly played some role in ousting Bakiev. In Kyrgyzstan, according to the *New York Times*, Russia used the lessons it learned in 2003–2005 to achieve its goal in 2010. But Russia appears to have learned well the lessons of the so-called color revolutions in Georgia, Ukraine, and Kyrgyzstan in the past decade. In those uprisings, which overthrew governments allied with Russia but that had become alienated from their own populations, the West provided open support for opposition elites and free media.

> This time, the Russians staked out a remarkably similar position and used it to their advantage. In Kyrgyzstan, an American diplomat said, the Russians 'had a color revolution of their own color."
>
> Russia's use of so-called soft power mirrored a long policy of American support for civil society in the former Soviet republics, under programs like the Freedom Support Act and financing for nongovernmental groups. Just five years ago that support, including U.S. financing for a publishing house in the Kyrgyz capital, Bishkek, which produced reports of corruption, was credited with preparing the ground for the previous Kyrgyz uprising, the so-called Tulip Revolution. (Kramer (2010)

Azerbaijan 2005

The October 2005 elections in Azerbaijan were the beginning of the end for the momentum generated by the three post-Soviet Color Revolutions. From the vantage point of mid-2005, Azerbaijan looked like a possible location for the next Color Revolution. Like Georgia, Ukraine, and Kyrgyzstan, Azerbaijan was governed by a nondemocratic regime with a history of fraudulent elections, there was still sufficient political space for opposition political parties to emerge and organize. The 2005 elections in Azerbaijan were parliamentary elections, like those that had led to the downfall of Shevardnadze in neighboring Georgia. Moreover, like Georgia and Ukraine, Azerbaijan had sought to orient itself toward the west and to build strong ties with the U.S. and Europe.

By mid-2005 a unified opposition block of political parties had emerged. The Azadliq (Freedom) block brought together Azerbaijan's three largest opposition parties—the Azerbaijan Popular Front Party, Musuvat, and the Azerbaijan Democratic Party—into an electoral alliance. The unity of the Azeri opposition compared favorably to that of neighboring Georgia in the 2003 elections, where the major opposition parties ran separately and continued bickering well into the post-election demonstrations. Throughout the summer and early fall 2005, the Azadliq block led demonstrations in Baku, at times mobilizing tens of thousands of Azeri demonstrators. These were far larger than any pre-election demonstrations in Tbilisi, Kiev, or Bishkek.

The leaders of the Azeri opposition sought to emulate the Rose and Orange Revolutionaries, traveling to Georgia, Ukraine, and elsewhere with some frequency and consulting with Americans who had been active in democracy assistance efforts in Georgia and Ukraine during that period. The Azeri government was aware of these efforts and sought to restrict the influence of the model from neighboring Georgia on the election in Azerbaijan. The arrest of youth activist Ruslan Basirli, on charges of colluding with Armenia to overthrow the government of Azerbaijan, in August 2005 shortly after returning from Georgia, sent this message very clearly. Basirli was charged with participating in an Armenian plot to overthrow the government of Azerbaijan, but the occurrence of the arrest after a trip to Georgia made it clear that too much communication with Georgian activists by opposition figures would not be well received by the government.

The similarities between Azerbaijan and Georgia, Ukraine and Kyrgyzstan were unmistakable, contributing to the potential, or hope as some saw it, of a Color Revolution in Azerbaijan. However, the many differences between Azerbaijan and the other cases as well contributed to the failure of a Color Revolution to occur in Azerbaijan.

One major difference between Azerbaijan and at least Georgia and Ukraine was that the election itself, although a parliamentary election, was not really national in nature. Because there was no party list element to the election, it was very difficult for national leaders or campaigns to emerge. Instead, the parliament would consist of 125 single mandate seats. Given Azerbaijan's population of roughly eight million people, this meant that each district had a population of only 64,000, a sufficiently small number e that social and kinship networks generally outweigh political parties and local issues are more salient than national ones. Additionally, small districts of this kind make it possible for the candidates and governments to know the voters well thus making threats and intimidation easier.

The election in Azerbaijan, like the one in Kyrgyzstan earlier that year, was more of a national election for city council than a true parliamentary election. The district sizes were small even by the standards of many city councils. New York City, for example, has roughly the same population as Azerbaijan but only a 51-member city council.

The electoral system made it more difficult to leverage the election into a democratic breakthrough, but it had not been an insurmountable barrier for the Tulip Revolution. The primary reason the government of Azerbaijan was able to prevent a Color Revolution was the relative strength of the state in Azerbaijan. In the first years of the new century, Azerbaijan under the leadership of first Heydar and then Ilham Aliev (père et fils) was not run democratically, and it was quite corrupt, but it was not weak the way the Shevardnadze, Akaev, and Kuchma regimes were because it was buttressed by money generated from Azerbaijan's substantial oil wealth.

Aliev was able to keep the government running, spread enough wealth around to keep enough of the people happy that the opposition support would be limited, and, perhaps most important, keep the security forces paid and loyal. This was perhaps the most important difference between Azerbaijan in 2005 and, for example, neighboring Georgia in 2003. The threat of state violence was far greater in Azerbaijan where the security forces were well compensated, deeply entrenched in the government, and had demonstrated a willingness to use force not just in 2003, but in various demonstrations during the spring and summer 2005.[7] During the months leading up to the election, the government of Azerbaijan showed a willingness and ability to use violence to maintain their grip on power. Shortly before the election occurred, the government restated its willingness to do what was necessary to maintain stability in Azerbaijan. For the citizens of Azerbaijan the message was clear and credible.

In Georgia, Ukraine, and Kyrgyzstan, by contrast, in the months leading up to the election, the governments gave little indication that they were willing, or perhaps even able, to rely on the use of force to stay in power. Therefore, the threat of violence was far smaller, making it easier for opposition leaders to organize demonstrations and for ordinary people to participate in these demonstrations and to otherwise show support for the Color Revolutions.

Azerbaijan shares a border with Georgia, which makes movement of news and information between the two countries quite easy and common. Accordingly, in Azerbaijan the Rose Revolution was scrutinized by both the opposition and the government. While the government sought, successfully, to learn from what it viewed as Shevardnadze's mistakes, the opposition sought to emulate the Georgian opposition.

Aspects of the Azeri opposition movement including efforts to unify the opposition, branding the campaign with a color, in this case Orange, and planning a post-election strategy borrowed heavily from the Rose Revolution. Additionally, in Azerbaijan the youth group Yeni Fekir (New Idea) was consciously modeled on Kmara, the Georgian youth group.

For the Azeri opposition, one of the most striking and decisive differences between Georgia and Azerbaijan was the role played by international actors, notably the U.S. The Azeri opposition viewed the U.S. as having played a critical role in the Rose Revolution, both in helping opposition politicians such as Saakashvili and Zhvania and in counseling President Shevardnadze to refrain from using force and ultimately to step down. This view was not entirely accurate, but it was in powerful contrast to the way the U.S. conducted itself in Azerbaijan. In Azerbaijan, the U.S. did not encourage the opposition and was noticeably silent regarding election fraud both before and after the election.[8]

The Azeri opposition saw the U.S. role in the Rose Revolution as greater than it was, but their assessment of the U.S. role in supporting fair elections and democracy in Azerbaijan in 2005 was more accurate. Western criticism of Aliev's government before and after the election was relatively muted, largely because of U.S. interests in the ample fossil fuel resources possessed by Azerbaijan. The U.S. put far more pressure on Shevardnadze's government in the period leading up to the 2003 election than it did on Aliev's government as the 2005 election in Azerbaijan approached. For example, there were far fewer high level delegations to Azerbaijan in the months preceding the 2005 election than there were to Georgia in 2003. President Bush had even dispatched former secretary of state Jim Baker as his personal representative to implore Shevardnadze to conduct the election fairly and to try to broker a deal between the government and the opposition regarding the makeup of the Georgian Central Election Commission. Nothing comparable to this took place in Azerbaijan.

Similarly, the increased U.S. funds surrounding the election in Ukraine were not matched in Azerbaijan. Total democracy-related assistance from the U.S. was roughly $48 million to Ukraine in fiscal year 2005, but only about $8.9 million in Azerbaijan. This seems equivalent given the relative size of each country, but given the often centralized nature of democracy work during elections, this interpretation is misleading.[9] While the Azeri opposition may have viewed the western support for opposition movements in Ukraine, and particularly Georgia, as greater than it actually had been, there was no mistaking the message that the west, notably the U.S., sent regarding the election in Azerbaijan.

The failure of the nascent Color Revolution in Azerbaijan should not be reduced to a narrative that suggests that the west lost its desire for courage or its willingness to take risks in the name of spreading democracy. Although many in the Azeri opposition believed this narrative, it oversimplifies the role and intentions of the west in Georgia and Kyrgyzstan as well as the influence of the U.S. in general. The strength of the Azeri state and the willingness of its leaders to use force, the nature of the election system, and the weaker level of civil society development all contributed at least as much to the failure of a Color Revolution to emerge in Azerbaijan.

Nonetheless, the actions of the U.S. were different from those in the Color Revolution countries. Although this was probably not a decisive factor, it contributed to the political environment in Azerbaijan making it easier for the government to crack down on, and created more barriers for, the opposition.

Belarus

The presidential election in Belarus on March 19, 2006, saw President Alexander Lukashenko, to the surprise of no one, reelected easily. Lukashenko received 82.6 percent of the vote, the second place candidate, Alexander Milinkievic only 6 percent. Western election monitoring organizations were in broad agreement that there had been widespread fraud of every kind before, during, and after the election and that, while Lukashenko may have won, his margin of victory was nothing near the numbers that were reported.

Despite the fact that these candidates offered voters a genuine choice, the authorities subsequently failed to ensure equal conditions for a meaningful contest. The treatment of candidates by State authorities exhibited a decisive advantage for the incumbent president, Mr. Lukashenko, and raised doubts regarding the authorities' willingness to tolerate political competition based on equal treatment before the law and by the authorities.

Despite the fact that these candidates offered voters a genuine choice, the authorities subsequently failed to ensure equal conditions for a meaningful contest. The treatment of candidates by State authorities exhibited a decisive advantage for the incumbent President, Mr Lukashenko, and raised doubts regarding the authorities' willingness to tolerate political competition based on equal treatment before the law and by the authorities.

State power was employed arbitrarily against opposition candidates, thwarting their campaign efforts. Throughout the campaign, opposition campaign workers were routinely harassed, detained and arrested. Due to harassment by State authorities, campaign representatives reported that as the campaign progressed, it became increasingly difficult to recruit volunteers campaign staff.

Civil and political rights guaranteed by the Constitution were disregarded, including freedoms of expression, association, and assembly, and the right to access, gather, and disseminate information.[10]

Following the closing of the polls, crowds estimated in the tens of thousands gathered in the center of Minsk to protest the election fraud. Within a few days, however, these crowds had almost entirely dissipated and even the slightest doubt that Lukashenko would stay in power was no longer realistic.

The 2006 election in Belarus occurred in a very different geopolitical environment than any of the Color Revolution elections. Unlike the Shevardnadze, Kuchma, or Akaev regimes, the Lukashenko regime had fallen into strong disfavor with the west, particularly the U.S., years before the election. U.S. interest in getting rid of Lukashenko was explicit and could be traced back to at least 2002. The U.S. had suspected Belarus of cooperating with Saddam Hussein's regime in Iraq, offering military expertise and training to a regime that had been targeted by the U.S. government as supporting anti-American terrorism. In the "us versus them" framework of the early Bush years, Belarus had become part of "them" and, by doing so, a target of the U.S.

U.S. views toward Belarus were made clear at a conference in November 2002 hosted by the American Enterprise Institute, a think tank with strong ties to the Bush administration. The name of the conference, "Axis of Evil: Belarus—The Missing Link," spoke for itself. Radek Sikorski, a Pole who has served in numerous high profile positions in his country, summed up the spirit and goal of the conference, commenting "The message from this conference to Lukashenka is: 'President Lukashenka, be careful, because if your buddy in Baghdad gets thrown out, we will find the evidence of what you've been up to with him.'"

The keynote speaker at that conference was powerful U.S. senator, John McCain, who stated the American position on Lukashenko when he said "Thanks to Lukashenko's leadership, Belarus now joins a group of nations, including Iraq, Iran, and North Korea, that are both isolated in the modern community of nations and face a newfound American commitment to change the way they do business or go out of business."

After the Bulldozer Revolution, the Serbia model of electoral revolution became relevant in Belarus. By 2006, however, the Color Revolution model had made it even more significant. The failed Color Revolution in Belarus earned the name the Blue Jeans (occasionally Denim) Revolution. In keeping with the other Color Revolutions, the events in Belarus were really named not for a color, but for an object associated with a color. In most regards, however, the Blue Jeans Revolution had more in common with the events in Azerbaijan, than with those in Georgia, Ukraine, or Kyrgyzstan, because it resulted in failure. As in Azerbaijan in 2005, the election in March 2006 did not lead to resignations, regime change, or democratic promise.

Again, as in Azerbaijan, the Blue Jeans Revolution ended because a sufficiently strong state could raise the plausible fear of force to dissuade demonstrators from coming to the streets. Lukashenko clearly spelled out consequences which anybody participating in, or supporting post-election demonstrations would face. "Any attempt to destabilize the situation will be met with drastic action. We will wring the necks of those who are actually doing it and those who are instigating these acts. Embassies of certain states should be aware of this. They should know that we know what they are up to. They will be thrown out of here within 24 hours." As early as 2005, Lukashenko had made his views on Color Revolutions, and their applicability in Belarus clear, stating, "In our country there will be no pink or purple or even banana revolution. . . . All (those) colored revolutions are pure and simple banditry" (Karajkov 2005). Additionally, the Lukashenko regime was sufficiently popular that an uprising was very unlikely.

Belarus, like Azerbaijan, was the neighbor of a state where a successful Color Revolution had occurred. Georgia and Ukraine, however, even before the Rose and Orange Revolutions, were considerably different from Azerbaijan and Belarus. They were freer and more open: citizens enjoyed greater civil liberties, the media were less restricted, and civil society was stronger. One of the key lessons of the failure of Color Revolutions in Belarus and Azerbaijan was that such revolutions succeed in semidemocracies where the state is weak and freedoms exist. They are far less able to flourish in more authoritarian contexts like Azerbaijan and Belarus.

The failure of the Blue Jeans Revolution was the last gasp of the Color Revolution movement. The failure in Azerbaijan was bad in this regard, but that in Belarus was worse because in the years since the Rose Revolution Belarus had received a great deal of attention from western democracy promoters. Supporters of Color Revolutions could brush off defeat in Azerbaijan by arguing that the west had not really tried all that hard there. A similar argument could not be made about Belarus, where 2006 was the culmination of years of effort by Europe and the U.S. to get rid of Lukashenko[11]

By spring 2006 Belarus was one of the few countries in the world, certainly the only one in the former Soviet Union, for which the U.S. government had a more or less public policy of seeking regime change. Nothing even remotely like this had existed in Kyrgyzstan, Georgia, or Azerbaijan in the years and months leading up to successful or failed Color Revolutions in those countries. Even in Ukraine, where support for Yushchenko by the west was more explicit, and where democracy organizations had received more direct support and encouragement from western governments, the situation was not truly comparable to that of Belarus.

A *New York Times* magazine article provocatively titled "Bringing Down Europe's Last Ex-Soviet Dictator" describes an environment where

> Following popular uprisings against authoritarian leaders in Georgia, Ukraine and Kyrgyzstan, those who would like to break Lukashenko's iron grip, from President Bush to leaders across Europe, have thrown their support—and money—behind Milinkevich and an array of democratically minded activists determined to wake up a populace considered too passive, or too afraid, to challenge the state.

The article also captured the extent and nature of western commitment to regime change in Belarus:

The money, like the organizations themselves, has now gone underground or abroad. In December, 50 representatives of foreign ministries and international groups that support democracy gathered in Vilnius, the capital of neighboring Lithuania, to try to coordinate—and divide up—millions of dollars of aid. Thomas C. Adams, the State Department's aid coordinator for Europe and Eurasia, described the meeting to me as a gathering of "the Belarussian freedom industry."[12]

The extent and overt nature of Western opposition to Lukashenko's regime raised the stakes as the election approached, but the reality of the political situation there muted these expectations somewhat. Belarus was not a semi-democratic state where freedoms of assembly and speech were at least somewhat honored. It was an authoritarian regime where all efforts to change the government, even through political campaigns, were met with harassment, arrests, attacks in the media, and occasionally violence.

The failure of the Blue Jeans revolution was a failure of the Color Revolutions to expand beyond Georgia, Ukraine, and Kyrgyzstan, but it was also, as in Azerbaijan, a misapplication of the model. Color Revolutions depended on weak states where there was some freedom. One quick way to see this contrast is that in 2006, which is based on research from 2005, Belarus had Freedom House scores for "Freedom of Expression and Belief" and "Associational and Organizational Rights" of 3 and 0 respectively.[13] Azerbaijan's scores, also based on research from 2005, were not significantly better at 7 and 3.[14]

Without some ability to contest an election and make a plausible argument that the opposition had won, Color Revolutions would not have been possible. Similarly, a media climate that could expose and prepare the population for the inevitability of election fraud and report on post-election events was also a fundamental component of Color Revolutions. If the population in Georgia or Ukraine had been as afraid of state violence as those in Belarus and Azerbaijan, Color Revolutions would not have been possible in those places either. The failure of the Color Revolution in Belarus therefore, must be partly attributed to the failure of western powers to understand what made the first three Color Revolutions successful. The model never could have worked in Belarus and was the wrong strategy altogether.

After Belarus, the tenor and rhetoric of democracy assistance in the former Soviet Union changed. The U.S. no longer sought to bring about regime change through electoral breakthroughs. Since that time, elections in Azerbaijan, Armenia, and elsewhere have occurred with almost no talk by the west of potential democratic breakthroughs. The backlash against the Color Revolutions, however, has not receded, so the environment for making this kind of change has become extremely difficult, further discouraging anybody from trying.

The failure of attempted Color Revolutions in Azerbaijan and Belarus in 2005 and 2006 was followed by problems of democratization in all three successful Color Revolution countries that became increasingly difficult to ignore. This also contributed to the withering away of Color Revolutions as viable models for political change or democratic breakthroughs in the former Soviet Union or elsewhere.

Belarus 2010

The 2010 presidential election in Belarus occurred in a domestic political climate similar to that in 2006. Lukashenko continued to govern Belarus as an authoritarian regime with strict limits on freedoms, civic life, media, and political competition. As in 2006, the outcome of the election was never in doubt as Lukashenko's political control as well as genuine support among a substantial proportion of the population all but guaranteed his reelection. He ended up with 80 percent of the vote, beating his closest rival by more than 77 points.

Following the election, thousands of demonstrators gathered in Minsk to protest the outcome. The Belarusian government, to the surprise of nobody, moved quickly, arresting opposition candidates and activists, violently dispersing the demonstrations, expelling the OSCE, and threatening further consequences. Lukashenko's remarks the day after the crackdown were understated, but firm "There will not be any more tolerance of attempts to destabilize the situation in the country." Lukashenko also showed little sympathy for Uladzimir Nyaklyaeu, one of his opponents, who was beaten to the point of needing hospitalization, but was taken from his hospital bed to jail: "Should a current president know where a former presidential candidate is? Excuse me, but if you want to see him—he is in the detention center" (RFE/RL 2010).

Lukashenko, despite signals—including his public disagreements with Russia's leaders and his refusal to join Russia in recognizing independence for Abkhazia and South Ossetia—that he was slowly moving closer to the west in 2006–2010, was just as committed to his authoritarian rule in 2010 as he had been four years earlier. In Belarus, little had changed during this period, but the election and the Belarusian government's complete intolerance of any post-election demonstrations were met with very little response from the west. During the brief time the demonstrations were happening before the crackdown, admittedly only a few hours, there was no talk in the west of democracy or Color Revolution. Moreover, after the crackdown, as Belarus reinforced its authoritarian credentials and hurried to re-cement its relationship with Russia, there was also very little attention from the U.S. and Europe. By 2010, Color Revolutions, democratic breakthroughs, and the like had become something of the distant past, no longer a model or a goal, as yet another authoritarian post-Soviet regime demonstrated it could do what it needed to stay in power.

Other Lessons Learned

Authoritarian and semi-authoritarian leaders like Putin, Aliev, and Nazerbayev were not the only leaders who learned important lessons from the Rose Revolution. These lessons—wariness of NGOs, the need to manipulate election laws well before elections, the dangers of relatively free media—were also internalized by at least two beneficiaries of Color Revolutions. Both Bakiev and Saakashvili began to make changes to the laws and politics of their countries not too long after their ascent to power that looked similar to policies pursued by leaders throughout the region who enjoyed, at least in the eyes of the west, far less impressive democratic credentials.

Yushchenko did not pursue a similar path in Ukraine. This was caused by and, contributed to, the survival of a political opposition following the Orange Revolution. In Ukraine, the advances of freedoms of speech and assembly as well as of relatively free and fair elections, beginning with the redo of the runoff between Yushchenko and Yanukovich in January 2004, became entrenched, rather than reversed, during Yushchenko's presidency. Ironically, this contributed to the defeat of the Orange forces and Yanukovich's victory in the 2010 election.

Georgia and Kyrgyzstan were different. In these countries the new leadership took steps to consolidate power, preclude the emergence of serious political opposition, and limit freedoms of media and association similar to those taken throughout the region. The failure of Georgia and Kyrgyzstan to build on the initial democratic gains of the Rose and Tulip Revolutions has been addressed in Chapter 6, but these democratic shortcomings take on added significance when viewed in the context of broader regional trends.

The Kyrgyz government's policies on freedom of assembly since the

Tulip Revolution demonstrate this. In August 2008, ignoring a ruling by the Kyrgyz Supreme Court, President Bakiev amended the Law on Assembly severely limiting freedom of assembly. The amendment that "require(s) assembly organizers to notify local authorities 12 days in advance of any planned event, regardless of the size, does not enumerate grounds for 'reasonable disagreement' by the authorities, and allows provincial governors excessive powers to interfere with the planning of public assemblies" (HRW 2009) would not have been out place in Russia or Kazakhstan and is not consistent with the democratic aspirations of the Tulip Revolution.

The Bakiev regime sought to assert similar control over the media. A 2008 broadcast law gave the president direct power to appoint the executive directors of the state run television and radio stations. This meant that public broadcast outlets would become state broadcast outlets. The law also required that at least 50 percent of the broadcasts by any station be in either Kyrgyz or Russian, 50 percent be material produced by that station, and 60 percent have a Kyrgyz author or performer.

While all these policies had a direct impact on any station seeking to communicate with a non-Kyrgyz audience, the second and third provisions affected all stations. Media outlets in Kyrgyzstan have sufficiently few resources that they rely heavily on broadcasting programs produced outside the country. Limiting their ability to do this meant that stations were not able to broadcast as many programs and restricted their ability to broadcast critical programs which had been produced outside the country (Reporters Without Borders 2008). None of these restrictive laws were enough to keep the Bakiev regime in power, but the efforts they made to do this were apparent.

Throughout this period, Georgia remained more democratic and free than Kyrgyzstan. Additionally, the government of Georgia has been far more adroit and subtle at manipulating institutions to solidify their hold on power. The post-Rose Revolution government is too sophisticated to pass heavy-handed legislation explicitly aimed at limiting freedoms of media or assembly. However, it has succeeded in enacting similarly restrictive policies by relying on executive orders, financial pressure, and, when necessary, a state security apparatus far stronger than before the Rose Revolution.

Although achieved through subtler techniques, the result, while not nearly as draconian, has been similar in Georgia to what it was in Kyrgyzstan and the region more broadly. The media are less free. While there is still considerable freedom of assembly there, it is understood that surveillance is widespread and beatings occur once the cameras have gone. The government has worked both to reduce the potential impact of the nongovernmental sector and to ensure that no serious opposition parties emerge.

The Georgian government has relied on several different approaches, although less frequently through changing laws, to achieve these goals. No Georgian law restricts the media as overtly as laws in Kyrgyzstan and elsewhere in the region; and while the media are freer in Georgia than in much of the region, the government still asserts substantial control, particularly over electronic media. Through placing strong government allies in key media positions, harassing owners of independent media outlets, and using public outlets for the promotion of the government, the Georgian government has stripped Georgia's media of its freedom.

The Georgian treatment of Imedi television, particularly since November 2007, demonstrates how the government is able to exert influence over the media without resorting to laws that explicitly rein in media freedom. By 2005–2006, Imedi was the last remaining television station with a national reach that was not under the formal or informal control of the government. To a great extent this was due to its powerful and wealthy owner, Badri Paterkatsishvili. However, as Paterkatsishvili's relations with the government soured, the station became more fervently and vocally anti-government.

The government's reaction, following the crackdown on the demonstrations beginning November 7, 2007, was to violently raid Imedi headquarters, destroying equipment and rendering the station largely inoperable. The station resumed broadcasting in an extremely limited capacity in mid-December.[15] This all but assured that there would be no genuine independent television in the weeks preceding the snap presidential election of January 2008.

Following Paterkatishvili's death in February 2008, the ownership of Imedi was contested for several years.[16] The political inclinations, however, were unambiguous. Following Paterkatsisvhili's death, Imedi ceased being critical of the government. In July 2009, Giorgi Arveladze, a close associate of Saakashvili who had previously served as general secretary of the UNM, chief of staff to President Saakashvili, and minister of economics, was made director general of Imedi. By 2010, Rustavi-2 (a fervently pro-Saakashvili station) and Imedi had "come to look like identical franchises, utilizing the same journalists, incorrect news stories, and innuendo" (Welt 2010). Imedi encountered further controversy when it broadcast a hoax news story featuring a fake Russian invasion of Georgia, scaring many in

Georgia and demonstrating the strong ties between Imedi and the Georgian government.

The Response

The crackdown on NGOs, harassment of opposition political forces, and manipulation of laws and institutions throughout the former Soviet Union following the Color Revolutions as regimes sought to buttress themselves against possible similar events was a blow to democracy and human rights. During this period Russia began to emerge as a formidable force, seeking, with significant success, to staunch the growth of democracy. While many of these tactics are clear-cut human rights violations or authoritarian gestures, the specific issue of restricting foreign NGOs is more complicated.

The issue may not be as significant because the role of foreign organizations in Color Revolutions has been somewhat overstated by authoritarian leaders, but restricting these organizations is not a simple straightforward human rights violation comparable to, say, shutting down an uncooperative newspaper or beating up demonstrators.

The leaders of the semi-authoritarian regimes who feared Color Revolutions were not entirely wrong about foreign NGOs. While these organizations were only very rarely engaged in deliberate efforts to overthrow the government, in most cases the organizations working for democracy raised an implicit threat because democracy would have meant a radical change to domestic political arrangements. Similarly, democracy assistance is, generally speaking, a policy that powerful states implement in weak ones. This framed the relationship between post-Soviet regimes and the west that could not help but create rancor in leaders of countries like Kazakhstan, Uzbekistan, and most significantly, Russia.

Democracy assistance by the U.S. and Europe has contributed to the spread of democracy throughout Eastern Europe, South America, and elsewhere over the last several decades, but at bottom it is still an involvement by one state, or group of states, in the domestic politics of another state. It is difficult to imagine the U.S., for example, tolerating the degree of involvement in its domestic politics that U.S.-supported organizations had in Ukraine, or even Georgia and Kyrgyzstan in the years preceding the Color Revolutions.

Vladimir Putin, speaking in July 2005, when the Color Revolution movement was at its peak, stated very clearly: "We are against overseas funding for the political activities (of NGOs) in Russia. I categorically object. Not a single state that respects itself does that, and we won't allow it either."[17] Putin was slightly wrong here, as many self-respecting states seeking to become democratic have welcomed such activities. He was, however, right in that no self-respecting authoritarian, or semi-authoritarian, state would welcome this type of involvement.

The frustration many in the west felt because of the pushback against democracy NGOs specifically should be tempered by the recognition that even when democracy assistance is well-intentioned, it is still a tool of the powerful against the not powerful. For countries like Russia, stopping democracy NGOs was a way to stop the U.S. and Europe from treating them like a weak defeated country. It is significant that U.S. democracy assistance in China, the world's most powerful nondemocratic country, is virtually nonexistent and was in 2005 as well. For Putin, U.S. democracy assistance was a reminder that in the west's eyes Russia was more like, for example, Armenia, not China.

Reaction to Color Revolutions Outside the former Soviet Union

Although Georgia, Ukraine, and Kyrgyzstan are all formerly part of the Soviet Union, the Color Revolutions have roots and impacts beyond the region. The Bulldozer Revolution in Serbia was an important model for the Rose Revolution and, indirectly, for the Orange and Tulip Revolutions as well. The events in Georgia, Ukraine, and Kyrgyzstan were not lost on authoritarian leaders outside the former Soviet Union. Authoritarian regimes from various points of the world took note and began to be more wary of foreign NGOs working in democracy assistance. A number of countries sought to pass laws restricting the activities of NGOs similar to those passed in Russia and much of Central Asia.

In 2005 both NDI and IRI were expelled from Ethiopia shortly before elections. Similarly, in 2007 NDI was expelled from Bahrain. In both cases the governments feared that NDI or IRI was involved in efforts to foment Color Revolutions. In many other countries where these organizations have remained, they have had to operate under more difficult circumstances facing increased harassment, monitoring, and the like.

The Color Revolutions, at first glance, seem to have been peripheral to China. Although Kyrgyzstan shares a border with China and not Russia, these events were clearly part of the story of post-Soviet political development, occurring in countries that had little in common with China. Most obviously in all three cases, national elections were leveraged into democratic breakthroughs. China, as a far stronger and more authoritarian state, does not have elections at the national level, so the chance of a Color Revolution occurring in China would be quite small.

Nonetheless, the Chinese took steps to insulate themselves against possible Color Revolutions beginning in 2005. A 2005 report by Chinese president Hu Jintao entitled *Fighting the People's War Without Gunsmoke* sought to lay out the Chinese government's fears about Color Revolutions and create a strategy for combating them.[18] The report precipitated a crackdown in China in which "government censorship was ratcheted up. Officials closed or restricted many popular online public bulletin boards and ordered all Web sites and blogs to register with the government.... Perhaps the most telling sign of China's concern has been its crackdown on nongovernmental organizations (NGOs)" (Yongding 2005).

The possibilities of another Color Revolution were raised again following the election fraud committed by Mahmoud Ahmadinejad of Iran in June 2009 as part of his effort to secure his reelection. The widespread street demonstrations in Teheran following the announcement of results were similar to demonstrations in Tbilisi and Kiev in 2003 and 2004. The events in Teheran quickly earned the nickname Green Revolution because protestors chose the color green as their symbol. Demonstrators also relied on Twitter and other social networking sites to share information and to get information out of Iran to western news agencies, but the Twitter Revolution became the name more closely associated with Moldova, not Iran.

The outcome in Iran, of course, looked quite different from the Color Revolutions. The regime violently cracked down on the demonstrators, killing and injuring many, as Ahmadinejad conceded nothing. In this regard, Iran fits the pattern of Belarus and Azerbaijan as a country where the regime was too strong for a Color Revolution to occur, even when some of the other elements were in place. Since those events, the Iranian regime has become even more repressive. However, cracks in the leadership, ongoing small protest movements, and the weak economy make the future of the Iranian regime far from clear. It may yet be that the last tweet of that Twitter revolution has not been sent.

Since 2003–2005, the period during which all three post-Soviet Color Revolutions occurred, a subtle transformation has occurred in how Color

Revolutions are perceived. This has particular bearing for China. In the years since the Color Revolutions, these events have been described as part of a strategy, frequently a western backed strategy, for ending authoritarian rule. However, the Color Revolutions, with the possible exception of Serbia, did not bring an end to authoritarian governments. They brought down semidemocratic governments.

Nonetheless, this sleight of taxonomic hand was significant and relatively widespread. Way (2008) in an article exploring the "Real Causes of the Color Revolutions," refers to these events as "postcommunist authoritarian turnovers" (2008: 55). Chupryna (2008) argued that "Ukraine and Georgia share the history of 'color' revolutions that ended the rule of authoritarian leaders." Bunce and Wolchik (2006a: 283) point out, accurately with regards to democratic breakthroughs in the formerly Communist world, including the Color Revolutions, that "not all of these revolutions succeeded in the overarching goal of creating authentic democratic orders." However, they then misstate the impacts of the Color Revolutions by claiming, "they did succeed in one respect: removing authoritarian leaders from political power."

Presenting Color Revolutions as having played a role in ousting authoritarian as opposed to semidemocratic leaders not only gets the history wrong, but suggests policy directions that are also wrong. The Chinese government may have been, and continue to be, genuinely worried about a Color Revolution, but the chance of something like a Color Revolution occurring in China is quite small.[19] The freedom Saakashvili, Zhvania, Bakiev, Kulov, Yushchenko, Timoschenko, and other political and civic leaders exploited to make the Rose, Tulip, and Orange Revolutions does not exist in China, at least at this time. Similarly, the Chinese state, again for the moment, is far stronger than the pre-Color Revolution state in Georgia, Ukraine, or Kyrgyzstan. The absence of elections in China further underscores this.

Azerbaijan and Belarus are much better, although still flawed models for China and Iran then either Georgia or Ukraine are. The willingness of the Chinese and Iranian states to use force to repress public demonstrations, as shown most chillingly in Teheran in 2009 and Tiananmen in 1989, demonstrates this. Seeking to pursue Color Revolution scenarios in these types of country is a mistake, as it will more likely end in bloodshed than in a democratic breakthrough. The Chinese and Iranian regimes are far from invulnerable, but the Color Revolution model will not be the one that brings either regime down.

The most significant democratic breakthroughs since the Color Revolutions were, of course, in North Africa in early 2011. In a period of only a few months, semi-authoritarian and authoritarian regimes in Egypt, Tunisia, Syria, Bahrain, and elsewhere were either overthrown or threatened by demonstrators demanding dignity, freedom, and democracy. Like the Color Revolutions, these breakthroughs are ripe with democratic potential, but it is too early to know whether this potential will be met.

There are some similarities between the Color Revolutions and the 2011 events in North Africa: the large and mostly peaceful crowds in places like Egypt and Tunisia, the feeling of inevitability around Ben Ali and Mubarak's resignations, and the enormous sense of hope and possibility surrounding these events. There were also, however, key differences suggesting that although some of the post-Color Revolution challenges and obstacles confront post-transition Egypt or Tunisia, the Color Revolution model was not applicable in North Africa. The Color Revolutions were all catalyzed by fraudulent elections, leading some to speak of an "electoral breakthrough" model of democratization.[20] Elections, while an important part of the political environment, were peripheral to the demonstrations and mobilizations which ousted leaders in the Middle East in 2011. None of these demonstrations began following a fraudulent election or in response to an election related issue.

Regimes in the Middle East proved themselves to be considerably more willing and able to use force to defend themselves than were those in Georgia, Ukraine or Kyrgyzstan. In Egypt, the violence only lasted a few days before some in the military split from Mubarak and refused to use violence against demonstrators, before reasserting their primacy in post-Mubarak Egypt. In Libya, Syria, and Bahrain the violence was more sustained leading to a few deaths in Bahrain, considerably more in Syria, and a civil war in Libya.

The regimes overthrown, or threatened, in the Middle East were not semidemocracies with significant civic freedoms and some degree of electoral competition like those in Ukraine, Georgia, and Kyrgyzstan in the years leading up to the Color Revolutions. Instead, they were significantly more repressive semi-authoritarian regimes where citizens enjoyed far less freedom and where, in most cases, there had been little history of electoral competition of any kind. The violent responses of these regimes were consistent with their previous intolerance of dissent.

Accordingly, while lessons from the Color Revolutions, which the west learned the hard way in the former Soviet Union, such as the dangers of viewing a democratic breakthrough as anything more than only an opportunity for democratization, the need to hold leaders who pledge their belief in democracy accountable to their words, the difficulty in building multiparty systems where none have existed in the past, and the legacy of decades of corruption and abuse of power are still relevant in North Africa, the Color Revolution model itself does not explain these events.

CHAPTER 8

Misreading Democratic Breakthroughs: U.S. Policy After the Color Revolutions

THE WESTERN POWERS—and especially the United States—played an important role in the stalled or even reversed development of democracy in Georgia, Ukraine, and Kyrgyzstan after the Rose, Orange, and Tulip Revolutions.[1] For the first several years following the revolutions, U.S. policy contributed to the failure of democracy to consolidate in Kyrgyzstan and Georgia for a similar set of reasons. However, U.S. policy regarding Ukraine was more complex, and the overall impact less clear.

U.S. policy was different in each country, but began with an initial set of flawed assumptions across all three countries, leading to unrealistically high expectations. The Color Revolutions were, at best, democratic breakthroughs, but U.S. policy treated them as broader, democratizing events. Leaders of the Color Revolutions, especially those from Georgia and Ukraine, were feted in western capitals almost immediately after taking office. Yushchenko and Saakashvili received extensive praise from the U.S. government and positive coverage from the western media. Their democratic credentials and desire to quickly consolidate the democratic gains of the Color Revolutions were never challenged. While this attention and media coverage was probably inevitable in the months immediately following the dramatic events in Tbilisi and Kiev, U.S. policy makers seemed to unquestioningly accept this narrative as well.

The Color Revolutions were dramatic events with compelling story lines filled with clear villains such as Akaev, Kuchma, Yanukovich, and Shevardnadze, crowds of demonstrators that, while varying in size and disposition, were usually peaceful and occasionally quite large, and, in the case of Georgia and Ukraine, attractive young leaders who said all the right things. In these ways they looked like other democratic breakthroughs in the region, notably those in Eastern Europe in 1989, but also in Serbia in 2000. However, these images and storylines were allowed to overshadow the questions which these events should have raised.

The years between the end of the Soviet period and the Color Revolutions were difficult ones for democracy for all three countries. Although the Color Revolutions grew out of political systems that were not entirely unfree and where there was space for elite-based civil society, the legacy of the Soviet period was still strong and the challenges facing democracy were clear. The weakness of grassroots civil society, lack of a tradition of sharing power or peaceful transitions from one leader to another, and lack of a well-functioning state all were indicators of the challenges facing democracy after the excitement of the Color Revolutions faded away.

While the initial U.S. policies in each country overestimated the democratic advances brought about by the Color Revolution, these policies were also not crafted to reflect the conditions and challenges in each country. In Georgia, an impatient reform-oriented government was initially torn between at least a rhetorical understanding of the value and importance of democracy, and an intolerance for the delays democracy would have meant for their reform agenda as well as for most voices critical of the government. In Kyrgyzstan, it quickly became clear that the Tulip Revolution was about power and access to wealth more than democracy. In Ukraine, the Orange Revolution left the country deeply polarized although with the potential for a functioning multi-party system. This may be easier to see several years after the events, but evidence that there were problems with democratic development emerged shortly after the Color Revolutions in each country

After the events that brought Yushchenko, Saakashvili, and Bakiev to power, a great deal of work remained to be done with regard to democracy in Ukraine, Georgia, and Kyrgyzstan. Correspondingly, these initial months, and perhaps even years, were times of great potential in each of these countries. In the beginning, all three new leaders sought stronger relationships with the west, pledged continued democratization, and enjoyed widespread financial and political support from the west. In Kyrgyzstan and Georgia, this was supported by widespread popular support for the new government. In all three countries a palpable sense of hope was in the air for the first time in years.

Kyrgyzstan

Perceptions about the democratic character and potential of the Tulip Revolution were driven by the timing, and branding, of the events as much as they were by the events themselves. Had the Tulip Revolution occurred in 2002 and had the leaders not adapted the word and symbol of the Tulip, its links to democracy would have been viewed much more tenuously. However, because it occurred only a few months after the Orange Revolution, and because its centerpiece was a stolen election, the Tulip Revolution fit the model reasonably well and was treated accordingly.

While the Tulip Revolution may have temporarily helped move democracy forward in Kyrgyzstan, little about the events, or the period immediately following these events, suggested that these gains would be easy to maintain, or that the changes occurring in Kyrgyzstan were in any way fundamental or revolutionary. Additionally, unlike Yushchenko in Ukraine or Saakashvili in Georgia, Bakiev represented neither a generational shift nor a profound shift of his country's geopolitical orientation.

The Tulip Revolution was a potential democratic breakthrough because it changed the mood, however briefly, in Kyrgyzstan to one where there was more hope and, at least at the elite level, renewed faith in democratic processes. Ordinary people also saw that through voting and mobilizing they could change their country and its leadership. Helping turn this potential breakthrough into a meaningful and enduring democratic advance would not have been a simple or brief task. It would have required a comprehensive democracy assistance strategy with a timeframe of at least several years.

The general inability of U.S. assistance to implement multi-year democracy strategies notwithstanding,[2] U.S. policy in Kyrgyzstan following the Tulip Revolution substantially overstated the gains made in spring 2005 and deemphasized democracy assistance. More ominously, as Bakiev's government began to slide toward semi-authoritarianism, the U.S. not only said very little but provided insufficient support to domestic organizations seeking to stop this slide.

While the U.S. can be criticized for not speaking out strongly enough after bad elections and worse electoral environments in 2009, this is only one part of the U.S. policy on democracy in Kyrgyzstan. In the days leading up to the 2009 election which saw Bakiev handily reelected,

> The United States ... remained largely silent in response to this wave of violence, apparently wary of jeopardizing the status of its sprawl-

ing air base, on the outskirts of this capital, which supports the mission in Afghanistan. Indeed, the Obama administration has sought to woo the Kyrgyz president since he said in February that he would close the Manas base.

In June, President Obama sent a letter to Mr. Bakiyev praising his role in Afghanistan and the campaign against terrorism. Mr. Bakiyev allowed the base to stay, after the United States agreed to pay higher rent and other minor changes.

The lack of criticism of Mr. Bakiyev underscores how the Obama administration has emphasized pragmatic concerns over human rights in dealings with autocratic leaders in Central Asia. (Levy 2009)

The misreading by the U.S. of the democratic nature of the events of spring 2005 led to more serious mistakes with greater impact on Kyrgyz democracy. The major obstacles facing democracy in Akaev's Kyrgyzstan did not disappear with the Tulip Revolution. On the contrary, they remained largely the same. The same institutions that were weak before the Tulip Revolution, including political parties as well as legislative bodies and the rule of law, remained that way following Bakiev's election. Similarly, the influence of regional identities and clans or kinship networks did not go away, but continued to raise difficulties for any hopes of a democratic transition in Kyrgyzstan.

Instead of seeing the Tulip Revolution as an opportunity to increase the investment in Kyrgyz democracy by taking advantage of the initial openness of the new government, increasing support to civil society development, and working closely with the newly elected government on the further democratization and opening of the government, the U.S. viewed the events as more of an end point in the Kyrgyz transition to democracy. Redoubling democracy assistance after a high profile democratic breakthrough may seem counterintuitive, but it was clearly necessary in Kyrgyzstan and probably in most other cases as well. The failure to do this, especially when linked to an unwillingness to speak out against blatant examples of government backsliding from democratic commitments, means that whatever opportunities were created by the Tulip Revolution were squandered by the U.S.

U.S. policy in Kyrgyzstan during the years following the Tulip Revolution, as well as the years immediately preceding those events, was driven almost entirely by concerns about maintaining the base at Manas, which was critical to the ongoing U.S. effort in Afghanistan. Accordingly, the U.S. was extremely hesitant to do anything that might jeopardize U.S.-Kyrgyz relations. This, as well as the good relations the Bakiev regime enjoyed with both Moscow and Beijing, substantially limited the leverage the U.S. had with Kyrgyzstan.

The policy of supporting an increasingly authoritarian regime in exchange for access to a small, but extremely important, air force base was a short-term strategy, but it may turn out to have been a mistake for the U.S. Although the U.S. managed to stop Kyrgyzstan from turning the base over to Russia during summer 2009, it is not yet known for certain what the attitude of the Kyrgyz government toward U.S. base access will be. Accordingly, the U.S. is no less susceptible to the whims of the new Kyrgyz government than it was it was to the old one during summer 2009.

The Tulip Revolution was a less distinctive break from the past than either the Rose or Orange Revolutions. In Kyrgyzstan, the new regime was led not by young west-leaning reformers, but by former Communist insiders who were similar to their predecessors. In Georgia and Ukraine, while the need for more democracy work still held true after the Color Revolution, the nature of that work was different from what it had been under the previous regime, but in Kyrgyzstan the nature of the needed work was the same.

Before and after the Tulip Revolution, Kyrgyz democracy was hindered by weak political institutions, freedoms of media and assembly, which, while greater than those in much of Central Asia, were not near the levels in Ukraine or Georgia, and powerful corruption and kinship networks that made rule of law very weak. The new regime, unlike that of Saakashvili or Yushchenko, did not seek to change any of this. Bakiev was reasonably successful in this project, creating a regime that shared many of the democratic shortcomings of the late Akaev era. The best way to view the Tulip Revolution was not as a change of regimes but as a change of leaders, which led to making little change with regards to democracy in Kyrgyzstan. It was not possible to have known this at the time of the Tulip Revolution, but it was not difficult to have known this only a few months after those events. The conflation of the impact of the Tulip Revolution on democracy in Kyrgyzstan is an outgrowth of taking too short a view toward politics there.

The problems facing Kyrgyz democracy in the middle of the last decade, like those in many parts of the world, were not the kind that could be changed quickly because of one election. At best, one election could have created a better legal and legislative climate for the development of democracy, but the events of 2005 did not even accomplish that. The Tulip Revolution, at first, however, created an opening for democracy assistance. The new regime was initially more receptive to U.S. assistance and democratic pressure than its predecessor, but the failure of the U.S. to act quickly in this regard led to a missed opportunity.

Georgia

U.S. policy toward post-Rose Revolution Georgia suffered primarily from misreading the extent to which those events had brought democracy to Georgia and from strong personal ties between the new Georgian leadership and American foreign policy elites from both sides of the aisle, which obscured some of the realities in Georgia. Over time, these once bipartisan ties took on a more partisan bent as the Saakashvili government seemed to cast its lot with the neoconservative elements in Bush's foreign policy team.

The U.S. policy in Georgia failed in several ways. Today, despite years of pledging support to Georgia's territorial integrity, the chances of restoring Abkhazia and South Ossetia to Georgia are more remote than they were in the darkest years of the Shevardnadze presidency. Georgian democracy, after a period of stagnation between about 2004 and 2008, now appears to be backsliding. Moreover, Georgia, particularly since the military defeat at the hands of Russia in 2008 has become even more dependent on foreign, notably American, assistance than before the Rose Revolution.

Ironically, the damage U.S. policy did to Georgia was grounded not in hostility or disdain but in the best of intentions. The U.S. did not seek to weaken Georgian democracy, make it more dependent on the U.S., and make territorial integrity little more than a dream. In fact, it sought to do the precise opposite, but there was an extraordinary disconnect between intentions and outcomes in Georgia. Shortly after the Rose Revolution, the U.S. moved to a policy of working to strengthen the Georgian government. This approach was based on the accurate assessment that the Rose Revolution could only succeed if the Georgian state was strengthened and revitalized after being run into the ground by the kleptocratic Shevardnadze regime. However, with regard to democracy, this approach was based on the considerably more dubious notion that the primary engine for both state building and democracy was the Georgian government. The U.S. simply failed to see the obvious problems that would arise if the state received ample support while civil society was neglected. This became clear shortly after the Rose Revolution, when state strengthening began to be accompanied by restricting democratic space.

As the Georgian government moved farther away from the initial democratic promise of the Rose Revolution, it encountered almost no resistance from the U.S. government. Importantly, whatever concerns the U.S. government raised privately, publicly it continued to trumpet Georgia as a democratic success story long after that view had been discredited. This included not only President Bush's unfortunate use of the phrase "beacon of liberty" to describe Georgia in 2005, but additional statements from U.S. leaders throughout the post-Rose Revolution period and a complete unwillingness by the Bush administration to say anything critical regarding the state of democracy in Saakashvili's Georgia. Additionally, during the Georgia-Russia war, Georgia's democratic credentials were invoked by the Bush administration to explain U.S. support for Georgia. This was a tactical mistake because that support should have been based on international law and support for Georgian sovereignty, both of which would have put the U.S. on more solid rhetorical ground.

Most striking was the failure of the U.S. to strongly condemn the Georgian government after the crackdown on demonstrators on November 7, 2007. The State Department statement the day after the crackdown began, "The United States welcomes the Georgian Government's decision to hold early presidential elections and a referendum on timing of parliamentary elections." To be fair, the statement went on to say "At the same time, we continue to urge the Government of Georgia to lift the state of emergency and restore all media broadcasts" (U.S. Department of State 2007a). Nonetheless, it is extraordinary that the day after fire hoses, tear gas, and other means were used to break up peaceful demonstrations, the official position of the U.S. government was to thank the Georgian government for holding early elections—elections that could not be held in anything approaching a fair media environment given that the major independent television station, Imedi, had just been destroyed by government forces.

The degree to which the U.S.-Georgia relationship was personalized, particularly during the Bush administration, was extreme, but not new. Strong personal ties between Saakashvili's predecessor, Eduard Shevardnadze, and the U.S. leadership had been key to Georgia receiving ample American assistance during those years. Those ties were, of course, founded on Shevardnadze's years as Soviet foreign minister, but benefitted him as president of Georgia as well. The value of these ties was not lost on Saakashvili, Zhvania, and other leaders of post-Rose Revolution Georgia who had been close with the former Georgian president.

The close ties were grounded in the Saakashvili government's rhetorical commitment to American values, support for American foreign policy regarding Bush's Global War on Terror, and the U.S. war in Iraq. These relationships became more important because as the Bush administration drew to a close it became increasingly unpopular globally, allowing the Georgian government to emerge as one of the few that were willing to be not only an ally but a friend.

The ties were strengthened by the personal rapport developed not only at the highest levels between Bush and Saakashvili, but also among members of both administrations at all levels. The images of Bush and Saakashvili enjoying a *supra* (traditional Georgian feast) in Tbilisi's old city in 2005, followed by Bush briefly joining the Georgian dancers on stage captures this affinity well.

During much of the post-Rose Revolution period, it was very common in Washington to hear U.S. government officials, diplomats, and powerful nongovernmental figures punctuate serious discussions about Georgia policy with mentions of close personal relationships and even the English language skills of various members of the Georgian leadership. Similarly, no visit to a Georgian government official was complete without some name-dropping about how tied in that government official was to the Bush administration. This sentiment was made most clear during the few months following the November 7 crackdown, when it was not unusual in Washington to hear the view, and often the phrase "Misha had a bad week, but now he's okay" to explain away the crackdown.[3]

These deeply personal ties contributed to the inability of the U.S. to act on more realistic assessments of Georgian democracy and thus to the U.S. failure to revisit the premise that the Georgian government was an engine for democracy in Georgia. This also, however, contributed to a climate in which official statements urging Georgia to avoid a conflict with Russia during the months preceding the 2008 Russia-Georgia war could be safely ignored by the government of Georgia. It instead sought out individuals within the U.S. government who would look more kindly on the confrontational Georgian policy during summer 2008, which helped facilitate the war with Russia. Unfortunately, the nature of these relationships also misled the Georgian government into believing that the U.S. would provide more support than it did once the war began. Asmus (2010) is very sympathetic to the Georgian position but also captures the Georgian belief that the U.S. and the West betrayed it, first by not accelerating Georgia's admittance into NATO and then by failing to aid Georgia once the war started.

Ukraine

U.S. policy in Ukraine was less harmful than in either Georgia or Kyrgyzstan. Although the U.S. overestimated the extent to which the Orange Revolution made Ukraine a democracy, this did not lead directly to policies as destructive as those in Georgia and Kyrgyzstan.

The persistence of the pre-revolution political leadership in the form of Yanukovich and the Party of the Regions not only contributed to a different kind of political development in Ukraine, but also required a different kind of policy from the U.S. Because the alternative was never distant, the pressure on Yushchenko and Timoschenko to succeed, and the imperative for the U.S. to help them succeed, was far greater than similar pressure on Saakashvili or Bakiev. Therefore the U.S. had to become deeply involved in Ukraine to ensure this success and keep the forces of the old regime at bay. At least that is what seemed to be the case in 2005. Timoschenko and Yushchenko both failed to deliver on the economic promise of the Orange Revolution, so control of parliament and the office of prime minister fluctuated between the Orange Revolutionaries and their opponents after 2005. In 2010, Yanukovich redeemed his 2004 defeat by narrowly defeating Timoschenko in a runoff and becoming president of Ukraine.

In Ukraine, as in the other two Color Revolution countries, the U.S. viewed the new leadership as the primary engine of democracy, but because of the more serious political competition in Ukraine, it could not simply support the government as it did in Georgia and Kyrgyzstan. For much of the period following the Color Revolution there was no cost to the U.S. associated with supporting the regimes of Saakashvili and Bakiev. No powerful political forces existed who might have been angry about this, and the U.S. could easily conflate support for the countries, the states and the regimes.

In Ukraine, there was a cost associated with unequivocal support for the new Yushchenko regime. It risked increasing anti-American, and correspondingly, pro-Russian sentiment in the southern and eastern part of the country. The U.S. wanted Yushchenko to succeed, but had to do so in a way that did not entail getting involved in domestic politics so as to be seen as too closely aligned with the Orange forces. In short, this meant that the U.S. had to work with the Ukrainian state, not just with the Color Revolution regime. Immediately following the Orange Revolution, the ties between the leaders of that movement and the American government were strong and personal, albeit not to the extent as with Saakashvili. The temptation to make the same mistake of overpersonalizing the relationship was undoubtedly strong, but the U.S. rarely succumbed.

At times, it seemed as if the U.S. erred in the other direction and did not offer sufficient support to the new Ukrainian leaders. Like the other Color Revolutionaries, Yushchenko inherited a broad range of political and economic problems but did not come into power with a mandate comparable to that enjoyed by Bakiev or Saakashvili. Instead, he sought to govern over a divided country: one half was excited with the prospect for change, but almost one half approached the new government warily and with a fair amount of skepticism.

Yushchenko needed help more urgently than Bakiev or Saakashvili because his presidency, and indeed the Orange experiment, occurred under the scrutiny of a powerful political opposition. Even in 2005, it could have been foreseen that the political cost for the Orange forces of failing to deliver on the promise of the Orange Revolution would have been defeat by the Party of the Regions, while the cost to, for example, Saakashvili, for failing to deliver on these promises, at least with regard to domestic politics would not be as grave. The size of Ukraine compared to that of Georgia or Kyrgyzstan made helping Yushchenko's government more difficult as well. The problems facing Ukraine, although in many respects not as dire as those facing Georgia after the Rose Revolution, were on a much larger scale. Therefore, the U.S. could not provide the broad support for Ukraine that it could for Georgia.

The U.S. relationship with Georgia can be faulted for being too reliant on personal relationships, which often led to faulty decision making in both Tbilisi and Washington.[4] The relationship between Yushchenko and the Bush administration was different. Pifer (2009) points out that

> after Yushchenko became president at the start of 2005, President George W. Bush and Vice President Dick Cheney each visited Kiev once and hosted Yushchenko in Washington twice. By comparison, President Bill Clinton and Vice President Al Gore visited Kiev five times in 1994–2000, and Kuchma made many more visits to Washington and the United States.

Pifer also argues,

> In part because of its intermittent contact, the Bush administration did not have particular influence with Yushchenko. Despite urgings by both Bush and Cheney in September 2008, Yushchenko did not ease off attacks on Tymoshenko and restore a more coherent line between the presidency and cabinet of ministers.

It seems unfair to fault the Bush administration for being too close to Saakashvili and not close enough to Yushchenko, but there is an appropriate level of personal connections and relationships between friendly heads of state for which the U.S. should strive. This level was exceeded with regard to Georgia, but not met with regard to Ukraine.

The need to work differently with Yushchenko than with either Saakashvili or Bakiev was further complicated because the Orange Revolution raised a different challenge for American policy makers than did similar events in Kyrgyzstan or Georgia. Unlike the case of the other two Color Revolution countries, the new leadership in Ukraine did not have a monopoly on political power, nor were they even overwhelmingly popular. Yushchenko had come to power in a highly contested and competitive election, whereas Bakiev and Saakashvili had won in landslides.

Accordingly, it was easy for outsiders to view the post-Orange Revolution political arrangements in Ukraine as a reasonably clear two, or perhaps two and a half, party system, as almost all voters either supported Yanukovich's block, or the Timoschenko-Yushchenko coalition. There were, however, two major flaws in this analysis. The first was that the Timoschenko-Yushchenko Orange coalition was neither strong nor enduring. It had come together during the months preceding the Orange Revolution, but was grounded in electoral necessity. Once the electoral necessity of 2004 faded away, the competition between the two principals made the coalition unsustainable.

The second flaw was that this approach tended to overstate the extent, particularly immediately following the Orange Revolution, to which the Party of the Regions was simply one of two parties competing for political power in Ukraine. The party, which as recently as 2004 had relied on heavy election fraud to win a close presidential election, did not rush to embrace clean politics after the defeat. For much of Yushchenko's presidency, the Party of the Regions ran most of eastern Ukraine in a way not conducive to democratic development. The party had significant influence on the economic life of the region. Factory directors were expected to support the party and deliver their workers' votes. While the existence of the Party of the Regions made the possibility of a two-party system stronger in Ukraine than in Kyrgyzstan or Georgia, it was an overstatement to view that as having already occurred by 2006 or so.

Ukrainian politics since 2004 have been less parsimonious than suggested by a simple division between two major blocks. Instead, for much of that period Ukraine was dominated by three blocks led by Timoschenko, Yanukovich, and Yushchenko. Each of these blocks enjoyed a strong base of support for much of this time, but a stable governing coalition was entirely elusive. Ideology during Yushchenko's presidency was vague as each of the three major principals was at times willing to take on different coalition partners to stay in power. This dynamic made it impossible for the Orange leaders to consolidate an illiberal state, but it also rendered Ukraine virtually ungovernable.

The U.S. continued to work on democracy assistance in Ukraine following the Orange Revolution as well. Probably the clearest gains for democracy in Ukraine from 2004 to 2010 were in the areas of media freedom, which remained vibrant as the Orange leaders did not crack down on media comparable to those in Kyrgyzstan and Georgia. Similarly, civil society remained free and open, another significant accomplishment of the period.

Significantly, the U.S. offered very little direct support to the Orange forces in elections after 2004. The notion that victory for Yushchenko was victory for democracy and defeat for Yushchenko was defeat for democracy, which was the U.S. and Europe's policy in 2004, rapidly dissipated after that initial election. In parliamentary elections in 2006 and again in 2007, western involvement focused far more on process than on seeking to influence the outcome. The problem with this approach was not so much one of democracy as one of politics. Although post-Orange Revolution politics were clearly dominated by three blocks, which in the initial months following the Orange Revolution could reasonably have been viewed as two blocks, this development was a barrier to greater Ukrainian democracy. As long as the country remains polarized between orange and blue forces, political paralysis, or at least stagnation, will be unavoidable. This was true in 2005, and remained true through 2011. U.S. democracy policy embraced this political division when a more strategic approach would have been to weaken it by strengthening other political actors and voices. Seeking to nurture political forces that created common ground around economic or social issues between voters in the west and the east through exchanges, workshops, public information campaigns, and other guidance might have moved Ukraine out of its post-Orange Revolution political morass, but these policies were never seriously pursued.

On the other hand, embracing the rise of what appeared to be a two-party system doomed Ukraine to be stuck in that two-party framework. This contributed to the cycle of election-deadlock-new election that continued from 2005 to 2010. Every election since 2004 has been extremely close, with similar patterns of support emerging for the orange and blue factions. It is only a slight exaggeration to say that these elections were essentially the same as the Orange Revolution election. The difference of a few points for one side or the other, which determined the winner each time, was never enough to really move Ukrainian politics forward.

The extent to which this policy is viewed as successful rests largely on how the 2010 election in which Yanukovich was elected president is viewed. While some analysts initially viewed the victory as evidence that the Orange Revolution had failed,[5] many observers took the opposite view, arguing that because Yanukovich's victory occurred in a peaceful and legal process, through a free and fair election, it was evidence of the success of the Orange Revolution.[6]

If Yanukovich's victory is proof of the strength of Ukrainian democracy, then the U.S. approach to the Ukrainian election through the whole election period was the right one. It demonstrated a commitment to process with regard to elections and a concrete rebuttal to those who believe that the U.S. only supports democracy when it means electing pro-American governments. The administration could have worked harder to help defeat Yanukovich and elect Timoschenko, sought to present the inevitable election problems in Ukraine as evidence that the elections were not free and fair, threatened policy consequences for Ukraine if Yanukovich won, or supported Timoschenko's claim that Yanukovich's victory was illegitimate. The U.S. could have weighed in more heavily on the Orange side in national elections in 2006 or 2007 as well. However, any of these actions would have been ineffective, further undermined U.S. credibility, and made it more difficult for the U.S. to work with the new Ukrainian government.

The Obama administration, in a quiet and understated way handled the politics of the 2010 Ukrainian election very well and drove the post-election narrative very effectively. Yanukovich's election, while on the surface a victory for Moscow, was quickly presented, and understood, as a victory for democracy and, implicitly, the west.

The election itself probably, at least in the short term, was a victory for democracy. It was conducted freely, fairly, and peacefully. The Ukrainian people accepted the outcome , and a peaceful transition of power ensued. The election can be seen as a good sign for Ukrainian democracy, but that does not mean that the years of Yushchenko's presidency do not represent a lost opportunity for Ukraine.

During Yanukovich's tenure in office the electoral deadlock that made governance so difficult is unlikely to change. Nor is the nature of the dominance of the Party of the Regions in eastern Ukraine likely to change. However, the hope and excitement which characterized the first months following the Orange Revolution have dissipated. Ukrainians are unlikely to see Yanukovich's presidency as an opportunity to continue to push the country further to democracy, but more likely to see it as the latest iteration of post-Orange Revolution political stalemate.

Impact and Limits of U.S. Involvement

The flawed U.S. response to the Color Revolution in Georgia and Kyrgyzstan, and to a lesser extent Ukraine, contributed to the failure of the Color Revolutions to make a lasting impact on democratic development in Georgia and Kyrgyzstan. This is less true in Ukraine, where it is still too early to write off the potential democratic impact of the Orange Revolution.

Simply identifying the mistakes made by U.S. policy makers is not proof that better U.S. policy would have led to more democratic outcomes, particularly in Kyrgyzstan and Georgia. While the failure of democracy to develop in those two countries, and the U.S. role in that failure, suggests that the Color Revolutions were missed opportunities, it also raises the question of whether or not they were opportunities at all.

The Color Revolutions may not have been democratic breakthroughs but part of the increasingly complicated and labyrinthine path of post-Soviet political development in all three of these countries. Because the language and narrative around the Color Revolutions has emphasized democracy and change, the extent to which the Color Revolutions have been about continuity and semidemocracy has been obscured.[7] Even the term "Color Revolution" does this, as it is very difficult to describe any kind of revolution as being about continuity. This is not to suggest that the Color Revolutions, in any of these countries, had no effect, but that the impacts may have been different from what first seemed to be the case, particularly with regard to political development.

In Ukraine, the Orange Revolution has had a lasting impact of civil and media freedoms, at least for a few years; and has helped move Ukraine toward consistently better elections. It also changed politics in Ukraine as it brought it out into the streets. The initial demonstrations following the fraudulent election in November 2004 were enormous and groundbreaking, but following that election street, demonstrations became relatively common in Ukraine. Almost any time Yanukovich's forces wanted to stress a point or raise concern about Yushchenko or Timoschenko, they too mobilized demonstrators.

While this might be viewed as a democratic breakthrough, it is more of a new semidemocratic development. Leaders on all sides began to view street demonstrations not as an organic expression of discontent, as may have been the case in 2004, but as a tool to be used by political elites to put pressure on political opponents. The evidence suggesting that most demonstrators in the years since 2004 have been paid supports this notion.[8] The Orange Revolution, according to this view, did not make Ukraine a democracy, although it might have made it more liberal. It did, however, make Ukraine a more complex semidemocracy.

In Georgia and Kyrgyzstan, the Rose and Tulip Revolutions are better understood not as democratic breakthroughs, but as additional chapters in the fluctuation between strong and weak states and between liberal and illiberal regimes. In Kyrgyzstan, Bakiev's regime continued a repressive trend in Kyrgyz politics that had begun during the later years of Akaev's presidency. It now looks as if the new regime will not move in a similarly repressive direction. In Georgia, Saakashvili's government quickly moved to strengthen the Georgian state while restricting some of the media and civic freedoms of the previous regime.

In both these countries it is not clear whether the events of the post-Color Revolution period signify the longer-term direction in which the country is going or are part of a cycle that will soon lead to a period of liberalization. In Kyrgyzstan, this will be largely determined by the actions of the new government. It is not clear, however, whether the current government in Georgia will hold onto power for decades, evolve into a more cyclical pattern of winning and losing power as seems to be the case in Ukraine, or perhaps even collapse as occurred in Kyrgyzstan.[9]

At the time the Color Revolutions happened, the change outshone the continuity. It was not easy to look at the peaceful street demonstrations, democratic promises, and sense of hope in all three countries and conclude that nothing important was happening. However, even as those events were occurring, another story was emerging as well. The Color Revolutions in all three countries were battles between different groups of political insiders with strong ties to the old regime. In Georgia and Kyrgyzstan, the rapid coalescing of political elites around the new president indicated that at the elite level there was an understanding that not much was going to change about how the government did business. The failure of any significant political opposition to emerge in time for the presidential elections in Kyrgyzstan in 2005 or Georgia in 2004 indicated that the one-party paradigm was still strong but had been reset. In Ukraine, the political developments made it clear that the Orange Revolution did not change the existing state of political competition.

The U.S. response to the Color Revolutions focused on the elements of change to the preclusion of recognizing any elements of continuity. This was most apparent in Georgia, where, for example, U.S. policy did not reflect that Georgia was still a semidemocratic country with a need for strong civil society: one that relied on foreign money and expertise for nurturing CSOs. Similarly, in Kyrgyzstan, by the time U.S. policy began to reflect that Bakiev's regime signified leadership change but not regime change, the new system had already hardened into a semi-authoritarian state. In Ukraine, although democracy has not fallen too far off track, Yushchenko's victory was treated as bringing some kind of finality to Ukraine's geopolitical direction that has not yet occurred.

During the late Shevardnadze years, Georgia had become a one and a half party system, with a weak economy, heavily dependent on foreign aid with a disorganized political opposition that had few ideological differences with the government. Kyrgyzstan during the last years of Akaev's rule had become an illiberal regime, dominated by the family and trusted associates of the president with elections stolen, corruption widespread and dissent not tolerated. Under Kuchma, Ukraine had become a highly polarized country with weak rule of law, strong ties between the state and private sector, and uneven democratic development. All these things, of course, can be said about Georgia, Kyrgyzstan, and Ukraine today and throughout most of the post-Color Revolution period. Too often this apparent continuity did not drive U.S. policy as much as the perception of change did.

This raises the question of what might have been expected of U.S. post-Color Revolution policy. By substantially overstating the extent of the initial democratic breakthrough, the U.S. all but guaranteed failure for its policy and indeed for the Color Revolutions themselves. The answer to the question whether different U.S. policies in these countries, based on a different set of assumptions, would have led to more successful outcomes is unclear and varies depending on the country.

In Georgia, a policy based on a more realistic understanding of the extent to which the new government was committed to democracy and of the unchanged need for substantial democracy support from the U.S. might have led to more democracy. Had the Georgian government leaders, for example, learned soon after the Rose Revolution that they would be held to their words regarding their democratic intentions, they might have been less likely to move away from democracy. Instead, they learned the opposite lesson—that moving away from democracy, whether through restricting media, rewriting the constitution, or pressuring judges, would bring about no consequences from their American patrons.

The situation was not so clear regarding Ukraine and Kyrgyzstan, where the U.S. enjoyed less leverage. Had the U.S. downplayed the democratic breakthrough aspect of the Tulip Revolution and continued to focus more acutely on Kyrgyzstan's ample democratic shortcomings, it is likely that Bakiev's government would have distanced itself from the U.S., preferring to build relationships with powers less concerned with democracy, a policy that would not have led to more democracy either. It might, however, have put the U.S. in a better position when Bakiev's regime collapsed.

Had the U.S. viewed the Orange Revolution as a temporary victory by one, albeit more democratic, side in Ukraine, rather than a paradigm changing event in that country, a policy focusing more on the longer-term problems of democracy in Ukraine, including the intense regional division, cronyism, and weak rule of law might have been pursued. This policy, rather than one oriented around an understanding of a two-party system in Ukraine, might also have been more fruitful, but it would have been a long term strategy.

Conclusion

Although the U.S. made mistakes in Georgia, Kyrgyzstan, and Ukraine, it is not certain that better U.S. policy would have led to more successful outcomes for the three Color Revolutions. Moreover, in recent years U.S. policy has been a little more nuanced. Although remaining hamstrung by its reliance on the base at Manas, the U.S. eventually realized that Kyrgyzstan under Bakiev was not moving toward becoming more democratic. The Obama administration also avoided the temptation to get involved and choose sides in the 2010 Ukrainian presidential election, has begun to tone down the personalized nature of U.S.-Georgia ties, and takes a more sober view of democratic developments in that country.

The reality that the U.S. could have done worse does not obscure the fact that mistakes were made or that more than six years after the most recent Color Revolution little progress has been made with regard to state building or democracy in these countries. Bakiev's lack of interest in democracy as well as the proximity and political influence of both China and Russia, combined with the concrete and narrow, but high priority, American need for access to the Manas base, meant that it would have been very difficult for the U.S. to pursue a different path in Kyrgyzstan. Pressure from the U.S. could have easily been ignored. Building meaningful democratic institutions would have been very difficult in Kyrgyzstan given how weak these institutions had been during the Akaev regime and in broader historical context. To some extent, the U.S. got lucky in Kyrgyzstan because its base-centric policy there almost backfired twice. In summer 2009, the Kyrgyz government came very close to breaking its lease with the U.S. and essentially turning over the base to Russia. Less than a year later, that regime was ousted by opponents who at the very least did not face opposition from Moscow. In the former case the U.S. was able to buy its way out of the problem; in the second case it seems to have narrowly escaped losing Manas to an anti-American government.

The same cannot be said for Georgia or Ukraine. In both countries, the Color Revolutions represented openings, perhaps only briefly, that might have led to meaningful and enduring change, but these opportunities were not fully exploited. The Orange and Rose Revolutions represented opportunities to accelerate democratization not because these events themselves were extraordinary democratic breakthroughs, but because they were moments when political elites changed, the old regime was temporarily discredited, and there was openness to doing things differently at both the elite and grassroots level.

In Georgia, the opening was made greater because the rhetoric of the new administration, which enjoyed extremely widespread support from the population, stressed the need for greater democracy. The U.S. mistook this rhetoric for genuine commitment and ability and began to make policy mistakes accordingly. Immediately following the Rose Revolution, it would have been possible to combine strong support for the Rose Revolution and democracy by focusing on the promise, rather than the leaders. For example, speaking out against the new constitutional reforms and initial repression of political media in 2004, while still supporting the overall themes of the Rose Revolution, would have sent a different message to the people and government of Georgia. Criticizing the government in the context of an overall program of support would have made it difficult for the government to ignore it. Similarly, knowing that the U.S. was genuine in its support for democracy, rather than just the new government, might have empowered ordinary people and political elites to articulate their concerns. Instead, at least at first, ordinary people were largely silenced and political elites repeated the patterns with which they were most comfortable, consolidating support around a new one party system.

Although political division and a strong opposition remained following Yushchenko's assumption of the presidency of Ukraine in 2005, the Orange Revolution still represented a moment when significant change was possible. A major U.S. effort to ensure the success of the Orange Revolution government would have increased Ukrainian support for the Orange Revolution, further discredited the claims of opponents, and strengthened ties between Ukraine and the west. This not only would have required many resources, but needed to occur while the excitement and national adrenaline surrounding the Orange Revolution was still strong. The window in which to do this had closed within a year, if not sooner, of Yushchenko becoming president. Instead, the country returned to the governmental weakness and bickering that had been, and remains, the norm in Ukraine.

The shortcomings of U.S. policy arose from several obvious failings. In all three cases, the Color Revolutions were treated as the end rather than the beginning of a process. Additionally, great faith was placed in individual leaders, which strengthened the perception that democracy was farther ahead than it was. In Georgia, the faith placed in Saakashvili and his team facilitated a U.S.-Georgia relationship that was far too oriented around personal relationships.

The shortcomings also arose from at least one less obvious failing. Post-Color Revolution policy suffered because the Color Revolutions were not placed in a proper political or developmental context. The excitement and hope surrounding the events themselves created a feeling that something dramatic was happening. It was extremely difficult to have been part of these events and not feel that way. The three leaders of the Color Revolutions were, at first glance, starkly different from their predecessors. Lost in this excitement was a sense of perspective that might have led to different initial views of the Color Revolutions.

The first decade of the twenty-first century was a time when the "transition paradigm" (Carothers 2002) wound down in many parts of the world, not least the former Soviet Union. The Color Revolutions were, at the time, viewed as breathing new life into this framework, suggesting that democratic development was still possible in the former Soviet Union. This may still be true, but the Color Revolutions will not be the vehicle for it. The ideological desire for the transition paradigm to live on, and the short-term political desire for a success story somewhere blinded policy makers, particularly in the U.S., to the perhaps less obvious, but at least equally important, narrative of continuity that also is central to the Color Revolutions.

Akaev, Kuchma, and Shevardnadze, like those who replaced them, were all initially viewed as reformers who spoke of democracy and the need for stronger ties with the west. They all presided over mixed systems with elements of democracy existing alongside obvious democratic shortcomings. Through some combination of incompetence, dishonesty, corruption and political circumstance, all three of these leaders were failures by the time of the Color Revolutions. By comparing Saakashvili, Yushchenko, and Bakiev to their predecessors late in their careers after failure was already upon them, the U.S. missed an important part of the narrative, one which emphasized continuity between the regimes. Several years after the dramatic events of 2003–2005, it is possible to view the Color Revolutions differently. They no longer seem like a sharp dividing line in the post-Communist history of any of these countries. It is unlikely that historians even a few decades from now will point to the Rose, Orange, or Tulip Revolutions as critical moments in the independent history of Georgia, Ukraine, or Kyrgyzstan. While it may not be fair to expect policy makers in the west to have grasped that right away, for the most part, they have ignored evidence throughout the period of the Color Revolutions that this was true. Akaev, Kuchma, and Shevardnadze were almost immediately relegated to the dustbin of history, where they were viewed as post-Soviet dictators governing over authoritarian regimes. This not only was an inaccurate portrayal, but it lowered the democracy bar for their successors. Saakashvili, for example, has, for the most part, created a more open regime than post-Communist leaders in Uzbekistan, Belarus, or Azerbaijan. However, Shevardnadze's regime was also quite different than that of Karimov, Lukashenko, or the Aliyevs.

There had been other moments of potential in these three countries during the post-Communist period. The first few years after Shevardnadze returned to stabilize Georgia after Gamsakhurdia's presidency, much of Akaev's term and even the time in Ukraine when Yushchenko served as Kuchma's prime minister brought similar, if less intense, feelings of hope for these countries. By ignoring this entire context, observers could easily project too much onto the Color Revolutions and make the corresponding policy mistakes.

CHAPTER 9

The End of an Era

THE COLOR REVOLUTIONS have receded into the past. They are no longer an important political factor in the former Soviet Union, nor have they precipitated, or are likely to precipitate, meaningful democratic advances. However, for a few brief years, they were important not only throughout the former Soviet Union, but beyond. Democratic activists throughout the region, as well as in countries like Lebanon or Iran, were inspired by the events of 2003–2005 in Georgia, Ukraine, and Kyrgyzstan. Every time an election was stolen somewhere leading to public demonstrations, talk of Color Revolution heated up. None ever happened after 2005, but the Cedar, Twitter, and Green Revolutions were viewed as possibilities in Lebanon, Moldova, and Iran. However, when authoritarian and semi-authoritarian regimes fell in North Africa in 2011, it was the fall of Communism in 1989–1991, not the Color Revolutions, to which most comparisons were made.

Equally significant, authoritarian and semi-authoritarian leaders, not only from Minsk to Almaty, but from Teheran to Beijing and Addis Ababa to Caracas, took steps to make sure Color Revolutions would not happen in their countries. Long after the last successful Color Revolution occurred, the fear persisted. There seems to be something of a contradiction here. If Color Revolutions had such a relatively minor effect on democracy and political development, why did they persist as a model, and as a perceived threat? One reason is that although Color Revolutions proved to have little to do with democracy, they clearly were effective means of ousting nondemocratic leaders, even if, as in the Kyrgyz case, that meant replacing them with equally authoritarian leaders. Thus, while Color Revolutions had little democratic effect, this should not be interpreted to mean they also had little effect on domestic political arrangements in the countries in which they occurred.

Did the Color Revolutions Happen?

It is easy, at least in the case of Georgia and Kyrgyzstan, to dismiss the notion that Color Revolutions were democratic breakthroughs. Even in Ukraine, where democracy moved forward between late 2004 and 2010, it occurred in a way that was more incremental than revolutionary. Color Revolutions cannot be unambiguously described as lost opportunities either. A third conclusion might be that with the benefit of a few years perspective, it turns out that the Color Revolutions were not opportunities for democratic breakthroughs at all, and that, in general, they were not as important as thought of at the time.

One way to approach this question is to ask whether the change between Shevardnadze's and Saakashvili's Georgia, Akaev and Bakiev's Kyrgyzstan, and Kuchma's and Yushchenko's Ukraine was more or less than what might be seen in a typical political transition in a western democracy such as the U.S., UK, or France. This is a useful approach because it recognizes that even in stable regimes there is some degree of change. As mentioned in the introduction, there are some transitions of power in Western democracies that led to greater policy changes than the Color Revolutions did. The election of Franklin Roosevelt in 1932, Ronald Reagan's victory in 1980, or the victory by the Conservatives that Margaret Thatcher headed in the UK in 1979 all created changes in their respective countries that led to more significant policy outcomes than those that occurred after the Color Revolutions. However, many Western elections, even when an incumbent party loses, bring only minor change. Kennedy and the Democrats taking over after Eisenhower and the Republicans in 1960 or Carter's victory over Ford in 1976 are examples of such elections in the U.S. The Color Revolutions may be most appropriately seen as having had the impact on their respective countries of a moderately strong electoral change in a western country.

The tendency to focus on change and the impact of specific events is certainly understandable, particularly given the excitement, imagery, and spin surrounding the Color Revolutions. However, it is clear now that the Color Revolutions were as much a story about continuity and the difficulty of making meaningful enduring political change as they were about change itself. A central lesson of the Color Revolutions, particularly the Orange and Rose Revolutions, where generational change was a large part of the transition, is that political habits, styles, and even regimes that are residues of the Soviet period are indeed very difficult to change.

Saakashvili, Zhvania, and to a lesser extent Burjanadze in Georgia were viewed as the hope for Georgia's future long before they came to power and before they broke with Shevardnadze. Not only did they say the right things about democracy and development, but they were young,—barely old enough to have done any political work during the Soviet period. Yushchenko and Timoschenko were not Western darlings for quite as long before coming to power, but during the 12-18 months before the Orange Revolution they occupied a similar place in the western view of Ukraine. While not as young as their Georgian counterparts, they seemed young, particularly when compared to Kuchma and Yanukovich, neither of whom would have looked out of place sharing a photo op with Nikita Khrushchev.

The limited impact the Orange and Rose Revolutions had suggests not only that making change is more difficult than it might have seemed in the halcyon days of Georgia in January 2004 or Ukraine a year later, but that by the first years of the twenty-first century, the post-Soviet regimes—even the more liberal ones in places like Bishkek, Tbilisi, and Kiev—had hardened into something that would endure more than just an electoral defeat for an incumbent.

Just as democracies can only be consolidated when power changes hands peacefully (Linz and Stepan 1996), these nondemocratic regimes can also be consolidated when power changes hands peacefully, but the basic regime is not altered. This model is most applicable to Kyrgyzstan, where the Akaev and Bakiev regimes were similar, even in the way they eventually were brought down, but certainly has bearing on Ukraine and Georgia as well. In the former, the stability was tempered by increased liberalization, while in the latter it was tempered by temporary state strengthening and restricting freedoms. These are important but not regime changing developments, making the Color Revolutions not about regime change at all, but part of the larger ebb and flow of post-Communist regimes.

According to this view, the Color Revolutions were not successes, democratic breakthroughs, disappointments, or lost opportunities. Instead, this approach suggests that they did not happen at all. The actual events of 2003-2005 in the three countries in question obviously occurred, but the Color Revolution paradigm was flawed from the beginning and did not hold up to the passage of time. In Ukraine, for example, the transition from Kuchma to Yushchenko to Yanukovich, when viewed holistically, represents as much continuity as change. Neither the events of January 2004, as dramatic and symbolically laden as they were, nor the governance of Yushchenko, were lasting turning points for Ukraine that demarcate a clear break with the past. There were, of course, differences in the coalitions that elected these three presidents, as well as in the goals, policies, and governance of Kuchma and Yushchenko. Yanukovich will also differ in this respect from his predecessor, but these differences occurred within a regime which, while far from entirely static, has remained somewhat consistent throughout these years.

An even stronger argument can be made regarding Kyrgyzstan, where the Tulip Revolution was categorized as a Color Revolution more because of its temporal proximity and shared Soviet legacy with Georgia and Ukraine than for the nature of the events themselves. Any change to the Kyrgyz regime between the late Akaev period and the post-Tulip Revolution period is minor compared to the consistently repressive and semi-authoritarian nature of the regime. It is too early to know if the new government will succeed in fundamentally changing the regime either. The names and relationships of the primary leaders have changed, but this speaks more to elite competition than to meaningful political change.

The Rose Revolution seems to have caused the most change as the old regime was, as in Kyrgyzstan, swept away but, the new regime tried to do things differently. This was especially evident in the early years of the regime, when the government had some demonstrable successes in fighting corruption, improving the business climate, and strengthening the state. Nonetheless, the similarities of the pre- and post-Rose Revolution political systems in Georgia should not be overlooked. Both systems were characterized by one-party dominance, few ideological differences between parties or within the ruling party, a weak legislature—although it was even weaker under Saakashvili—a highly personalized and informal style of governance that made the president stronger, and a dependency on foreign assistance that allowed Georgia to develop into what meets Beblawi and Luciani's definition of a "second-grade" rentier state.[1]

The argument that the Color Revolutions did not really happen is in fact easily rebutted by the rather obvious observation that these events did, in fact, occur and that had they not occurred, politics in Georgia, Ukraine, and Kyrgyzstan would have been much different. The first half of this assertion is obviously true, but the second part is less obvious and all but impossible to test. Georgia might have slipped into a more authoritarian system if the 2003 election had been successfully stolen, but it is just as likely that the country would have stumbled along until 2005, when a popular reform oriented politician would have won the election. The most likely candidate for that role would have been Mikheil Saakashvili, who would have been the leader of the opposition in the parliament in that particular alternate universe. Similarly, had there been no Orange Revolution, Viktor Yanukovich would have presided over a divided Ukraine. He might have tried to move it in a more authoritarian direction, but would have had no guarantee of success. This is more or less where Ukraine is today. In Kyrgyzstan, had Akaev remained in power the old kleptocrats would have been in power, rather than the newer ones, but that seems to be a distinction without a difference.

Ó Beachain and Polese (2010) rest their belief in the significance of the Color Revolutions on the argument that "the capacity to inspire people to contest fraudulent elections or unpopular political decisions had not dissipated . . . Colour Revolution movements were remarkable for their patient organization, strategic thinking and ability to attract and retain a network of dedicated activists" (242–43).

These assertions are true, but are not a legacy of any great significance. While the capacity to "contest fraudulent elections," or more generally, "unpopular political decisions," is good, neither of these originated with the Color Revolutions. Similarly, even if their assertions about organization and strategic thinking are taken at face value, these attributes may have made the Color Revolutions remarkable, but far from unique. At any given moment, dozens of political movements around the world have these characteristics.

The events in North Africa in early 2011 may raise a similar set of questions. When Mubarak in Egypt and Ben Ali in Tunisia resigned, contributing to a wave of protests for greater dignity and freedom throughout the Middle East, much of the world looked on incredulously as these events, similarly to the Color Revolutions, were celebrated in the West as democratic breakthroughs. As with the Color Revolutions, these events, while extremely inspiring, are far better understood as opening the door to greater democracy than as democratization itself. Moreover, the forces of continuity will likely remain very powerful in North Africa as they have in Georgia, Ukraine, and Kyrgyzstan.

The International Impact

The Color Revolutions may have had little lasting impact on the domestic politics of the countries in which they occurred, but they were not entirely domestic political occurrences. The perception that western countries, most notably the U.S., were involved in conceiving and implementing the Color Revolutions is, as has been shown, widespread both among the leadership and population of much of the former Soviet Union, as well as among the radical European and American left. Regardless of the accuracy of this perception, the perception itself is strong and has had an impact on the U.S. role in the region. Additionally, the Color Revolutions have created or perhaps exacerbated tension between the U.S. and Russia. This has been particularly acute regarding the NATO aspirations of Georgia and Ukraine as well as the close relationship between the U.S. and Georgia more generally.

Because of the perceived role of U.S. democracy assistance in the Color Revolutions, barriers have been erected in the former Soviet Union and beyond that make it harder for the NGOs and companies that work on democracy assistance to function around the world. Additionally, the democracy assistance project became conflated not just with regime change, but with regime change seeking to install pro-American leaders. This has contributed to the increasing cynicism and doubt surrounding democracy assistance internationally and in the U.S.

The Color Revolutions occurred during a time when the U.S.-Russia relationship was evolving; Russia itself was growing and becoming a more powerful international actor; and issues involving Russia were simply not the highest priority for an administration focused primarily on wars in Iraq and Afghanistan or combating Jihadist terror. This changed in August 2008 when war broke out between Russia and Georgia, with the strongly pro-Georgian position taken by the Bush administration and the general rancor toward Russia from that time, but this is not a fair reflection of the policy during most of the time Bush was in office. This led to a problem because just as the U.S. was congratulating itself on the success of the Color Revolutions and trumpeting a new wave of democracy, Russia began to push back. The U.S. seemed unprepared for the strength of this opposition because the democracy narrative, not the Russia narrative, had dominated American thinking about the Color Revolutions.[2]

Although the Color Revolutions have been characterized as both a triumph of U.S. democracy assistance and a demonstration of U.S. influence in the region, they were in many respects the apex of U.S. influence in the former Soviet Union. Since 2005 the region and the power of the U.S. has changed sufficiently that the possibility of the U.S. being able to have an impact on political change in the region, even a role as modest as that which the U.S. played in Georgia or Kyrgyzstan, seems unlikely. It is equally difficult to imagine any country in the region proclaiming an unambiguously pro-western orientation like that announced by Saakashvili or Yushchenko upon coming to power.

The Color Revolutions are not the only cause of tension between the U.S.

and Russia during the last few years, but these events contributed to new flashpoints in the already complicated U.S.-Russia relationship. NATO expansion, for example, had been a source of contention between the U.S. and Russia since Hungary, the Czech Republic, and Poland were brought into NATO in 1999 less than a decade after the first Bush administration had promised NATO would not expand to include former Soviet republics or allies. Nine other countries have joined NATO since that time, contributing to the Russian fear that NATO is an anti-Russian alliance. However, the stronger move toward bringing Georgia and Ukraine into NATO, which began following the Rose and Orange Revolutions, and has not yet been consummated, raised a qualitatively different set of concerns for Russia.

Between the end of the initial post-Soviet period and the time of the Rose Revolution an equilibrium had begun to characterize political development in the region. Semi-democratic or semi-authoritarian regimes of variously repressive degrees had stabilized most of the countries in the region. The Baltics, by this time, had become reasonably consolidated democracies, but no other country in the region was on a fast, or even not so fast, path to democracy. For Russia this meant that while the U.S. continued to have a presence in the region, the regimes themselves, often stewarded by former Communist apparatchiks, remained in spirit and political orientation closer to Russia. In this context western rhetoric about democracy, implicitly linked to a western orientation, and western efforts to achieve this goal were not very potent, so were tolerated by Russia.

The Color Revolutions, beginning in Georgia, but reaching their height in Ukraine, smashed this equilibrium and raised serious threats to Russia's presence in the region. This naturally led to increased tensions between the U.S. and Russia. From today's perspective this may seem like an overreaction, but in early 2005 the Russian perspective was very different. In Russia's view at that time, American-backed revolutions had brought pro-American leaders to power in both Georgia and Ukraine and threatened to do the same in Kyrgyzstan, Azerbaijan, and perhaps the entire region. From that perspective, Russia's decision to push back against the Color Revolutions was certainly understandable.

Russian-American relations in the post-Color Revolution period have been marked by a fundamental difference in how recent events are perceived. The U.S. sees these events through a narrative of democratization, while Russia views them as being primarily about influence in the region. The U.S. narrative about democracy has little value inside the region, where the articulated demand for democracy is weak and where, in most countries, belittling democracy is as popular as calling for it. Outside the region, this narrative proved a very flimsy frame on which to hang support for Georgia and Kyrgyzstan as democracy did not flourish after the Rose and Tulip Revolutions.

These differing narratives make it difficult for the U.S. and Russia even to have a discussion about Georgia and Ukraine. The U.S. often wants to focus on the democratic progress made by Ukraine and Georgia, but Russia does not care about or believe in this progress. Russia for its part wants to focus on increasing American influence in the region, but the U.S. only sees this behavior as promoting and protecting democratic development. This is most clear with regards to NATO where U.S. policy does not reflect Russian fears of NATO and the Russian leadership does not care about the value of NATO as a democratizing force.

Prospects for Democracy in the Former Soviet Union

The period immediately following the Color Revolutions represented a peak in democratic prospects in the former Soviet Union not seen since the first heady days after the collapse of the USSR. Democratic breakthroughs in Georgia, Ukraine, and Kyrgyzstan spanned three different regions and thousands of miles, but the similarities in style and outcomes as well as the very evident replicability of the Color Revolutions suggested that a new wave of democracy might just sweep the whole region. This occurred in a global context where Iraq's first elections in 2005 proved to be a bright spot in what until that time had been a dismal U.S. experience in Iraq, and talk of the Arab spring from the earlier part of the decade was beginning to be reignited.

The failure of Yushchenko, Saakashvili, or Bakiev, as well as their supporters and colleagues, to turn these democratic breakthroughs into meaningful and enduring steps toward greater democracy is not simply the failure of another round of Communist era semi-authoritarian hacks, and raises larger questions about the future of democracy in the region. The post Color Revolution governments, particularly of Georgia and Ukraine, from the western vantage, represented the best and the brightest their countries had to offer. Many were trained in the west, were English speaking, or were young enough not to have come of age politically in the Soviet period. These were the leaders positioned to move their countries forward and put the Soviet legacy firmly to rest. Their failure to do this suggests that the impact of this Soviet legacy was underestimated and that the U.S. and its allies, still lack a cohesive set of policies for lifting these countries out of the morass of semi-authoritarian, corrupt and unfree regimes.

Several years after the last Color Revolution, feelings about the future of democracy in the former Soviet Union are quite different from those in 2005. By 2009, the region's democratic hopes were at a low point of the post-Soviet period, but this cannot all be attributed to the failure of the Color Revolutions to live up to their early democratic promise, because the hardening of semi-authoritarian regimes in the region is also one of the causes of the current democratic despair.

The failure of the Color Revolutions is nonetheless significant. The electoral breakthrough model at the core of all three Color Revolutions proved to be an exciting but ineffective way to further democracy. Additionally, the reaction to the Color Revolutions by semi-authoritarian leaders throughout the region means that electoral breakthroughs are significantly less likely than they seemed to have been in 2003–2006. Even in the years immediately following the Color Revolutions, activists and their supporters in Azerbaijan, Belarus and elsewhere held the electoral breakthrough model in enough regard to seek to replicate it. Although these efforts failed, the belief in the model was significant. Today, nobody is discussing possible Color Revolutions in the region. Even after Lukashenko stole yet another election in Belarus in 2010, the demonstrations were again broken up quickly amid arrests and harassments. While there was some outrage in the U.S. and Europe, there was little talk of Color Revolution. To the extent that Color Revolutions still inspire anybody, it is outside the former Soviet Union.

The regimes that are in place in of Central Asia, the South Caucasus, and Russia can no longer be described as transitional. Many of them are in their second generation of semi-authoritarian leadership and have experienced relatively smooth, if largely undemocratic, transitions. Oppositions, to the extent they exist at all, are beleaguered, weak, and have little access to media, financial support, or any other resources and are not popular with ordinary people. The conditions that made the Color Revolutions possible do not exist anywhere in the region and are unlikely to come back anytime soon.

The hope for democratic change, indeed the future in general remains an even greater challenge in Georgia, Ukraine, and Kyrgyzstan themselves. Although these three countries are still freer than most of their neighbors, the experience of the Color Revolutions has been disruptive, confusing, and traumatizing for their people and institutions. While some commonalities exist between the Color Revolutions and the countries in which they occurred, at least on the surface, Georgia, Kyrgyzstan, and Ukraine find themselves in political positions that are very different from each other. Kyrgyzstan under Bakiev was almost indistinguishable from other semi-authoritarian regimes in the region run by a handful of prominent kleptocratic famlies. The assertion that the Color Revolution simply brought a new group to power and gave them an opportunity to steal money and lead corruption rings far truer in Kyrgyzstan than in Georgia or Ukraine. However, unlike similar regimes in the region, Bakiev could not remain in power very long. Given that the nature of the current regime is still not fully known, there is still a possibility for change in Kyrgyzstan, but if it occurs it will be in spite of, and in reaction to, the post-Tulip Revolution government.

Georgia is still more liberal than Kyrgyzstan, but politics in Georgia are distinguished not by greater democracy than its neighbors, but by greater rhetorical emphasis on democracy. In addition, Georgia's regime is given to strange and erratic behavior, including television programs showing a fake Russian invasion, grandiloquent and unrealistic promises for the future, and the larger than life personality of Saakashvili himself.

While Yanukovich's election in Ukraine may not herald the end of the Orange Revolution and hopes for democracy in that country, it is not exactly a sign that the Orange Revolution was a great success either. Yanukovich's victory was possible not necessarily because the Orange Revolution failed, but it would never have occurred if the leaders of the Orange Revolution had succeeded. It is still too early to know how his presidency will affect Ukraine's political development.

Beyond Transitions

The Color Revolutions turned out not to be harbingers or catalysts of change or new regime types. They were not the beginning of something new in Georgia, Kyrgyzstan, and Ukraine or in the former Soviet Union more generally. Ironically, the Color Revolutions were more of an end of a period than a beginning of one. Instead of being democratic breakthroughs as they were first thought, the Color Revolutions may have been the last gasp of the transition period in Georgia, Ukraine, and Kyrgyzstan. The most significant political development in the former Soviet Union in the decade from roughly 2000 to 2009 was not the advance of democracy. It was the end of the transition period. Carothers (2002) pointed out the declining value of the transition model relatively early in this period, but at that time, some of the countries in the former Soviet Union could still plausibly be described as transitional.

By 2010 this was clearly no longer the case. The Baltic countries were consolidated democracies well before 2010. The remaining twelve countries, with the exception of Ukraine and Moldova, had become consolidated authoritarian or semi-authoritarian regimes. This was true of Georgia and Kyrgyzstan, despite the experience of the Rose and Orange Revolutions. The democratic façade and slightly more liberal political climate in Georgia were differences of spin and degree, but did not mask an underlying political system which was dominated by one group, with little opportunity for meaningful political contestation and a media and civic climate that could not be reasonably described as free. In Kyrgyzstan, even the façade was no longer in place by the end of the decade, and the government itself followed soon after.

The picture with regard to democracy was not as gloomy in Ukraine, which had not become a semi-authoritarian regime by the end of the decade. Democracy was stronger in Ukraine and Moldova than in the rest of the non-Baltic former Soviet Union by 2010, but that does not mean Ukraine was still transitioning. Yanukovich's election in 2010 demonstrated that alternation of power is possible in Ukraine, but democratic institutions and rule of law remain weak while the economy is still heavily influenced by crony capitalism and corruption. These are textbook features of semi-democracies (Carothers 2002), not necessarily of countries in transition. In this framework the Orange Revolution is more accurately seen as helping to consolidate semi-democracy in Ukraine, not as bringing about real democracy.

All three countries experienced a revolutionary event, but none experienced revolutionary outcomes. This has become clear as the years have passed since the Color Revolutions and suggests that the regimes in place in Georgia, Ukraine, and Kyrgyzstan were considerably more resilient than they first seemed. It turned out that a few thousand, or in the case of Ukraine a few hundred thousand, demonstrators, some courageous leaders, and support from key international actors was enough to bring down the governments, but not to bring about enduring or meaningful regime change.

Although the initial post-Soviet transition period is over in all three of these countries, the current regimes will not last forever, nor is there any guarantee of stability in Georgia, Ukraine, or Kyrgyzstan. Future instability, however, should not be mistaken for transition but would more accurately be described, as were the Color Revolutions themselves, as part of the ebb and flow of politics in these semi-democratic or semi-authoritarian regimes.

Democratization After the Transition

Ironically, the Color Revolutions, which were first viewed as reinvigorating democratic aspirations both in the former Soviet Union and globally, because of their failure to lead to substantive democratic outcomes, are further evidence that the transition period has passed. It is not, however, clear what has replaced it. The end of the transition period has not brought stability, at least in the case of the Color Revolution countries. Kyrgyz instability was again front page news in April 2010 when the disillusioned Tulip Revolutionaries forced Bakiev and his supporters out of office in a set of events that at least looked something like a Tulip Revolution, and which was precipitated by hikes in utility and cell phone fees rather than by a fraudulent election.

Ukraine and Georgia, at least on the surface, both seem considerably more stable than Kyrgyzstan. Yushchenko left office peacefully after losing an election, while Saakashvili's regime has never really been threatened by domestic political forces. However, low level instability has been a fact of political life in both Georgia and Ukraine since the Rose and Orange Revolutions. The possibility of this mild instability becoming more significant is never far from the surface in either country.

Yanukovich's victory in 2010 may not have been the defeat of the Orange Revolution which some immediately thought it to be, but there is no doubt that Yanukovich could not only orient Ukraine more toward Russia, but also seek political support from Russia and begin to change Ukrainian politics to more resemble Russian style "sovereign democracy." If this happens, it will almost certainly provoke tension in western Ukraine, where Yanukovich remains unpopular.

In Georgia, government efforts to control this instability through increasingly strong, and at times quirky, manipulations of media, exercise of censorship, and harassment of opposition political forces, have generally, to paraphrase former mayor of Chicago Richard M. Daley, not created instability, but preserved it.[3] Efforts to bring moderate change through constitutional processes such as elections proved not only fruitless, but futile, within the first few years of the Rose Revolution, meaning that unplanned transitions remain the only way to make even moderate political change in Georgia. This suggests that while the Georgian regime can be described as stable; the stability will not last. Moreover, when it ends, it will likely give way to quick and radical change rather than gradual change through, for example, a transition of presidential power to a Saakashvili opponent in 2013.

The Color Revolutions fizzled out in the years between 2005 and 2007 as Georgia and Kyrgyzstan moved closer to becoming semi-authoritarian regimes complete with media repression, harassment of political opposition, and violent crackdowns on demonstrators. In Ukraine, the energy and excitement of the Maidan seemed to dissipate more gradually as Yushchenko's lethargic presidency gradually sapped away the hopes the Orange Revolution had held for many in Ukraine. 2010 brought about more symbolically clear evidence of the end of the Color Revolutions as elections and coups forced Yushchenko and Bakiev from the presidencies of their respective countries. In Georgia there was no similarly dramatic break.

The end of the Color Revolutions closed a chapter in the history of the entire former Soviet Union, not just the three countries that experienced them and also meant the end of a period in which the dream—primarily in the West—that these countries could relatively easily evolve into market based economies and democracies was still alive. Western powers now seem resigned to regimes that are either undemocratic, unstable, or both in that part of the world. There was no more clear evidence of this than the relative silence that greeted Roza Otunbayeva and other leaders of post-Bakiev Kygyzstan. Nobody in the West spoke of them as democratic or feted them in Washington or Brussels. Instead, they were treated as simply more of the same. Perhaps they are.

Appendix: Studying Color Revolutions

Academic research on the Color Revolutions generally falls into one of several different areas: case studies of various individual Color Revolutions, pieces written either by participants or by observers offering guidance to would be Color Revolutionaries, explanations of what made the Color Revolutions possible, and efforts to place the Color Revolution phenomenon in a broader comparative or analytical context.

Georgia

Only a handful of books focus entirely on the Rose Revolution, including Karumidze and Wertsch (2006), Wheatley (2006), Areshidze (2007), and Mitchell (2008). Karumidze and Wertsch provide some useful interviews and background from the period immediately following the Rose Revolution. They interviewed many of the key players from both the Georgian and American side, so offer good insight into what these individuals were thinking during or shortly after the events of the winter of 2003–2004. However, this work does not seek to offer a great deal of analysis or to place the Rose Revolution in a broader context.

Wheatley (2006) offers a more in-depth analysis of the events Rose Revolution with particular emphasis on the origins of the Rose Revolution in the context of Georgia's post-Soviet political development. This work, however, is a study of Georgian political evolution since 1991, rather than an examination of the Rose Revolution per se.

Areshidze (2007) is also based largely on interviews. However, unlike Karumidze and Wertsch, who offer a very positive, almost celebratory view of the Rose Revolution, Areshidze is much more negative. He views the Rose Revolution as a step backward for Georgian democracy that undermined the positive developments of the Shevardnadze years. Areshidze's book was written a few years after the Rose Revolution, so this view is buoyed by his analysis of some of the problems with democracy in Georgia since the Rose Revolution. Areshidze is, however, not a neutral observer in this as he worked as a close advisor to the New Rights Party which did not support the Rose Revolution and was the only opposition party in the first post-Rose Revolution parliament.

Mitchell (2008) focuses entirely on the Rose Revolution, rather than on post-Soviet Georgian politics more broadly. In that book I examine the role of U.S. democracy assistance and democratic development in Georgia after the Rose Revolution in some detail, but I do not probe the evolution of the U.S.-Russia relationship since the Rose Revolution.

In addition to these books, several articles in scholarly or policy journals have addressed various aspects of the Rose Revolution. King (2004), Fairbanks (2004), Dolidze (2007), Mitchell (2004, 2006, 2008, 2009), Kupchan (2006), Kandelaki (2006), and others have written on various aspects of the Rose Revolution including its origins, impact on the region, and continued democratic development.

Other aspects of the impact of the Rose Revolution have been explored as well. Legvold and Coppetiers (2004) examined the Georgia-Russia relationship in the aftermath. Mitchell and Cooley (2008), Simes (2008), Sestanovich (2008), King (2008), Cornell (2009) and Asmus (2010) have written specifically about the 2008 war between Russia and Georgia, while Blank (2008), Cornell (2002), King (2001), Hunter (2006), and Fairbanks (1995) have written about Georgian politics and the conflicts in Abkhazia and South Ossetia.

Ukraine

The Orange Revolution has also generated book length case studies and edited volumes. Aslund and McFaul (2006) offer one of the most useful of these volumes. Their work brings together Ukrainian and foreign scholars offering different angles and analyses of the Orange Revolution. Issues such as the Russian and western role in the Orange Revolution, the evolution of Ukraine's political opposition, and the role of various parts of Ukrainian civil society are explored in various parts of this book.

D'Anieri (2007) offers a detailed analysis of Ukrainian politics since the Orange Revolution examining the ongoing tension between the different political forces in Ukraine as well as the challenges facing the government of Viktor Yuschnenko. Wilson (2005) and Aslund (2009) are among the other book length studies of the Orange Revolution.

Kyrgyzstan

Less has been written about Kyrgyzstan than about the other two Color Revolution countries. Marat (2006) provides a good overview of the events leading up to, and immediately following, the Tulip Revolution. While this book offers a substantial level of detail and good descriptions of events in Kyrgyzstan in 2005-2006, it does not provide much analysis. Nor does it seek to place the Tulip Revolution in a broader context of democratic development or post-Soviet politics.

Other than Marat's, there are almost no book length treatments of any aspects of the Tulip Revolution. This may be due to the speed with which the Tulip Revolution lost its democratic promise or the general lack of interest in Central Asia compared to Ukraine and Georgia. The Tulip Revolution is the most tenuous of the Color Revolutions, and this is reflected in the literature, or absence thereof.

Other scholarly work on the Tulip Revolutions includes articles by Radnitz (2006) and Khamidov (2006). Radnitz offers useful valuable analysis of the Tulip Revolution, focusing on the events of spring 2005 as well as the failure of the new government to live up to the democratic promise of the Tulip Revolution. Khamidov's work looks more narrowly at the role of youth activists in the Tulip Revolution.

Fuhrmann (2007) examines the mobilization of the Kyrgyz people that contributed to the Tulip Revolution. He points out that "Without a significant NGO presence, the leaders of the demonstrations mobilized thousands of protesters across three different cities and coordinated the actions of several anti-Akiev factions" (16). Furhmann identifies two distinct kinds of social capital, imported and indigenous, which contributed to mobilization during the Tulip Revolution. As suggested by their names, "imported" refers to the "western" notion of civil society based on associations and even NGOs, while "indigenous" social capital refers to "ceremonies, trust and reciprocity" (18).

Engvall (2007) compares the Akaev regime to its post-Tulip Revolution successors, arguing that the two regimes share key similarities particularly around the issue of statehood where both regimes proved largely unable to consolidate the state or even provide a raison d'être for Kyrgyz statehood. Under Bakiev's leadership, according to Engvall "the political situation in Kyrgyzstan is one in which no group, let alone any individual, can claim to be in control . . . but the balance of power resulting from their inability to neutralize one (an)other is the source of some degree of stability." This suggests unequivocally that the Tulip Revolution had little, if anything, to do with democracy.

Comparative Studies

There have been fewer efforts to look at the Color Revolutions in a comparative and analytical context. These works have included a range of scholarly and journalistic efforts. MacKinnon (2007) presents a journalistic account focusing mostly on Serbia, Georgia, and Ukraine. McKinnon argues that all three of these breakthroughs were the work of a broad U.S. supported effort to replace leaders unfriendly to the U.S. with more western-oriented leaders. As evidence of this he draws on the similarities between political events in all three of these countries as well as similar roles played by U.S. democracy assistance organizations such as the NDI, IRI, and the NED as well as local NGOs such as Otpor, Kmara, and Pura.

McKinnon argues that the Color Revolutions were a U.S. based conspiracy. His book is a good example of this sentiment which is believed by many both in the west and in the former Soviet Union. His argument, however, suffers from a dependency on interviews with only a few people, asking the reader to assume links that are not really apparent and a tendency to quote from, for example, public websites and imply nefarious behavior when there is little evidence that it exists. He also overlooks the desire for democracy or change, from the people in places like Georgia and Serbia, or even the ability of these people to determine their own futures, all of which were central to the Color Revolutions.

A more thoughtful and measured look at the idea that Color Revolutions are the result of western planning or conspiring is offered by Herd (2005). He describes the view, held relatively broadly among political elites in Russia and other former Soviet states, that "These revolutions (Georgia, Ukraine and Serbia) all have certain features in common . . . a youth protest movement with catchy slogans and logos" (4) and that "This understanding of the role of national, international and non-governmental organizations as willing and able to act in concert suggests that other post-Soviet states will be targeted for regime change . . . in accordance with a secret strategic blueprint for change" (4).

Herd concludes that "This idea, though weak, is grounded in fact. . . . However, the assertion that international organizations, foreign countries and NGOs act in concert to achieve a grand strategy of transforming the CIS states into democracies by exporting catalytic revolutions rests on assumptions that are hard to credit" (13). His analysis captures the nuance of the situation well.

McFaul (2005) wrote one of the first serious efforts to study the Color Revolutions. Written before the Tulip Revolution, this article draws primarily on the Serbian, Georgian, and Ukrainian cases. In this piece McFaul argues that these Color Revolutions mark a significant break from the semi-democratic regimes which had governed those countries in the post-Communist years and thus mark an evolution away from the post-Communism. He argues that these three events have four key similarities:

> First, in all three cases, the spark for regime change was a fraudulent national election. . . . Second, the democratic challengers deployed extraconstitutional means solely to defend the existing, democratic constitution rather than to achieve a fundamental rewriting of the rules of the political game. Third, each country for a time witnessed challengers and incumbents making competing and simultaneous claims to hold sovereign authority. . . . Fourth, all of these revolutionary situations ended without mass violence. (6)

In a 2007 article McFaul adds a fourth shared characteristic "the conclusion of these electoral revolutions triggered a significant jump in the degree of democracy" (2007: 50). The degree to which this last point can be applied to all of the countries is debatable. Georgia and Kyrgyzstan did not see significant democratic advances after their respective Color Revolutions. McFaul's 2007 article is, however, primarily about Ukraine where the Orange Revolution clearly moved that country, at least initially, in a more democratic direction. The extent to which these advances will be reversed due to the result of the 2010 presidential election is still not known.

In the 2005 article McFaul outlines seven factors which contributed to the success of the Color Revolutions in Serbia, Georgia and Ukraine:

1) a semi-autocratic rather than fully autocratic regime; 2) an unpopular incumbent; 3) a united and organized opposition; 4) an ability quickly to drive home the point that voting results were falsified; 5) enough independent media to inform citizens about the falsified vote; 6) a political opposition capable of mobilizing tens of thousands or more demonstrators to protest electoral fraud, and 7) division among the regime's coercive forces. (2005: 7)

This list is a good starting point but there are some aspects of it which should be examined more closely. Additionally, it is useful to examine the Tulip Revolution in the context of these seven factors. McFaul suggests, but does not make explicit the role of strong civil society which played a key role in the Color Revolutions. To some extent, this is captured in the first factor about semi- rather than fully autocratic regimes, but it could have been more explicit. More significantly, McFaul overlooks a central point, the weakness of the state. This is particularly pertinent to Kyrgyzstan and Georgia, where the state simply did not have resources to put an end to the post-election movements, even if the leaders had wanted to use violence.

McFaul's third point regarding the unity of the opposition, by his own admission, applies more to Ukraine and Serbia than to Georgia and Kyrgyzstan. In both Georgia and Kyrgyzstan, there was little pre-election unity. In fact, some of the most intense campaigning in Georgia occurred between opposition parties. More significantly, the early days of the November 2003 demonstrations in Georgia were characterized by strong competition between Mikheil Saakashvili's National Movement and Zurab Zhvania and Nino Burjanadze's Burjanadze Democrats. In Georgia, unity came at the last possible minute only when it became clear that Shevardnadze might actually resign. In Kyrgyzstan, it is not clear that it was ever there.

Tucker (2007) probes the impact of stolen elections on mobilizing people and overcoming the collective action problem in non-democratic states. He argues that while in general, most citizens would benefit from political change, in non-democratic countries, it takes a catalytic event, such as a stolen election to bring enough citizens onto the streets.

Bunce and Wolchik (2006) and Kuzio (2006) focus on the role of youth activists in the Color Revolutions. These works are a useful exploration of this important aspect of the Color Revolutions but seems to extrapolate the Slovakia, Serbia, and Ukraine experience onto Georgia in a way that is not entirely accurate. It is inaccurate to suggest, for example, that the Georgian youth group Kmara, had an impact comparable to Otpor in Serbia. In many respects, Kmara played a relatively minor role and, Bunce and Wolchik point out, was much closer to the political leadership, notably Saakashvili's National Movement than Otpor, the Ukrainian group Pura, or the Slovakian youth activists were to opposition political leadership in their own countries.

The focus of Bunce and Wolchik (2006) is the diffusion of the "electoral revolution" model of democratic breakthrough in the post-Communist countries. They identify the roots of this model in earlier electoral events in the Philippines in 1986 and Chile in 1988. They also argue that the electoral model which became the Color Revolutions in the post-Communist world began in the late 1990s in Serbia, Bulgaria, Romania, and Russia. While they are probably right about the roots of the Color Revolutions, it is striking how few people involved in these events see any antecedents before Serbia in 2000.

Their analysis in this article as well as in Bunce and Wolchik (2006a) focuses a substantial amount of attention on the role of democracy promotion organizations in the diffusion of the electoral model. This might be construed to indicate a belief that these organizations played a very large role in the Color Revolutions, but their conclusion "international democracy promotion is important only at the margins" (301), is a more accurate description of the roles played by these organizations.

Beissinger's (2007) emphasis is also on the diffusion of the Color Revolutions. He tracks these events from Serbia in 2000 through to Kyrgyzstan in 2005. Beissinger views the Color Revolutions as being "modular" events because they were "based in significant part on the prior successful example of others." He stresses that the "emulative characters of these revolutions is evident in the transnational linkages connecting them" (262).

While Beissinger's assertion that "each of these (Color) revolutions drew inspiration and expertise from previous cases, and each has inspired a rash of emulative activity. At the same time, each was based on local initiative and local sources of dissatisfaction" (2007: 262), is, for the most part, accurate, it is possible to overstate the extent of the modular aspect of the Color Revolutions. The "emulative" aspect varied in each of the Color Revolutions. While the Georgians borrowed somewhat from the Serbs, particularly with regard to Otpor and Kmara, other ideas from the Bulldozer Revolution, such as the unified opposition and use of western support, did not translate into the Rose Revolution. The Orange Revolution had the strongest modular aspect borrowing heavily from the Georgian and Serb cases. The failure of Color Revolutions after Kyrgyzstan, notably in Belarus and Azerbaijan, demonstrate the limits of diffusion in the face of different state structures and state strength

Beissinger also offers his own definition of Color Revolutions identifying six shared characteristics.

1) the use of stolen elections as the occasion for massive mobilizations against pseudo-democratic regimes;
2) foreign support for the development of local democratic movements;
3) the organization of radical youth movements using unconventional protest tactics prior to the election in order to undermine the regime's popularity and will to repress and to prepare for a final showdown;
4) a united opposition established in part through foreign prodding;
5) external diplomatic pressure and unusually large electoral monitoring; and
6) massive mobilization upon the announcement of fraudulent electoral results and the use of nonviolent resistance tactics taken directly from the work of Gene Sharp, the guru of nonviolent resistance in the West. (2007: 261)

This definition overstates the role of the west, particularly in points two, four and five, as well as the extent of opposition unity. The role of Sharp's work in the Color Revolutions probably applies more to Ukraine and Serbia than to Georgia or Kyrgyzstan. In general, Beissinger's definition reveals one of the major problems with many of the Color Revolution analyses as he extrapolates from Ukraine and Serbia, the best known and most studied cases, onto the other cases. Foreign support, for example, varied substantially between these two sets of cases.

In an earlier (2006) piece, Beissinger criticizes the U.S. approach of seeking to continue to diffuse the Color Revolutions, asserting that this undermines the cause of democracy because it makes it likely that democracy will become viewed as "a tool of external statecraft," that is to say a U.S. policy goal rather than a domestic political system. He also points out that "Even in Serbia, Georgia and Ukraine the long term stability of democratic change produced from these revolutions is in doubt"

Ó Beachain and Polese's (2010) edited volume on the Color Revolutions also seeks to define Color Revolutions and explore the extent to which they should be viewed as revolutions. They identify five variables which both characterize Color Revolutions and help describe them. First, they explore the "character of the state on the eve of the protests," concluding that "Relatively democratically oriented elites are more likely to allow the preconditions for a Color Revolution to take root by allowing the development of a civil society" (7–8).

The second variable they identify is the opposition, claiming that "a compact opposition is a sine qua non (of Color Revolutions) for a number of reasons" (8). This is a frequent characterization of Color Revolutions, but seems to rely on an interpretation of events in Georgia that ignores the heated rivalry between Saakashvili and Zhvania which not only continued during most of the period of the demonstrations, but was frequently apparent during Zhvania's tenure as Prime Minister serving at the pleasure of President Saakashvili.

Ó Beachain and Polese identify "external influences" as their third variable, but wisely point out that "It would be an erroneous assumption that the U.S. and the E.U., by pumping money into a country, can by themselves change the destiny of individual post-Soviet countries." (8) However, they qualify this assertion by their fourth variable, that foreign powers "concentrate on civil society." This emphasis on civil society may not be best viewed as a variable because it doesn't vary all that much. In most non-democratic countries, particularly during the period of the Color Revolutions, the U.S. and EU concentrated their assistance on civil society. The primary cause of different levels of civil society development between, for example, Kyrgyzstan and Kazakhstan or Georgia and Armenia was not support of the west for civil society, but absorptive capacity and legal environment in each of the countries involved.

Their fifth variable, "the people," seeks to understand to which ordinary people were engaged in the political process and "how motivated do individual activists become . . . and how much are they willing to risk." Obviously, any answer to this question needs to address the issue of why as well. Nonetheless, it is apparent that even if all the other structures are in place, a Color Revolution cannot occur if the people do not want it and are not willing to take some risks to get it.

Way's (2008) provocatively titled article "The Real Causes of the Color Revolutions" examines structural factors. Specifically, he notes that the relative strength of the state in the pre-revolutionary system is the key factor for determining where and when Color Revolutions were successful: "regime collapses have resulted more from authoritarian weakness than opposition strength" (62). This analysis offers critical insight into what makes Color Revolutions possible, but it does less to explain what makes them happen.

Hale (2006) argues that the Color Revolutions must be understood in the context of "patronal presidentialism," which is predominant in much of the former Soviet Union. When a patronal president is "firmly entrenched in his or her office," according to Hale, "the president's ideological opponents will have a very hard time attracting any kind of material support." However, Hale asserts, "Whenever a patronal president is widely perceived to be on his or her way out, however, the situation changes dramatically." Color Revolutions have occurred when patronal presidents Shevardnadze, Akiev, and Kuchma have appeared to be on their way out. The Serbian case complicates this somewhat as Milosevic was not quite considered to be on his way out until the Bulldozer Revolution was well under way.

Hale observes that the contestation for power once the opposition forces see that the president is weak can be quite fierce, often with substantial public input as in Ukraine, Georgia, and Kyrgyzstan. This contributes to a sense that Color Revolutions are democratic breakthroughs because the period of the breakthrough has a democratic feel to it. While Hale's point about patronal presidents being vulnerable when they have made it clear they are leaving office is accurate, he overstates the case somewhat in his description of the scramble for power in that president's wake. While elements of the Georgian opposition in 2002–2003 certainly were vying for power among themselves, this was not an "extraordinarily fierce" battle, but more like what one might see in a partisan primary for governor or senator in the U.S. In Ukraine, the struggle for post-Kuchma power came down to a two candidate election followed by street demonstrations, but not violence. Krygyzstan is perhaps the case that fits Hale's model closely as Bakiev did not emerge as the anti-Akaev figure until considerably after the election and a bit of fighting within the opposition.

Hale's efforts to examine the post-Color Revolutionary countries through the prism of the patronal president model represent useful contributions to our understanding of Color Revolutions as well as an attempt to place them in a broader, and more analytical context. Hale also challenges the belief that Color Revolutions were democratic breakthroughs, arguing that "analysts may have exaggerated the degree to which the Colored Revolutions actually represent democratic turning points for the countries in which they occurred."

Tudoroiu (2007) share's Hale's view that the Color Revolutions did not lead to democratic gains, "Popular enthusiasm was replaced by disillusionment as the new leaders created a Bonapartist regime (Georgia), entered into open conflict with former revolutionary allies (Kyrygzstan) or had to openly accept cohabitation with leaders of the former authoritarian regime (Ukraine)" (316). Tudoriu attributes this to a failure of civil society, both before and after the respective Color Revolutions. He argues that the Color Revolutions were really "struggle(s) for power within the ruling elite." Both Hale and Tudoroiu represent a growing view among many scholars that the Color Revolutions, with the possible exception of Ukraine, were not democratic breakthroughs at all.

D'Anieri (2006) argues that the focus of Bunce and Wolchik and others on youth and civic angles of Color Revolutions exaggerates the people power aspect of these events. He argues that "elites and, in particular security services, play a much more significant role in these revolutions than has generally been appreciated" (332). D'Anieri's point is particularly valuable because it puts the focus back on the state rather than just on civil society. State weakness was one of the key ingredients to the Color Revolutions. This factor was far more decisive than the relative strength and sophistication of, for example, opposition coalitions in determining whether Color Revolutions were successful or not.

Radnitz (2010) takes a significantly different approach from most other scholars, focusing on the economic, rather than political, roots of the Color Revolutions. Beginning with the reminder that in earlier periods, capitalism was viewed as "the engine of democratization" (128), Radnitz looks at the extent of economic liberalization in various countries of the former Soviet Union arguing that in countries "where economic dispersion as partial—the intermediate case—the balance of power tilted neither toward the state nor toward capitalists. Important assets fell into private hands and could form the basis of an opposition" (132). Georgia, Ukraine, and Kyrgyzstan were all this intermediate area making contestation for political power and potent opposition alliances possible.

Notes

Chapter 1. Introduction

1. All three Color Revolutions have been described in greater detail elsewhere. For background on the Rose Revolution, see, for example, Mitchell (2004, 2008); Wheatley (2006); Wertsch and Karumidze (2006). For more background on the Tulip Revolution, see Radnitz (2006); Marat (2006). McFaul and Aslund (2006) and Wilson (2006) provide similar valuable background on the Orange Revolution.

2. For many the U.S. role in the Color Revolutions is taken for granted; see MacKinnon (2007); Engdahl (2009). This view can also be found on numerous left of center websites including Atlantic Free Press (http://www.atlanticfreepress.com/), Mostly Water (http://mostlywater.org), and NOW Truth (http://nwotruth.com). Others such as Mitchell (2008), Way (2008), and Silitski (2008) challenge this assumption and place the U.S. role in a broader context.

3. Not surprisingly, there is a good deal of debate about the best way to define the term "revolution." Perhaps the most clear and accessible definition is offered by Huntington (1968), who describes revolution as "a rapid, fundamental and violent domestic change in the dominant values and myths of a society, in its political institutions, social structure, leadership, and government activity and policies. Revolutions are thus to be distinguished from insurrections, rebellions, revolts, coups and wars of independence" (264)

Huntington's definition is thorough, easy to understand, and relatively noncontroversial. He does, however, set the bar for what events can be defined as revolutions somewhat high, limiting the applicability of this definition to a handful of historical events such as the Russian, Chinese, and French Revolutions.

For many reasons none of the Color Revolutions come close to meeting this definition. They were not violent and had little apparent impact on the dominant values and myths of society or its social structure. The impact on government and government activity may have been substantial in some cases, but was not exactly "fundamental."

The notion of revolutions having a transformative effect on society is also found in a definition offered by Skocpol (1979), "rapid, basic transformations of society's state and class structures." Again, the Color Revolutions seem not to meet this threshold because while there were some changes they were not as profound as this definition suggests. Skocpol offers a definition of "political revolutions" that "change political structures but not social structures" (4). This seems an appropriate term to describe the Color Revolutions, which, in varying degrees, changed political structures while having a far less significant effect on social structures.

Moore's (1966) dismissal of the revolutionary credentials of the American Revolution, "Since it [the American Revolution] did not result in any fundamental changes of the structure of society, there are grounds for asking whether it deserves to be called a revolution at all" (112), is directly applicable to the Color Revolutions and also suggests these events were not revolutions.

Moore and Skocpol's definitions place an emphasis on societal change that seems to preclude the Color Revolutions. Goldstone (1986) introduces an element of mass mobilization: "revolution depends on elites with independent resource who have substantial grievances against the state over taxation, corruption, attacks on the elite, or over the state's failure to stand up to foreign pressures . . . but a full-scale revolution only occurs through the conjunction of such opposition with widespread popular uprisings," which also raises questions about the Color Revolutions. The first half of Goldstone's definition largely applies to the Color Revolutions, but only the Orange Revolution had a component of widespread popular uprisings. The Rose Revolution, while probably enjoying widespread support, was largely by political elites. The Tulip Revolution did not even enjoy support comparable to the Rose Revolution.

Goldstone (1991) echoes a bit of Huntington, as he describes revolutions as "the forcible overthrow of a government followed by the reconsolidation of authority by new groups ruling through new political (and sometimes social) institution." Force and violence were largely absent from the Color Revolutions. Even the Tulip Revolution, the least peaceful of the three, cannot be said to be truly violent in nature.

On balance, most of this literature suggests that the Color Revolutions were not violent enough, did not bring about substantial enough societal change, and did not have a sufficient ideological component to be truly considered revolutions. Nonetheless, dismissing the revolutionary character of the Color Revolutions too quickly would be a mistake because the changing nature of revolutions should be taken into consideration as well.

Basing a definition of revolution too heavily on the French, Chinese, and Russian models not only limits the universe of revolutions too much to be analytically useful, but makes it necessary to create entirely new terms for political change in the last half of the twentieth century or much of the post-Colonial world. Not understanding any event since the Chinese Communist Revolution to be a true revolution is a bit like refusing to vote for anybody for the Baseball Hall of Fame because nobody in the last seven decades was as good as Babe Ruth.

Hatto (2000) argues that the definition of revolution should be an ongoing process reflecting that new kinds of revolutions occur that force us to rethink existing definitions: "one is reminded of the Channel gun that had to fire a different sized shell at each round owing to the wear on the bore. To be plain, it is clear that one's working conception of revolution must modify one's making or breaking of revolution, and one's making or breaking of it must in turn modify one's conception of it" (17). The Color Revolutions have certainly had their "wear on the bore," the nonviolent, electorally based ousting of corrupt semidemocratic regimes is, according to Hatto's approach, an important contribution to the development of the concept of revolution.

Fairbanks (2007), writing about the Color Revolutions highlights three elements of his definition of revolution "(1) A revolution must be fairly brief and well demarcated from the periods before and after it; ... (2) ... it must be achieved not only by leaders but by the energies of a broader group of people; ... (3) ... violence has been quite important for revolutions." Fairbanks provides a mixed answer to the question whether the Color Revolutions were truly revolutions. He points out that "the most obvious difference" between the Color Revolutions and his definition was the lack of violence in Georgia, Ukraine, and Kyrgyzstan. However, he also argues that the Color Revolutions, particularly in Georgia and Ukraine, "separate and symbolize two distinct periods" as distinct from the "foggy indeterminacy" of a transitional period.

4. See Goldstone (1991), Johnson (1966) or Skocpol (1979) for the role of ideology in revolutions.

5. The U.S. air force base at Manas is essential for transporting troops and supplies to Afghanistan. Thus, Kyrgyzstan is of great strategic import as long as the U.S. war in Afghanistan persists.

6. Beissinger's definition of Color Revolution includes six key attributes:

"1) the use of stolen elections as the occasion for massive mobilizations against pseudo-democratic regimes;

2) foreign support for the development of local democratic movements;

3) the organization of radical youth movements using unconventional protest tactics prior to the election in order to undermine the regime's popularity and will to repress and to prepare for a final showdown;

4) a united opposition established in part through foreign prodding;

5) external diplomatic pressure and unusually large electoral monitoring; and

6) massive mobilization upon the announcement of fraudulent electoral results and the use of nonviolent resistance tactics taken directly from the work of Gene Sharp, the guru of nonviolent resistance in the West" (261)

McFaul (2005) identifies only four defining attributes of Color Revolutions "First, in all three cases, the spark for regime change was a fraudulent national election. Second, the democratic challengers deployed extraconstitutional means solely to defend the existing, democratic constitution rather than to achieve a fundamental rewriting of the rules of the political game. Third, each country for a time witnessed challengers and incumbents making competing and simultaneous claims to hold sovereign authority. . . . Fourth, all of these revolutionary situations ended without mass violence" (6).

7. See, for example, Kandelaki (2004).

8. For more on ISFED, see Mitchell (2008).

9. See Mitchell (2004, 2008) for more on this.

Chapter 2. Pre-Color Revolution Regimes

1. Western Ukraine includes all the country west or north of Kiev, as well as a few oblasts just to the east of Kiev including Kirovohrad, Poltava, and Cherkasy Oblasts. Eastern Ukraine includes all the remaining areas east and south of Kiev.

2. Stalin's real name was the more Georgian sounding Dzhugushvili. Beria's family was from the west Georgian region of Samagrelo, where the name is still not uncommon. Montefiore (2004) describes the Georgian roots, and styles, of both men as well as the relation between them.

3. Georgia's Borjomi brand mineral water was one of the most recognized brands of any kind in the Soviet Union. It continues to be a major export for Georgia.

4. Kyrgyzstan's north includes the eastern two thirds of the country as well as the capital, Bishkek. The south includes the western third, the southern central part of Kyrgyzstan, and the city of Osh.

5. Data from www.electoralgeography.com. None of these data should be taken as entirely accurate because, as will be discussed later, there were not altogether free and fair elections. Election data reflect that fraud was committed throughout the election period. Nonetheless, the trends suggested by these results are clear.

6. Quote from Olcott's testimony at Kyrgyzstan's Revolution Causes and Consequences Hearing before the Commission on Security and Cooperation in Europe, CSES (2005).

7. Scalapino (1962) and Pye (1985) introduced the notion of a "one and a half party system" to refer to Japan and other parts of East Asia. Georgia, during the late Shevardnadze years was, on behalf, a weaker such system.

8. The multipartisan nature of Ukrainian politics since the Orange Revolution also creates an illusion of a stronger democracy than actually exists. The neat division between blue and orange or west and east is relatively easy for Western observers, analysts, and even diplomats to understand and often leads them to overstate the democratic character of these divisions.

9. Technically, Russia is not a neighbor of Kyrgyzstan as the two countries do not share a border, but Russia remains extremely important and casts a very large shadow there.

10. FBIS May 29, 1992, quoted in Spector (2004: 15). Note Akaev's reference to east (meaning China) as well as west.

Chapter 3. Electoral Breakthroughs

1. This chapter seeks to provide description and analysis of the primary events that contributed to or became the Color Revolutions. The descriptions are necessarily incomplete and somewhat brief. There are a range of sources that can provide better detailed descriptions of these events. For Georgia, Wertsch and Karumidze (2005), Areshidze (2007), and Wheatley (2005) provide good summaries. In addition, Mitchell (2008) offers an in-depth description of the Rose Revolution. Much of the Georgia sections in this chapter draw heavily on that work. Wilson (2005) and Aslund and McFaul (2006) both provide far more in depth description of the Orange Revolution than

offered here. Less is written about the Tulip Revolution, but Marat (2006) provides a good collection of pieces on those events.

2. In Georgia the election occurred on November 3, 2003, and Saakashvili was sworn is as president January 25, 2004; in Ukraine the first round of the election was November 21, 2004, and Yushchenko became president January 23, 2005; in Kyrgyzstan the election occurred on February 27, 2005, and Bakiev was inaugurated on August 14, 2005.

3. Only 225 seats would be elected because ten seats were not filled and were held open for representation from Abkhazia. People in Abkhazia, however, did not vote in that election because Georgia exercised no sovereignty over Abkhazia.

4. Rayon is a Soviet era term, probably best understood as the equivalent to a U.S. county.

5. This term referred, and refers, to bringing Abkhazia and South Ossetia back into Georgia.

6. For details on the nature of the election fraud see OSCE/ODIHR (2004a).

7. A PVT is a system designed to protect against fraud in post-election counting. Essentially, election monitors are stationed in a large random sample of polling places. These monitors stay in the polling places throughout the day and through the counting which occurs in the stations. They then phone or text the results in their station to a central headquarters. From this sample, it is possible to determine the overall vote results.

8. The results in the first round were Yushchenko (39.88 percent), Yanukovich (39.32 percent), Moroz (5.81 percent), Symonenko (4.97 percent), the remaining votes being divided among 20 candidates and a few write-ins. None of these received more than 2 percent of the vote. Symonenko was the candidate of the Communist Party, Moroz of the Socialist Party. After the first round, Moroz agreed to support Yushchenko in the runoff. This support was quite valuable to Yushchenko and led to Moroz becoming speaker of parliament after the Orange Revolution.

9. A telling detail about the Color Revolutions is that all three people who became president immediately following the events were political insiders who, at one time, enjoyed strong ties to the old regime. This suggests a dynamic that was not exactly revolutionary in nature.

10. While many Georgians, most notably its ethnic Armenian minority, watch Russian television primarily, the 2003 parliamentary elections in Georgia were less important to the Kremlin than the Ukrainian presidential election of 2004.

11. For more on election fraud in these elections see OSCE/ODIHR (2004b,c); and Committee of Voters of Ukraine 2004.

12. This meant that in Georgia two-thirds of the parliament were chosen on a ballot where people selected a party and seats were to be distributed based on which parties received the most votes, while in Kyrgyzstan members of parliament ran and were elected in individual districts.

13. Tip O'Neill, speaker of the U.S. House of Representatives in 1977–1987, famously said "all politics is local."

14. This referendum was passed in February 2003, so it is not possible that Akaev pushed this change through as a reaction to the Rose Revolution.

15. Abazov (2007) offers a clear summary of the parties, blocks and coalitions in this election.

16. For more on fraud in the 2005 election in Kyrgyzstan see OSCE/ODIHR (2005b).

17. The following table shows the official percentage results as well as those from the PVT and the exit poll for each major party.

	Official results	PVT	Exit poll
FNG	21	19	19
Revival	19	8	9
NM	18	27	26
Labour	12	17	18
BD	8	10	10
NR	7	8	7
Industry	6	7	5

18. Shortly after Shevardnadze's resignation, I asked a very senior NM leader whether the party would have called off the demonstrations if the government had accepted the PVT results and seated the new parliament accordingly. The leader said yes without a second thought. This was the arrangement a number of western diplomats were trying to facilitate. The failure of the Georgian government at that time to save their own skins by agreeing to that deal reveals just how lost and maladroit they had become.

19. Data from www.electoralgeography.com.

20. OSCE/ODIHR (2004c: 14).

21. Kelkel means "Renaissance and shining of the good" in Kyrgyz.

22. OSCE/ODIHR (2004d: 1).

23. OSCE/ODIHR (2005c).

24. Although it is obvious, it is worth restating that these elections were all scheduled months and years in advance. One of the victories of democracy in recent decades is that it is extremely difficult for nondemocratic leaders to avoid somewhat regular elections. Moreover, while these elections are often far from free and fair, they are not sham elections of the kind that occurred in, the Soviet Union or Saddam Hussein's Iraq. Even in deeply imperfect democracies, such as the kind discussed in this book, elections can offer some form of accountability for voters.

25. In early 2004, shortly after Saakashvili became president, a former European diplomat, who had served in Georgia during the Shevardnadze years, came to my Tbilisi office to be briefed on the events of the Rose Revolution. At one point, he interrupted my briefing to say "So, the former justice minister (Saakashvili) is now president and the former speaker of parliament and leader of the CUG (Zhvania) is prime minister, how is this a revolution again?" That question should be kept in mind when thinking about all three countries.

26. See Karatnycky in McFaul (2006).

Chapter 4. The U.S. Role

1. MacKinnon's (2007) work is only one of many that take this position. See also Hadar (2010); Lendman (2009); Raimondo (2006). These are just some examples of the views of the Color Revolutions that are widespread on the American left.

2. See MacKinnon (2007) and Frolov (2004).

3. See, for example, Kandelaki (2006).

4. Assertions that there was a U.S. backed conspiracy in the Rose Revolutions often remind me of the numerous meetings and discussions in which I participated preceding the 2003 Georgian election. During these meetings U.S. government personnel and representatives from foreign and domestic NGOs and donor organizations argued about elections, politics, and democracy, bringing to mind the late Abbie Hoffman's remark when put on trial as part of the Chicago Seven for conspiracy: "Conspiracy, we couldn't agree on lunch!"

5. Petrov and Ryabov in Aslund and McFaul (2006: 152).

6. Ibid., 153

7. Petrov and Ryabov also argue that Russian involvement, in addition to not being able to deliver a victory for Yanukovich constituted "The Kremlin's biggest foreign policy blunder since 1991 . . . the Kremlin's clumsy intrusion drove Russia even further into a dead end, while raising the stakes. The result was not simply a defeat but a scandalous humiliation" (145).

8. Soros, interview with *Los Angeles Times*, July 5, 2004, quoted in Holley (2004).

9. Soros, news conference, Tbilisi, June 1, 2005, Newsmax.com.

10. "Senator Lugar Says Ukraine Election Day Marred by Fraud, Abuse," statement during November 21 run-off election, November 22, 2004, http://www.america.gov/st/washfile-english/2004/November/200411221341411CJsamohT0.4353601.html.

Chapter 5. Russia

1. Interestingly, the Party of the Regions received political support from Russian and American political consultants. Prominent Republican political consulting firm Davis Manafort began advising the Party of the Regions in 2005 and continued through Yanukovich's election.

2. See, for example, Spiegel (2009),3. Georgia has demonstrated willingness to support NATO projects as well: by mid-2010 its 1000 troop commitment to the U.S.-led effort in Afghanistan was the third largest of any country.

4. Georgia's generous commitment of troops to Afghanistan, for example, was paid for by the U.S. See Civil.ge (2010).

5. The most comprehensive study of the war remains the Tagliavini Report (2009). Asmus (2010), Cornell (2009), and Mitchell and Cooley (2009, 2010) offer differing interpretations. De Waal's (2010) review of Asmus's book is also quite valuable.

6. U.S. assistance to Georgia increased from $110 million in 2003 to more than $220 million in 2006, stabilizing at around $130 million in 2008: USAID (2009) The financial support was bolstered by strong personal ties between the Bush and

Saakashvili governments (Mitchell and Cooley 2008) and ample U.S. assistance as Georgia built up its defense sector following the Rose Revolution.

7. For more on this see volume 1 of Tagliavini (2009).

8. According to a National Security Study by the International Republican Institute (IRI), in late September and early October 2008 (IRI 2008), fully 89 percent of the Georgian people viewed the performance of the Georgian military as "good" or "very good."

9. For example, Bunce and Wolchik (2006), Mitchell (2008), Way (2008), Beissinger (2005), Tucker (2007) all examine Color Revolutions from the democracy angle.

10. According to a poll by the Kyiv International Institute of Sociology in January and February 2010, 93 percent of Ukrainians viewed themselves as positively disposed toward Russia. National Radio Company of Ukraine (2010).

11. This remark was made after Georgia's defeat in Russia-Georgia, but proved at best premature. Civil.ge (2008a).

12. This is an extraordinary comment to make about the elected president of a neighboring country who had done almost nothing to hurt Russia during his tenure. Saakashvili seemed unfazed by this threat, responding that Putin "wouldn't have enough rope" Steavenson (2008: 64).

Chapter 6. Democracy After the Color Revolutions

1. The wave of popular demonstrations that brought down nondemocratic regimes in North Africa in 2011 were not precipitated or linked to elections, further weakening the electoral breakthrough model's relevance.

2. Ukraine Parliamentary Elections 26 March 2006, OSCE/ODIHR (2006b).

3. Ukraine Pre-Term Parliamentary Elections 30 September 2007, OSCE/ODIHR (2007).

4. Kyrgyz Republic Presidential Election 10 July 2005 OSCE/ODIHR (2005c).

5. OSCE/ODIHR (2009a).

6. For overviews of corruption in Bakiev's Kyrgyzstan see ICG (2010); Quinn-Judge (2010); Marat (2008).

7. For more on Okruashvili's allegations, see Asatiani (2007).

8. OSCE/ODIHR (2008a).

9. OSCE/ODIHR (2008b).

10. Ibid.

11. This point was stressed to me during interviews with numerous opposition political leaders and European diplomats in Tbilisi in 2009 and 2010.

12. Shashkin served about a year becoming minister of education in December 2009.

13. Former New York City parks commissioner and City Council member Henry Stern might disagree with this assessment because, he pointed out, "at least a rubber stamp leaves an impression."

14. See Mitchell (2009) on state building in Saakashvili's Georgia.

Chapter 7. Exporting Color Revolutions

1. For more on the domestic and international aspects of this backlash against democracy assistance during these years see Gershman and Allen (2006) and Carothers (2006).

2. In this regard, these leaders had a point. The independent status of many U.S.-based NGOs working in this kind of capacity overseas is not entirely clear. These democracy organizations have independent leadership structures and a fair amount of freedom to make their own decisions, but their financial dependence on the U.S. government is substantial and in any given country they tend to communicate very closely with the official American representation.

3. See Mitchell (2008) for a full discussion of the influence of democracy assistance efforts on the Rose Revolution.

4. Kahmi (2006); Karajkov (2005).

5. For background on Azerbaijan see Fuller (2005); for Belarus see Myers (2006).

6. See RFE/RL (2007).

7. See Human Rights Watch (2005). The briefing paper reports that "Opposition party members who attempted to gather for rallies or meetings that were not authorized by the authorities were subjected to mass arrests and beatings;" and "Police detained campaign workers for opposition and independent candidates, and warned them to stop their political work. On numerous occasions, campaign workers who were putting up campaign posters were detained, charged with public order offenses, and sentenced to several days in prison."

8. This observation is based on numerous conversations I had with civil and political leaders of the Azeri opposition in the months preceding the election 2005 working with the National Democratic Institute (NDI). During these trips, I was asked on more than one occasion by members of the Azeri opposition, "Why won't you (meaning the U.S.) do for us what you did for the Georgians?" This question was not entirely fair as the Georgians had mostly done for themselves during the Rose Revolution, but the sentiment behind it was significant.

9. Data from U.S. Department of State, Bureau of European and Eurasian Affairs. http://www.state.gov/p/eur/rls/rpt/.

10. OSCE/ODIHR (2006a: 4).

11. In general in the Caucasus countries, neither successful nor unsuccessful Color Revolutions did not receive strong western support while in the the Slavic countries both successful and unsuccessful Color Revolutions received strong support from the west.

12. Myers (2006). It is noteworthy that an article about potential political change in Belarus before the election had occurred would appear in a newspaper at all, further confirming that pre-election western involvement in Belarus was qualitatively different from that in other countries.

13. Freedom House awards scores of 0 to 16 for each of these areas. Higher numbers are given to countries that are freer.

14. These breakdowns of Freedom House numbers are not available for years before 2006.

15. For a description of these events, see Human Rights Watch (2007).

16. For more on the contestation of Imedi's ownership see Hagey (2010) or Civil.ge (2009a).

17. Quoted in Karajkov (2005).

18. This existence of this report was first asserted in *Open*, a Hong Kong-based magazine. The report itself is not available.

19. This is not to suggest the current Chinese government cannot be changed, but that whatever changes or ends the current Chinese regime will look quite different from events in Georgia, Ukraine and Kyrgyztan.

20. For example, Bunce and Wolchik (2007, 2009); Silitski (2010).

Chapter 8. Misreading Democratic Breakthroughs: U.S. Policy After the Color Revolutions

1. For research on stalled democratic development in Georgia see Mitchell (2006, 2008, 2009), Lanskoy and Areshidze (2008), or Kupchan (2006); on Ukraine see Myers (2007) or Spence (2008); on Kyrgyztan see Judah (2009) or Puddington (2009, 2010).

2. For more on this, see Mitchell and Phillips (2008).

3. Cooley and Mitchell (2008) offer the most thorough discussion of the personal nature of the U.S.-Georgia relationship and its impact on U.S. policy toward Georgia.

4. See Cooley and Mitchell (2008).

5. Some examples include Arutunyan (2010) and Halpin (2010a).

6. See Sammut (2010) or Halpin (2010b). The headline writers for the *Times* clearly had a change of heart over the eight days between Halpin's articles.

7. The word "democracy" appears in the titles of many books and articles about the Color Revolutions: *Democracy and Autocracy*, Areshidze (2007); *Revolution in Orange: The Origins of Ukraine's Democratic Breakthrough*, Aslund and McFaul (2006); *Regime Cycles: Democracy, Revolution and Autocracy in Post-Soviet Eurasia*, Hale (2005); *Democracy and Revolution*, Kuzio (2009); and *Uncertain Democracy*, Mitchell (2008) are just some examples.

8. Writing about the tension and demonstrations in 2007, Steven Lee Myers (2007) asserted "Protests abound, though often with paid protesters."

9. Although it is obviously unknown how long the current Georgian government will stay in power, its intentions are clear. For example, during his 2010 State of the Union address, Saakashvili commented, "there will be no tragedy in change of the authorities, but I want to tell you that it will happen slower than you imagine where there is a democracy replacement always happens we will achieve creation of such a system, wherein when it happens—be it after *50, 100 or 250 years*—it should amount to continuation of a course instead of end of the country" (emphasis mine), Civil.ge (2010b).

Chapter 9. The End of an Era

1. Beblawi and Luciani (1987: 49–61) define a second-grade rentier state as one that relies on external sources for most of its revenue. A first-grade rentier state relies on natural resources.

2. This was never the case among the Rose Revolutionaries themselves. During a December 2004 meeting with President Saakashvili, the president greeted me wearing an orange tie and made it clear that he understood the bearing of the Color Revolutions on U.S.-Russia relations and on Russia in general.

3. During the 1968 Democratic Convention Daley defended the Chicago Police Department by saying "the policeman isn't there to create disorder, the policeman is there to preserve disorder."

Bibliography

Abazov, Rafis. (2001). Can We "Correct" Democracy. Knowledge Net. http://www.tol.org/client/article/4940-can-we-correct-democracy.html.

———. (2007). The Parliamentary Election in Kyrgyzstan, February/March 2005. *Electoral Studies* 26: 507–33.

Ambrosio, Thomas. (2009). *Authoritarian Backlash: Russian Resistance to Democratization in the Former Soviet Union*. Burlington, Vt.: Ashgate.

Areshidze, Irakly. (2007). *Democracy and Autocracy in Eurasia: Georgia in Transition*. East Lansing: Michigan State University Press.

Ariel, Dominique. (2005). Is the Orange Revolution Fading. *Current History* 104, 684 (October): 325–30.

Arutunyan, Anna. (2010). The Orange Revolution Is History. *Moscow News*, January 18. http://themoscownews.com/news/20100118/55403666.html.

Asatiani, Salome. (2007). Georgia: The Ally Who Turned on Saakashvili. Radio Free Europe/ Radio Free Liberty, September 27.

Aslund, Anders. (2009). *How Ukraine Became a Market Economy and Democracy*. Washington, D.C.: Peterson Institute for International Economics.

Aslund, Anders, and Michael McFaul. (2006). *Revolution in Orange: The Origins of Ukraine's Democratic Breakthrough*. Washington, D.C.: Carnegie Endowment.

Asmus, Ronald. (2010). *A Little War That Shook the World: Georgia, Russia, and the Future of the West*. New York: Palgrave Macmillan.

Associated Press. (2005). Soros Downplays Role in Georgia. June 1.

Baisalov, Edil. (2005). Statement by the President of the Coalition for Democracy and Civil Society (Kyrgyzstan) Promoting Democracy Through Diplomacy: Hearing before the House Committee on International Relations. May 5.

Beblawi, Hazem, and Giacomo Luciani. (1987). *The Rentier State*. London: Croom Helm.

Beissinger, Mark R. (2005). Rethinking Empire in the Wake of Soviet Collapse. In Zoltan Barany and Robert Moser, eds., *Ethnic Politics After Communism*. Ithaca, N.Y.: Cornell University Press.

———. (2006). Promoting Democracy: Is Exporting Revolution a Constructive Strategy. *Dissent* (Winter): 84–89.

———. (2007). Structure and Example in Modular Political Phenomena: The Diffusion of Bulldozer/Rose/Orange/Tulip Revolutions. *Perspectives on Politics* 5, 2: 259–76.
Berman, Howard. (2009). Georgia's Unmet Promise. *Washington Post*, August 7.
Blank, Stephen. (2008). Russia and the Black's Sea's Frozen Conflicts in Strategic Perspective. *Mediterranean Quarterly* 19, 3: 23–54.
Bunce, Valerie J., Michael McFaul, and Kathryn Stoner-Weiss, eds. (2010). *Democracy and Authoritarianism in the Post-Communist World*. New York: Cambridge University Press.
Bunce, Valerie J. and Sharon L. Wolchik. (2006a). International Diffusion and Postcommunist Electoral Revolutions. *Communist and Post-Communist Studies* 39: 283–304.
———. (2006b). Youth and Electoral Revolutions in Slovakia, Serbia, and Georgia. *SAIS Review* 26, 2: 55–65.
———. (2007a). Democratizing Elections in the Postcommunist World: Definitions, Dynamics, and Diffusion. *St. Antony's International Review* 2, 2: 64–79.
———. (2007b). Transnational Networks, Diffusion Dynamics, and Electoral Revolutions in the Postcommunist World. *Physica A* 378: 92–99.
———. (2009). Opposition Versus Dictators: Explaining Divergent Election Outcomes in Postcommunist Europe and Eurasia. In Staffan Lindberg, ed., *Democratization by Elections*. Baltimore: Johns Hopkins University Press.
Bush, George W. and Mikhail Saakashvili. (2006). President Bush and Georgian President Saakashvili. U.S. Department of State. http http://rncnyc2004.blogspot.com/2006/07/president-bush-welcomes-president.html.
Carothers, Thomas. (2002). The End of the Transition Paradigm. *Journal of Democracy* 13, 1: 5–21.
———. (2006). The Backlash Against Democracy Promotion. *Foreign Affairs* 85, 2: 55–68.
Chupryna, Iryna. (2008). Color Guards. *Transitions Online*, January 23.
CIA World Factbook. (2011). Central Asia: Kyrgyzstan. https://www.cia.gov/library/publications/the-world-factbook/.
Civil.ge. (2007). "Ossetia a Matter of, at Most, Months"—Saakashvili. December 4.
———. (2008a). Medvedev: "Saakashvili Is a Political Corpse." September 3.
———. (2008b). Saakashvili Speaks of "Second Rose Revolution." September 24.
———. (2009a). Patarkatsishvili Family Disputes Imedi Sale. February 26.
———. (2009b). Saakashvili Speaks of Second Rose Revolution. April 23.
———. (2009c). Police Probe into Opposition Party Wiretapping. June 30.
———. (2010a). Georgia to Receive U.S. Funding for Afghanistan Operation. March 27.
———. (2010b). Saakashvili's State of the Nation Address. (2010). 26 February.
Commission on Security and Cooperation in Europe (CSCE). (2005). Kyrgyzstan's Revolution: Causes and Consequences. Hearing, 109th Cong., 1st sess., April 7.
Committee of Voters of Ukraine. (2004). Report of the Committee of Voters of

Ukraine on Observation of Voting and Vote Tabulation on November 21, 2004. December 2.
Cooley, Alexander. (2008). *Base Politics: Democratic Change and the U.S. Military Overseas.* Ithaca, N.Y.: Cornell University Press.
Cooley, Alexander and Lincoln Mitchell. (2009). No Way to Treat Our Friends: Recasting Recent U.S.-Georgia Relations. *Washington Quarterly* 32, 1: 27–41.
———. (2010). Engagement Without Recognition: A New Strategy Toward Abkhazia and Eurasia's Unrecognized States. *Washington Quarterly* 33, 4: 59–73.
Cornell, Svante. (2002). Autonomy as a Source of Conflict: Caucasian Conflicts in Theoretical Perspective. *World Politics* 54: 245–76.
Cornell, Svante and Niklas Nillson. (2009). Georgian Politics Since the August 2008 War. *Demokratizatsiya: The Journal of Post-Soviet Democratization* 17, 3: 251–68.
Crosston, Matthew. (2006). *Fostering Fundamentalism: Terrorism, Democracy and American Engagement in Central Asia.* Aldershot: Ashgate.
Cummings, Sally N. (2010). *Domestic and International Perspectives on Kyrgyzstan's "Tulip Revolution": Motives, Mobilization and Meanings.* New York: Routledge.
D'Anieri, Paul. (2005). What Has Changed in Ukrainian Politics? Assessing the Implications of the Orange Revolution. *Problems of Post-Communism* 52, 5: 82–91.
———. (2006). Explaining the Success and Failure of Post-Communist Revolutions. *Communist and Post-Communist Studies* 39: 331–50.
———. (2007). *Understanding Ukrainian Politics: Power, Politics, and Institutional Design.* Armonk, N.Y.: M.E. Sharpe.
Derlugian, Georgi. (1998). The Tale of Two Resorts: Abkhazia and Ajaria Before and Since the Soviet Collapse. In Beverly Crawford and Ronnie D. Lipschutz, eds., *The Myth of "Ethnic Conflict": Politics, Economics, and "Cultural" Violence.* Berkeley: University of California Press.
———. (2001). How Adjaria Did Not Become Another Bosnia: A Study in the Interplay of Historical Determination, Human Agency, and Accident in the Chaotic Transition. In George Katsiaficas, ed., *After the Fall: 1989 and the Future of Freedom.* New York, Routledge.
De Waal, Thomas. (2010). Missiles over Tskhinvali. *National Interest*, May–June.
Diuk, Nadia. (2002). Post-Election Blues in Ukraine. *Journal of Democracy* 13, 4: 157–66.
Dolidze, Anna. (2008). Georgia's Choice. *National Interest*, January 7.
Donovan, Jeffrey. (2002). Belarus: Conference in Washington Urges "Regime Change" in Minsk. Radio Free Europe/Radio Liberty. , November 15.
Engdahl, F. William. (2011). Egypt's Revolution: Creative Destruction for a "Greater Middle East." February 5. http://www.engdahl.oilgeopolitics.net/.
Engvall, Johan. (2007). Kygyrzstan: Anatomy of a State. *Problems of Post-Communism* 54, 4: 33–45.
Fairbanks, Charles H., Jr. (1995). Russia's Future. *Current* 374: 26–34.
———. (2004). Georgia's Rose Revolution. *Journal of Democracy* 15, 2: 110–24.
———. (2007). Revolution Reconsidered. *Journal of Democracy* 18, 1: 42–57.

Fish, M. Stanley. (2001). The Dynamics of Democratic Erosion." In Richard Anderson, Jr., M. Stanley Fish, Stanley E. Hanson, and Philip G. Roeder, eds., *Postcommunism and the Theory of Democracy*. Princeton, N.J.: Princeton University Press, Chapter 3.

Freedom House. (2003–2010). Georgia, Ukraine, and Kyrgyzstan. *Nations in Transit*. http://freedomhouse.org/template.cfm?page=1.

———. (2005). Belarus and Azerbaijan. *Nations in Transit*. http://freedomhouse.org/template.cfm?page=1.

Freese, Theresa. (2005). A Report from the Field: Georgia's War Against Contraband and Its Struggle for Territorial Integrity. *SAIS Review* 25, 1: 107–21.

Frolov, Vladimir. (2005). Democracy by Remote Control. *Russia in Global Affairs* 4 (October–December). http://eng.globalaffairs.ru/engsmi/976.html.

Fuhrmann, Matthew. (2006). A Tale of Two Social Capitals: Revolutionary Collective Action in Kyrgyzstan. *Problems of Post-Communism* 53, 3: 16–29.

Fuller, Liz. (2005). Azerbaijan: Baku Implicates Armenian Intelligence in Alleged Coup Bid. *Radio Free Europe/Radio Free Liberty*, August 5.

Ray, Julie and Neli Esipova. (2010). Ukrainians Likely Support Move Away from NATO. Gallup, April 2. http://www.gallup.com/poll/127094/Ukrainians-Likely-Support-Move-Away-NATO.aspx.

Georgia Update. (2009). Weekly Edition, April 23. http://georgiaupdate.gov.ge/en/doc/10010520/GU%20April%2023%202009%20gm.pdf.

Gershman, Carl, and Michael Allen. (2006). The Assault on Democracy Assistance. *Journal of Democracy* 17, 2: 36–51.

Goldstone, Jack. (1986). State Breakdown in the English Revolution: A New Synthesis. *Journal of Sociology* 92, 2: 257–322.

———. (1991). Ideology, Cultural Frameworks, and the Process of Revolution. *Theory and Society* 20, 4: 405–53.

Hadar, Leon. (2010). The Fading Colors of Pseudo-Revolutions. *Huffington Post*, April 9. http://www.huffingtonpost.com/leon-t-hadar/the-fading-colors-of-pseu_b_532139.html

Hagey, Keach. (2010). A Riddle for RAK in Georgia. *The National*, February 3.

Hale, Henry E. (2005). Regime Cycles: Democracy, Autocracy, and Revolution in Post-Soviet Eurasia. *World Politics* 58: 133–65.

———. (2006). Democracy or Autocracy on the March? The Colored Revolutions as Normal Dynamics of Patronal Presidentialism. *Communist and Post-Communist Studies* 39: 305–29.

Halpin, Tony. (2010a). Ukraine Braced for Conflict as Polls Signal End of Orange Revolution. *New York Times*, Sunday, February 8.

———. (2010b). Yanukovych Win Is a Triumph for Democracy, Not Russia. *New York Times*, Sunday, February 16.

Hatto, Arthur. (1949). "Revolution": An Enquiry into the Usefulness of an Historical Term. *Mind* 58 (232): 495–517.

Herbst, John. (2004). Testimony, Hearing Before House Committee on International

Relations, 108th Cong., 2nd sess., December 7. http://www.foreignaffairs.house.gov/archives/108/97187.pdf.

Herd, Graeme P. (2005). Colorful Revolutions and the CIS: "Manufactured" Versus "Managed" Democracy? *Problems of Post-Communism* 52, 2: 3–18.

Holley, David. (2004). The World: Soros Invests in His Democratic Passion; The Billionaire's Open Society Institute Network Is Focusing on Central Asia Now. *Los Angeles Times*, July 5, A6.

Human Rights Centre, Tbilisi. (2009). Note on Human Rights Situation in Georgia. http://www.ccprcentre.org/doc/CCPR/FU/Georgia_HRIDC.pdf.

Human Rights Watch. (2005). Azerbaijan Elections and After. November 18. http://reliefweb.int/sites/reliefweb.int/files/resources/25DB88BC2554F52C492570C0000C597E-hrw-aze-18nov.pdf.

———. (2007). Crossing the Line: Georgia's Violent Dispersal of Protestors and Raid on Imedi Television. December 19. http://reliefweb.int/sites/reliefweb.int/files/resources/F23E12B60802288A492573C9001999F1-Full_Report.pdf

———. (2009). Kyrgyzstan: Events of 2008. http://www.hrw.org/en/node/79353.

———. (2010). Annual Report on Georgia. January 25. http://humanrightshouse.org/Articles/13165.html

Hunter, Shireen T. (2006). *The Transcaucasus in Transition: Nation-Building and Conflict*. Washington, D.C.: CSIS.

Huntington, Samuel. (1968). *Political Order in Changing Societies*. New Haven, Conn.: Yale University Press.

International Crisis Group (ICG). (2004). Saakashvili's Ajara Success: Repeatable Elsewhere in Georgia? Europe Briefing.

———. (2007). Georgia: Sliding Towards Authoritarianism. Europe Report 189.

———. (2010). Kyrgyzstan: A Hollow Regime Collapses. Policy Note, April 27. http://www.crisisgroup.org/en/regions/asia/central-asia/kyrgyzstan/B102-kyrgyzstan-a-hollow-regime-collapses.aspx

International Republican Institute. (2008). Georgian National Study. September 23–October 1. http://www.iri.org/sites/default/files/2008%20November%2021%20Survey%20of%20Georgian%20Public%20Opinion,%20September%2023-October%201,%202008.pdf.

Jones, Stephen. (2006). The Rose Revolution: A Revolution Without Revolutionaries. *Cambridge Review of International Affairs* 19, 1: 33–48.

Judah, Ben. (2009). A Sinking Island of Democracy. *Transitions Online*. http://www.tol.org/client/article/20800-a-sinking-island-of-democracy.html

Kamhi, Alison. (2006). The Russian NGO Law: Potential Conflicts with International, National, and Foreign Legislation. *International Journal of Not-for-Profit Law* 9, 1: 34–57.

Kandelaki, Giorgi. (2006). Georgia's Rose Revolution: A Participant's Perspective. United States Institute of Peace, July. http://www.usip.org/files/resources/sr167.pdf.

Karajkov, Risto. (2005). NGO Bashing. Worldpress.org, November 13. http://www.worldpress.org/print_article.cfm?article_id=2298&dont=yes

Karatnycky, Adrian. (2005). Ukraine's Orange Revolution. *Foreign Affairs* 84, 2 (March–April): 35–52.

———. (2011). Yanukovych Report Card: One Year of Power. *New Atlanticist: Policy and Analysis*, February 24. http://www.acus.org/new_atlanticist/yanukovych-report-card-one-year-power.

Karumidze, Zurab and James Wertsch. (2006). *Enough! The Rose Revolution in the Republic of Georgia*. New York: Nova Science.

Khamidov, Alisher. (2006). Kyrgyzstan's Revolutionary Youth: Between State and Opposition. *SAIS Review* 26, 2: 85–93.

King, Charles. (2001). Potemkin Democracy. *National Interest* 64 (Summer): 93–105.

———. (2004). A Rose Among Thorns? Georgia Makes Good. *Foreign Affairs* 83, 2 (March–April): 1–6.

King, Neil. (2008). U.S.-Russia Relations Turn Cold over Fate of Georgia, Provinces. *Wall Street Journal* 252, 39 (August 21): A6.

Kramer, Andrew E. (2010). Before Kygyrz Uprising, Dose of Russian Soft Power. *New York Times*, April 18.

Kubicek, Paul. (2005). The European Union and Democratization in Ukraine. *Communist and Post-Communist Studies* 38: 269–92.

Kupchan, Charles A. (2006). Wilted Rose. Council on Foreign Relations op ed., January 30. http://www.cfr.org/georgia/wilted-rose/p9701

Kuzio, Taras. (2006). Civil Society, Youth, and Societal Mobilization in Democratic Revolutions. *Communist and Post-Communist Studies* 39: 365–86.

Kuzio, Taras. (2006). Is Ukraine Part of Europe's Future? *Washington Quarterly* 29, 3: 89–108.

———. (2011). How to Turn a Partly Free Ukraine into a Not Free Ukraine. Radio Free Europe/ Radio Liberty, February 15. http://www.rferl.org/content/commentary_partly_free_ukraine_to_not_free/2310282.html

Lanskoy, Miriam, and Giorgi Areshidze. (2008). Georgia's Year of Turmoil. *Journal of Democracy* 19, 4: 154–68.

Legvold, Robert and Bruno Coppieters. (2004). *Statehood and Security: Georgia After the Rose Revolution*. Cambridge, Mass.: MIT Press.

Lendman, Steven. (2009). Color Revolutions Old and New. *Global Research*, July 1. http://www.globalresearch.ca/index.php?context=va&aid=14168

Levy, Clifford J. (2009). Strategic Issues, Not Abuses Are U.S. Focus in Kyrgyzstan. *New York Times*, July 22.

Linz, Juan and Alfred Stepan. (1996). *Problems of Democratic Transition and Consolidation: Southern Europe, South America, and Post-Communist Europe*. Baltimore: Johns Hopkins University Press.

Luong, Pauline. (2002). *Institutional Change and Political Continuity in Post-Soviet Central Asia*. New York: Cambridge University Press.

Lynch, Dov. (2006). *Why Georgia Matters*. Paris: Institute for Security Studies.

MacKinnon, Marc. (2007). *The New Cold War: Revolutions, Rigged Elections, and Pipeline Politics in the Former Soviet Union*. New York: Basic Books.

Makhovsky, Andrei. (2010). Bakiev Says Russian Anger a Factor in Kyrgyz Revolt. Reuters, April 25.

Marat, Erica. (2008). March and After: What Has Changed? What Has Stayed the Same? *Central Asian Survey* 27 (3–4): 229–40.

McFaul, Michael. (2002). The Fourth Wave of Democracy and Dictatorship: Non-Cooperative Transitions in the Post-Communist World. *World Politics* 54: 212–44.

———. (2005). Transitions from Postcommunism. *Journal of Democracy* 16, 3: 1–19.

———. (2007). Ukraine Imports Democracy. *International Security* 32, 2: 45–83.

Mitchell, Lincoln. (2004). Georgia's Rose Revolution. *Current History* 103, 675: 343–48.

———. (2006). Democracy in Georgia Since the Rose Revolution. *Orbis* 50, 4: 669–76.

———. (2007). Beyond Bombs and Ballots. *National Interest* 88: 32–36.

———. (2008a). Democracy Bound. *National Interest* 95: 70–76.

———. (2008b). Dour Democrats. *Transitions Online*, March 26.

———. (2008c). The End of the Rose Era. *Transitions Online*, May 27.

———. (2008d). More Than Location: Crafting U.S. Policy for the Black Sea Region. *Journal of Southeast European & Black Sea Studies* 8, 2: 129–40.

———. (2008e). *Uncertain Democracy: U.S. Foreign Policy and Georgia's Rose Revolution*. Philadelphia: University of Pennsylvania Press.

———. (2009a). Compromising Democracy: Statebuilding in Saakashvili's Georgia. *Central Asian Survey* 28, 2: 171–83.

———. (2009b). Georgia's Story: Competing Narratives Since the War. *Survival* 51, 4: 87–100.

Mitchell, Lincoln and Alexander Cooley. (2008). No Way to Treat Our Friends: Recasting Recent U.S.-Georgian Relations. *Washington Quarterly* 32, 1: 27–41.

Mitchell, Lincoln, and David Phillips. (2008). Enhancing Democracy Assistance. *American Foreign Policy Interests* 30, 3: 156–75.

Montlake, Simon. (2009). China Snares NGOs with Foreign Funding. *Christian Science Monitor*, August 4.

Moore, Barrington. (1966). *The Social Origins of Dictatorsihp and Democracy: Lord and Peasant in the Making of the Modern World*. Boston: Beacon Press.

Morgan, David. (2008). U.S. Urges Ukraine NATO Membership, Action Unlikely. *New York Times*, November 11.

Myers, Steven Lee (2006). Bringing Down Europe's Last Ex-Soviet Dictator. *New York Times*, February 26.

———. (2007). Stalled by Conflict, Ukraine's Democracy Gasps for Air. *New York Times*, June 1.

National Radio Company of Ukraine. (2010). Ukrainians' Attitude Toward Russia Is Still Positive, Opinion Poll Says. Kyiv International Institute of Sociology, February 22. http://www.nrcu.gov.ua/index.php?id=148&listid=112113.

Nichol, Jim. (2006). Armenia, Azerbaijan, and Georgia: Political Developments and Implications for U.S. Interests. Congressional Research Service, November 16. http://digital.library.unt.edu/ark:/67531/metacrs10337/m1/1/high_res_d/RL33453_2006Aug31.pdf.

———. (2010). Central Asia: Regional Development and Implications for U.S. Interests. Congressional Research Service, November 22. http://www.fas.org/sgp/crs/row/RL30294.pdf.

Nodia, Ghia. (1995). Georgia's Identity Crisis. *Journal of Democracy* 6, 1: 104–16.

Ó Beachain, Donnacha. (2009). Roses and Tulips: Dynamics of Regime Change in Georgia and Kyrgyzstan. *Journal of Communist Studies and Transition Politics* 25, 2–3: 199–26.

Ó Beachain, Donnacha, and Abel Polese, eds. (2010). *The Colour Revolutions in the Former Soviet Republics*. New York: Routledge.

Olcott, Martha Brill. (2005). Kygyrzstan's Tulip Revolution. Carnegie Endowment for International Peace Web Commentary, March 28. http://www.carnegieendowment.org/publications/index.cfm?fa=view&id=16710

Organization for Security and Co-operation in Europe, Office for Democratic Institutions and Human Rights (OSCE/ODIHR). (1998). Ukraine: Parliamentary Elections, 29 March. http://www.osce.org/odihr/elections/ukraine/15030.

———. (1999a). Georgia: Election Observation Mission, Parliamentary Elections, Second Round, 14 November. http://www.osce.org/odihr/elections/georgia/15610. 15 November.

———. (2000). Ukraine: Presidential Elections, 31 October and 14 November 1999, Final Report. http://www.osce.org/odihr/elections/ukraine/15000. Amended Version, March 2000.

———. (2000a). Kyrgyz Republic: Parliamentary Elections, 20 February and 12 March 2000. Final Report. http://www.osce.org/odihr/elections/kyrgyzstan/15803, April 10.

———. (2000b). Georgia: Presidential Election, 9 April 2000, Election Observation Mission. http://www.osce.org/odihr/elections/georgia/15591.

———. (2001). Kyrgyz Republic: Presidential Elections, 29 October 2000. Final Report, 16 January 2001. http://www.osce.org/odihr/elections/kyrgyzstan/15802.

———. (2002). Ukraine: Parliamentary Elections, 31 March 2002. Final Report. http://www.osce.org/odihr/elections/ukraine/14947. May 27.

———. (2004a). Georgia Parliamentary Elections, November 2, 2003, Part 1. http://www.osce.org/odihr/elections/georgia/22206. January 28.

———. 2004b. Ukraine: Presidential Election Second Round, 21 November 2004. Election Observation Mission Report. http://www.osce.org/odihr/elections/ukraine/16566. November 22.

———. 2004c. Ukraine, Preliminary Statement on the First Round of the Presidential Election, 31 October 2004. http://www.osce.org/odihr/elections/ukraine/35656.

———. (2004d) Georgia, Extraordinary Presidential Election, 4 January 2004. http://www.osce.org/odihr/elections/georgia/24600.

———. (2005a). Kyrgyz Republic. Parliamentary Elections, 27 February. Needs Assessment Mission Report, 9–11 December 2004. http://www.osce.org/odihr/elections/kyrgyzstan/39192. 4 January 4.

———. (2005b). Kyrgyz Republic. Parliamentary Elections, 27 February and 13 March

2005, Election Observation Mission Final Report. http://www.osce.org/odihr/elections/kyrgyzstan/14835. May 20.

———. (2005c) Kyrgyz Republic, Presidential Election, 10 July 2005 http://www.osce.org/odihr/elections/17661.

———. (2006a). Belarus: Presidential Election 19 March 2006. Election Observation Mission Report. http://www.osce.org/odihr/elections/belarus/19395. June 7.

———. (2006b) Ukraine: Parliamentary Elections, 26 March 2006. Election Observation Mission Report. http://www.osce.org/odihr/elections/ukraine/19595. June 23.

———. (2007). Ukraine: Pre-Term Parliamentary Elections, 30 September 2007. Election Observation Mission Report. http://www.osce.org/odihr/elections/ukraine/29970. December 20.

———. (2008a). Georgia: Extraordinary Presidential Election, 5 January 2008. Election Observation Mission Final Report. http://www.osce.org/odihr/elections/georgia/30959. March 4.

———. (2008b). Georgia: Parliamentary Elections, 21 May 2008. Election Observation Mission Final Report. http://www.osce.org/odihr/elections/georgia/33301. September 9.

———. (2009). Kyrgyz Republic: Presidential Election, 23 July 2009. Needs Assessment Mission Report, 23–25 April. http://www.osce.org/odihr/elections/kyrgyzstan/37088. May 11.

———. (2009a) OSCE Election Observation Mission, Kyrgyz Republic, Presidential Election 23, July 2009.

Pannier, Bruce. (2010). Kyrgyzstan Relegated to the Back of the Freedom Class. Radio Free Europe/Radio Liberty, January 12. http://rferl.org/articleprintview/1927741.html.

Pevehouse, Jon C. (2002). Democracy from the Outside-In? International Organizations and Democratization. *International Organization* 56, 3: 515–49.

Pfifer, Steven. (2009). Reversing the Decline: An Agenda for U.S.-Russian Relations in 2009. Brookings Policy Paper 10, Brookings Institution, January.

Puddington, Arch. (2009). A Third Year of Decline. *Journal of Democracy* 20, 2: 93–107

———. (2010). The Erosion Accelerates. *Journal of Democracy* 21, 2: 136–50.

Pye, Lucian. (1985). *Asian Power and Politics: The Cultural Dimensions of Authority.* Cambridge, Mass.: Harvard University Press.

Quinn-Judge, Paul. (2010). When Patience Runs Out. *New York Times*, April 11.

Radio Free Europe/Radio Liberty. (2007). Pro-Putin Youth Group Looks to Preempt Post-Election Rallies. November 30. http://www.rferl.org/content/article/1079218.html.

———. (2010). Lukashenka Claims Victory Amid Mounting Criticism. December 20. http://www.rferl.org/content/belarus_lukashenka_election_vote_crackdown_fraud/2253668.html.

Radnitz, Scott. (2006). What Really Happened in Kyrgyzstan? *Journal of Democracy* 17, 2: 132–46.

———. (2010). The Color of Money: Privatization, Economic Dispersion, and the Post-Soviet Revolutions. *Comparative Politics* 42, 2: 127–46.

Raimondo, Justin. (2006). The Color Revolutions Fade to Black. *Antiwar.com*, September 30. http://original.antiwar.com/justin/2006/09/29/the-color-revolutions-fade-to-black/.

Ray, Julie. (2010). Kygyzstanis Favor Russia over U.S. Gallup, April 13. http://www.gallup.com/poll/127334/kyrgyzstanis-favor-russia.aspx.

Reporters Without Borders. (2008). President's Signature on Broadcast Law Puts Many Media Under Threat. http://rsf.org/spip.php?page=article&id_article=27501.

———. (2009). Censorship and Self-Censorship Help President's Reelection. July 27. http://rsf.org/spip.php?page=article&id_article=33986.

Institute for War and Peace Reporting}. (2009). Disappointment at Kyrgyz Media Law Changes. 27 April, RCA 574. http://www.unhcr.org/refworld/publisher,IWPR,,KGZ,49F7FF57c,0.html

Rice, Condoleezza. (2005). Remarks with the President of Georgia Mikheil Saakashvili on the signing of the Millennium Challenge Compact. U.S. Department of State. September 11. http://www.mcc.gov/pages/press/speech/speech-091205-sethnessgeorgiasigning

Sammut, Dennis. (2010). Ukraine's Election Was a Victory for the Colored Revolutions. Radio Free Europe/Radio Free Liberty. February 11.

Scalapino, Robert. (1962). *Parties and Politics in Contemporary Japan*. Cambridge: Cambridge University Press.

Senator McCain Speaks Out Against Belarus Regime: November 14 Speech in Washington. (2002). http://www.america.gov/st/washfile-english/2002/November/20021115174902lfenner@pd.state.gov0.4453089.html.

Sestanovich, Stephen. (2008). What Has Moscow Done? *Foreign Affairs* 87, 6: 12–28.

Silitski, Vitali. (2009). What Are We Trying to Explain. *Journal of Democracy* 20, 1: 86–89.

———. (2010). Into the Minsk Minefield. European Voice.com, October 11. Rehttp://www.europeanvoice.com/article/2010/11/into-the-minsk-minefield/69406.aspx.

Simes, Dimitri. (2008). Russian Roulette. *National Interest* 98: 4–7.

Skocpol, Theda. (1979). *States and Social Revolutions: A Comparative Analysis of France, Russia, and China*. Cambridge: Cambridge University Press.

Socor, Vladimir. (2007). Badri Patarkatsishvili: From Russian Businessman to Presidential Claimant. *Jamestown Foundation, Eurasian Daily Monitor*, December 21. http://www.jamestown.org/single/?no_cache=1&tx_ttnews[tt_news]=33267

Spector, Regine A. (2004). The Transformation of Askar Akaev, President of Kyrgyzstan. Berkeley Program in Soviet and Post-Soviet Studies Working Paper Series, University of California, Berkeley.

Spence, Matthew. (2008). Reviving the Democracy Agenda in the Former Soviet Union. Century Foundation, June 3. http://tcf.org/publications/2008/6/pb643

Spiegel, Peter. (2009). Rebuking Russia's Ambitions: U.S. Backs Ukraine for NATO. *Wall Street Journal*, July 22.

Statistical Abstract of the United States. (2009). U.S. Foreign Economic and Military Aid by Major Recipient Country: 2000 to 2006. Section 28, Foreign Commerce and Aid, Table 1259, p. 786. http://www.census.gov/prod/2009pubs/10statab/foreign.pdf.

Steavenson, Wendell. (2008). Marching Through Georgia. *New Yorker*, December 15.

Tagliavini, Heidi. (2009). Report of the Independent International Fact-Finding Mission on the Conflict in Georgia, Council of the European Union. September. http://www.scribd.com/doc/20427542/Tagliavini-Report-Georgia-Volume-I.

Tarnoff, Curt. (2002). The Former Soviet Union and U.S. Foreign Assistance. Congressional Research Service Issue Brief, May 20. http://fpc.state.gov/documents/organization/10896.pdf.

———. (2007). U.S. Assistance to the Former Soviet Union. CRS Report to Congress. http://www.fas.org/sgp/crs/row/RL32866.pdf.

Toft, Monica Duffy. (2003). *The Geography of Ethnic Violence: Identity, Interests, and the Indivisibility of Territory*. Princeton, N.J.: Princeton University Press.

Toursunof, Hamid. (2003). Kyrgyzstan: Akaev's Iron Constitution." *Transitions Online*, February 11.

Tucker, J. A. (2007). Enough! Electoral Fraud, Collective Action Problems, and Post-Communist Colored Revolutions. *Perspectives on Politics* 5, 3: 535–51.

Tudoroiu, Theodor. (2007). Rose, Orange, and Tulip: The Failed Post-Soviet Revolutions. *Communist and Post-Communist Studies* 40: 315–42.

USAID. (2005). Overview: Reaching for Democracy. *Democracy Rising*, September 2–3. http://www.usaid.gov/our_work/democracy_and_governance/publications/pdfs/democracy_rising.pdf.

———. (2006a). U.S. Overseas Loans and Grants: Kyrgyzstan. http://gbk.eads.usaidallnet.gov/query/do?_program=/eads/gbk/tablesByCountry&cocode=4KGZ

———. (2006b). U.S. Overseas Loans and Grants: Ukraine. http://gbk.eads.usaidallnet.gov/query/do.

———. (2006c). U.S. Overseas Loans and Grants: Georgia. http://gbk.eads.usaidallnet.gov/query/do.

———. (2006d). Final Project Report: Support to the New Government of Georgia. March. http://pdf.usaid.gov/pdf_docs/PDACH558.pdf.

———. (2009). Europe and Eurasia Regional Overview http://www.usaid.gov/policy/budget/cbj2009/101440.pdf

USAID/Caucasus/Georgia. (2001). Civil Society Assessment (including NGO Development , Media & Political Process). June. http://pdf.usaid.gov/pdf_docs/PNACT641.pdf

USAID/ Caucasus-Tbilisi Mission. (2003). *USAID/CAUCASUS-Georgia Country Strategy, FY 2004–2008*. http://pdf.usaid.gov/pdf_docs/PDABY768.pdf.

USAID/Georgia. (2002). *Democracy and Governance Assessment of Georgia*. http://pdf.usaid.gov/pdf_docs/PNACT370.pdf.

U.S. Department of State. (2000). Cumulative Funds Budgeted (FY 1992 to date) for

Major NIS Assistance Programs by Country as of 09/30/00. http://www.state.gov/documents/organization/101440.pdf.

———. (2001). FY 2001 Funds Budgeted for U.S. Government Assistance to Eurasia as of 12/31/01. http://www.state.gov/documents/organization/101440.pdf.

———. (2002). Funds Extended for U.S. Government Assistance to Eurasia During FY 2002, Including Emergency Response Fund and Emergency Supplemental. http://www.state.gov/p/eur/rls/rpt/eurasiafy08/23726.htm.

———. (2004). FY 2004 FSA Funds Budgeted for U.S. Government Assistance to Eurasia. http://www.state.gov/documents/organization/101440.pdf

———. (2005). FY 2005 Funds Budgeted for U.S. Government Regional Assistance Programs for Central Asia. http://www.state.gov/documents/organization/101440.pdf.

———. (2006). FY 2006 FSA Funds Budgeted for U.S. Government Assistance to Eurasia.: http://www.state.gov/documents/organization/101440.pdf.

———. (2007a). Georgia: Need for Restraint and Respect for Rule of Law, Press Release.

———. (2007b). FY 2007 FSA Funds Budgeted for U.S. Government Assistance to Eurasia. http://www.state.gov/documents/organization/101440.pdf.

———. (2008a). FY 2009 Foreign Operations Appropriated Assistance: Performance Report Highlights: Georgia. http://www.state.gov/p/eur/rls/rpt/eurasiafy08/117314.htm.

———. (2008b). FY 2009 Foreign Operations Appropriated Assistance: Performance Report Highlights: Kyrgyz Republic. http://www.state.gov/p/eur/rls/rpt/eurasiafy08/117316.htm.

———. (2008c). FY 2009 Foreign Operations Appropriated Assistance: Performance Report Highlights: Ukraine. http://www.state.gov/p/eur/rls/rpt/eurasiafy08/117321.htm.

———. (2008d). FSA FY 2003 Funds Budgeted for U.S. Government Assistance to Eurasia as of 12/31/03. http://www.state.gov/documents/organization/101440.pdf.

Way, Lucan. (2008). The Real Causes of the Color Revolutions. *Journal of Democracy*, 19, 3: 55–69.

Welt, Cory. (2010). The Imedi Ownership Scandal: Is State Control over National TV Becoming Clearer? *Democratic Georgia*, February 9. http://democraticgeorgia.blogspot.com/2010_02_01_archive.html.

Wheatley, Jonathan. (2006). *Georgia from national awakening to Rose Revolution: Delayed transition in the former Soviet Union*. Burlington, Vt.: Ashgate.

Wilson, Andrew. (2005). *Ukraine's Orange Revolution*. New Haven, Conn.: Yale University Press.

———. (2006). Ukraine's Orange Revolution, NGOs and the Role of the West. *Cambridge Review of International Affairs* 19, 1: 21–32.

Woehrel, Steven. (2005). Ukraine's Orange Revolution and U.S. Policy. Congressional Research Service. http://www.whs.mil/library/crs/crs%2007.20.05.5.pdf.

———. (2009). Ukraine: Current Issues and U.S. Policy. Congressional Research Service. http://www.fas.org/sgp/crs/row/RL33460.pdf.

World Bank. (2000). Corruption in Georgia: Survey Evidence. June. Working Paper 19276.

———. (2007). *World Development Indicators.* http://pdf.usaid.gov/pdf_docs/PCAAB166.pdf

Yongding. (2005). China's Color-Coded Crackdown. *Empowerment and Rights Institute,* October. http://www.erichina.org/english/foreignpolicy10-2005.htm.

Index

Page numbers with a t indicate tables.

Abashidze, Aslan, 46, 58, 128
Abkhazia, 24, 93, 98–99, 172, 201; and
  Belarus, 157; Gamsakhurdia regime, 25;
  Russian war over, 24, 95, 103–6, 110,
  112; Shevardnadze regime, 40. *See also*
  Georgia
Adams, Thomas C., 156
Afghanistan War, 74, 94, 192; Georgian
  troops in, 217n2; and U.S.-Kyrgyz air
  base, 9, 42, 170, 213n5
Africa, North. *See* Arab Spring
Ahmadinejad, Mahmoud, 163
Ajara, 24, 128; Revival Party, 36, 46, 47, 55,
  68, 216n17; and Saakashvili, 104
Akaev, Askar, 8, 9, 137, 140, 191; corruption
  under, 29–31, 30t; election fraud, 4,
  32–34, 53–56, 62–63, 70–71; foreign
  policy, 39–42; Freedom House score,
  116t, 117; political opposition, 37–39,
  52–55; regime, 24–29, 126–27, 139,
  182; resignation, 4, 14, 63, 96; U.S. view
  of, 27, 81, 185–86
Aliev, Ilham, 143, 144
Ambrosio, Thomas, 143–44, 147
Arab Spring (2011), 2, 15, 165, 187, 191,
  194, 218n1
Areshidze, Irakly, 200–201, 214n1
Armenia, 47, 92, 147, 149, 157
Arveladze, Giorgi, 160
Aslund, Anders, 201–2, 214n1

Asmus, Ronald, 174
Azerbaijan, 28, 92, 115, 156–57, 195;
  Aliev regime, 143; antirevolutionary
  strategies, 143–46, 151; elections of
  2005, 6, 148–52; pipeline through, 41

Bahrain, 165
Baker, Jim, 151–52
Bakiev, Kurambek, 14, 136–37, 140,
  183, 186; criticisms of, 116, 126–27,
  159; election, 4, 8–9, 14, 63–66, 68,
  115, 123–24; and Obama, 170, 183;
  resignation, 2, 198, 199; and Russia,
  96–97, 108, 125–26, 148
Baku-Tbilisi-Ceyhan (BTC) pipeline, 41
Baltic states, 27–28, 73, 101, 107, 197
Basirli, Ruslan, 149
Beblawi, Hazem, 220n1
Beissinger, Mark R., 12, 142–44, 206–7,
  213n6
Belarus, 28, 49, 74, 92, 115;
  antirevolutionary strategies in, 144,
  145, 157; Blue Jeans Revolution, 6,
  154–56; Lukashenko regime, 143, 152–
  58, 195; Patriotic Youth movement,
  148; and Russia, 157–58; U.S. view of,
  154–56
Ben Ali, Zine el Abidine, 2, 165, 191
Beria, Lavrenty, 21, 214n2
Berman, Howard, 139
Bloc of Yulia Timoschenko (BYT) Party, 14,
  35, 118–21

Blue Jeans Revolution, 6, 154–56. *See also* Belarus
Brownback, Sam, 27
Bulgaria, 77, 101, 206
Bulldozer Revolution, 69, 137, 142; as model for Rose Revolution, 3, 6, 12–13, 162; outcome of, 204–9; as U.S. plot, 75; youth organizations, 12–13, 69, 84, 85, 203–6. *See also* Serbia
Bunce, Valerie J., 12, 13, 69, 115, 164, 205–6, 210
Burjanadze, Nino, 3, 14, 46, 57, 67, 138, 205
Burjanadze Democrats (Georgia), 3, 13–14, 46, 57, 205, 216n17
Bush, George H. W., 16, 101
Bush, George W., 102, 141; and Belarus, 154–56; and Color Revolutions, 5–9, 151–52, 173–74; and Georgia, 9–10, 217n6; Russian policies, 74, 93–94, 98–100, 106–7; and Ukraine, 89, 176–77

Carothers, Thomas, 185, 196–97
Carter, Jimmy, 188
Castro, Fidel, 66
Cedar Revolution, 3, 6, 187
Cheney, Dick, 176
Chile, 206
China: Communist Revolution of, 66, 211n3; democratizing trends in, 146, 163, 164, 187; and Kyrgyzstan, 41, 126, 162–63, 171
Chupryna, Iryna, 164
Citizen Voters of Ukraine, 70
Citizens' Union of Georgia (CUG), 3, 36–39, 46–47, 55, 67–68
civil rights movement (U.S.), 13
civil society organizations (CSOs), 31, 32, 44, 68–71, 79, 127, 144, 182, 202
Clinton, Bill, 74, 106, 176
Coalition for Democracy and Civil Society (CDCS), 70, 82
Color Revolutions, 1–5, 10–15; Beissinger on, 206–7, 213n6; and China, 163, 164, 187; definitions, 3, 7–10, 211n3; democratization after, 115–40, 187–91, 198–99; democratization before, 11, 31–37, 42–43, 74–75, 82; electoral breakthroughs in, 44–72; expectations, 108–14; exporting, 141–43; foreign views of, 162–66; foreign policy before, 39–42, 80–81; Frolov on, 76–77; Lukashenko's view of, 154; mobilization against, 143–48; outcomes, 5–7, 15–16, 115–40, 158–61, 191–97; political parties under, 37–39; Russian role, 39–40, 75, 92–114; scholarship on, 200–210; strategies against, 143–62; U.S. role in, 5–7, 73–91, 151–52, 167–86, 211n2; and U.S.-Russian relations, 39–40, 74–75, 92–114; as U.S. plot, 75–79, 81. *See also individual countries*
Committee of Voters of Ukraine, 82, 84–85
Commonwealth of Independent States (CIS), 76, 124, 147, 204
Cooley, Alexander, 98, 201, 217n5, 220n3
corruption, 29–31; and election fraud, 32–37, 44–50, 53–56, 60–63, 70–71, 213n6; index of, 30t
Crimea, 20, 22, 26, 59, 99, 110. *See also* Ukraine
CSOs. *See* civil society organizations
Cuban Revolution, 66
CUG. *See* Citizens' Union of Georgia
Czech Republic, 101, 193

Daley, Richard M., 198, 221n3
D'Anieri, Paul, 12, 202, 210
democratization: after Color Revolutions, 115–40, 187–91, 194–99; before Color Revolutions, 11, 31–32, 42–43, 74–75, 82; misreading of, 167–86; strategies against, 141–66

Egypt, 2, 165, 191
Eisenhower, Dwight, 188
Engvall, Johan, 202–3
Estonia, 27–28, 73, 101, 107, 197
Ethiopia, 162, 187
European Network of Election Monitoring Organizations (ENEMO), 71

European Union, 28, 76, 100–101; and Georgia, 111–12; and Ukraine, 42, 121–22. *See also* Organization for Security and Cooperation in Europe

Fairbanks, Charles H., Jr., 213n3
Fish, M. Stanley, 43
For a New Georgia (FNG) Party, 46, 216n17
Ford, Gerald, 188
France, 188, 211n3
Franco, Francisco, 139
"freedom agenda," 73
Freedom House, 85, 87; civil liberties scores, 116–18, 116t, 122, 156
Freedom Support Act, 148
Frolov, Vladimir, 76–77
Fuhrmann, Matthew, 202

Gadhafi, Mu'ammar Muhammad al-, 165
Gamkrelidze, David, 46
Gamsakhurdia, Zviad, 24, 25
Georgia, 22–24, 75; and Afghanistan War, 217n2; corruption, 29–31, 30t, 36, 128, 137; economic problems, 21, 24–25, 29, 36; elections, 13, 29–30, 35–37, 47–48, 56–58, 70–71, 128–32; EU membership for, 111–12; foreign policy, 39–41, 80–81; Freedom House score, 116t, 117–18; and Iraq War, 80, 174; judicial system, 132–33; NATO membership for, 7, 95, 100–103, 111–12, 174; Orthodox Christianity, 17; political opposition, 13–14, 37–39, 44–48, 55–72, 132–35, 216n17; and Russia, 40–41, 95, 133–34; Russian invasion of, 24, 95, 103–6, 130, 173–74, 201; Soviet period, 18–21; tourist industry, 24, 29, 95; and United States, 40–41, 83–84, 98–99, 104, 110–11, 172–74, 191; warlords in, 24. *See also* Rose Revolution
German Marshall Fund, 85
Germany, 19–20, 23, 112
Goldstone, Jack, 8, 212n3
Gorbachev, Mikhail, 21, 27

Gore, Al, 176
Green Revolution, 163, 187. *See also* Iran

Hale, Henry E., 209
Hatto, Arthur, 212n3
Herbst, John, 88
Herd, Graeme P., 203–4
Hoffman, Abbie, 217n4
Hu Jintao, 163
human rights, 13, 31; Belarus, 155, 156; Georgia, 132–35; Kyrgyzstan, 33, 117, 157, 159, 170; NGOs, 132–34, 159, 219n7
Hungary, 27–28, 101, 193
Huntington, Samuel, 8, 211n3

Industry Party (Georgia), 35–36, 46, 216n17
International Republican Institute (IRI), 77, 85, 87, 144, 162, 203
International Society for Fair Elections and Democracy (ISFED), 13, 70, 82, 84
Iran, 94, 163, 164, 187
Iraq War, 74, 141, 192, 194; and Belarus, 154; and Georgia, 80, 174
Israel, 23, 120

Japan, political parties of, 214n7

Karatnycky, Adrian, 122
Karumidze, Zurab, 200
Kazakhstan, 23, 27, 92; antirevolutionary strategies in, 143–46; civil society in, 159, 161, 208
Kelkel (Kyrgyz youth organization), 11–13, 62–63, 69, 70, 216n21
Kennedy, John F., 188
Khamidov, Alisher, 202
Khrushchev, Nikita, 19, 103, 189
Kmara (Georgian youth organization), 12–13, 69–70, 84, 203–6
Kosovo, 98, 107
Kostenko, Yuri, 67
Kostunica, Vojislav, 13, 146
Krastev, Ivan, 93
Kravchuk, Leonid, 26
Kuchma, Leonid, 4, 8; corruption under,

Kuchma, Leonid, (cont'd)
  29–31, 30t; election fraud by, 32–35, 34t, 48–50, 60, 70–71; foreign policy of, 39–40, 42; Freedom House score, 116t, 117; political parties under, 37–39; regime, 24, 26, 28–29, 139, 182; U.S. view of, 88–89, 185–86; and Yanukovich, 49, 64–65; and \ Yushchenko, 49
Kulov, Felix, 4, 14, 33, 55, 63–64, 68, 96–97
Kuzio, Taras, 12, 13, 26, 122
Kyrgyzstan, 22–24; and China, 41, 126, 162–63, 171; corruption in, 29–31, 30t, 54; economic problems of, 23, 29, 198; elections, 32–34, 53–56, 61–64, 70–71, 123; foreign policy, 39–42, 80; Freedom House score for, 116t, 117; human rights abuses in, 33, 117, 157, 159, 170; independence, 27; Manas air force bas, 9, 42, 78, 80, 98, 126, 170, 183–84, 213n5; political parties, 37–39, 53–54, 123; and Russia, 41, 96–97, 108, 125–26, 148, 171; Soviet period, 18–19, 21–22; "Switzerland of Central Asia," 28, 33, 54; after Tulip Revolution, 115–18, 122–27, 136–40; and United States, 9, 41–42, 167–72. *See also* Tulip Revolution

Labor Party (Georgia), 35–37, 47, 56–57, 67–68, 216n17
Latvia, 28, 73, 101, 107, 197
Lebanon, 3, 6, 187
Libya, 165
Lithuania, 28, 73, 101, 107, 156, 197
Luciani, Giacomo, 220n1
Lugar, Richard, 88–89
Lukashenko, Alexander, 143, 144, 148, 152–58, 195
Luong, Pauline, 27

MacKinnon, Marc, 77, 203
Manas air force base (Kyrgyzstan), 9, 42, 78, 80, 98, 126, 170, 183–84, 213n5
Mao Zedong, 66

Marat, Erica, 202, 215n1
Marchuk, Yehven, 34t
McCain, John, 89, 154
McFaul, Michael, 12, 85, 201, 204–5, 213n6, 214n1
Medvedev, Roy Aleksandrovich, 107
Merkel, Angela, 112
Miles, Richard, 89
Milinkievic, Alexander, 152, 155
Milosevic, Slobodan, 80, 141–42, 209
Moldova, 76, 163, 187, 197
Moore, Barrington, 212n3
Moroz, Oleksander, 34t, 215n8
Mubarak, Hosni, 2, 165, 191
Munich Security Conference (2010), 106
Myers, Steven Lee, 219n12, 220n8

Natalashvili, Shalva, 47, 68
National Democratic Institute (NDI), 70, 71, 77, 82–85, 87; and Azerbaijan, 219n7; MacKinnon on, 203; opposition to, 144, 162
National Endowment for Democracy (NED), 77, 84, 142, 203
National Movement (NM) Party (Georgia), 3, 13–14, 37, 55–58, 83, 205–6, 216n17; and Citizens' Union of Georgia, 46; and United National Movement Party, 129, 131–32
Nazerbayev, Nursultan, 143, 144
NDI. *See* National Democratic Institute
New Rights Party (Georgia), 46, 67, 216n17
Nicaragua, 112
9/11. *See* September 11 attacks
North Atlantic Treaty Organization (NATO), 7, 28; expansion of, 74, 94, 98, 193; and Georgia, 7, 95, 100–103, 111–12, 174, 192; and Ukraine, 7, 42, 99–103, 109, 110, 112, 192
Nyaklyaeu, Uladzimir, 157

Ó Beacháin, Donnacha, 191, 207–8
Obama, Barack, 102, 170, 179, 183
Okruashvili, Irakli, 129
Olcott, Martha Brill, 28, 124

O'Neill, Thomas Philip "Tip," 53
Open Society Institute (OSI), 69, 84, 86, 144, 145
Orange Revolution, 1–5; elections before, 32–35, 34t; electoral breakthrough in, 44–45, 48–52, 55–72; expectations of, 108–14; exporting of, 141–43; foreign countries' views of, 162–66; foreign policy before, 39–42, 80–81; outcomes of, 9, 15–16, 115–22, 136–40, 158, 188–99; political parties before, 37–39; scholarship on, 201–10; U.S. policy after, 175–83; U.S. role in, 5–7, 78–91, 211n2; U.S.-Russian relations during, 92–114; as U.S. plot, 75–79, 81. *See also* Ukraine
Organization for Security and Cooperation in Europe (OSCE), 76, 100, 147; on Belarusian elections, 153, 157; on Georgian elections, 35–36, 64, 131–32; on Kyrgyz elections, 33, 39, 123–24; on Ukrainian elections, 34–35, 60, 121–22
Orthodox Christianity, 17
OSI. *See* Open Society Institute
Ossetia, South, 40, 93, 98–99, 172; and Belarus, 157; Gamsakhurdia regime, 25; Russian war over, 24, 95, 103–6, 110, 112; scholarship on, 201
Otpor (Serbian youth organization), 12–13, 69, 84, 85, 203–6
Otunbayeva, Roza, 14, 55, 68, 126, 190, 199
Our Ukraine Coalition, 14, 35, 49, 118–21

parallel vote tabulation (PVT), 13, 48, 57, 60, 68, 70; definition, 215n7; and exit polls, 216n17
Parliamentary Assembly of the Council of Europe (PACE), 76
Party of the Regions (Ukraine), 14, 99, 118–21, 140, 217n1
Patarkatsishvili, Badri, 130, 160
Patiashvili, Jumbar, 36
Philippines, 206
Pifer, Steven, 176
Poland, 27–28, 84, 101, 193

Polese, Abel, 191, 207–8
Poroshenko, Petro, 86
Pura (Ukrainian youth organization), 12–13, 69, 85, 203–6
Putin, Vladimir, 12, 40; antirevolutionary strategies, 143–44, 148, 161–62; and Saakashvili, 93, 103, 113, 218n12; and United States, 107; and Yanukovich, 4, 49, 75, 85

Radnitz, Scott, 11, 54, 202, 210
Reagan, Ronald, 16, 188
rentier states, 220n1
Revival Party (Georgia), 36, 46, 47, 55, 68, 216n17
Romania, 77, 101, 206
Roosevelt, Franklin D., 16
Rose Revolution, 1–5, 13–14, 200–210; and Bulldozer Revolution, 3, 6, 12–13, 162; elections after, 128–32; elections before, 29–30, 35–37; electoral breakthrough, 44–48, 55–58, 67–72, 128; expectations, 108–14; exporting of, 141–43; foreign countries' views of, 162–66; foreign policy before, 39–41, 80–81; outcomes, 10, 15–16, 115–18, 127–40, 158–61, 188–99; political parties before, 37–39; Serbia as model, 162; Soros on, 86; U.S. policy after, 172–74; U.S. role in, 5–7, 78–91, 151–52, 211n2; U.S.-Russian relations during, 92–114; as U.S. plot, 75–79, 81, 217n4. *See also* Georgia
Russia, 72; antirevolutionary strategies of, 143–44, 148; and Belarus, 157–58; and Commonwealth of Independent States, 76, 124, 147, 204; Communist Revolution, 211n3; democratizing trends in, 28, 49, 161–62, 195; election monitoring by, 147–48; and Georgia, 40–41, 95, 133–34; Georgian invasion by, 24, 95, 103–6, 130, 173–74, 201; influence on Color Revolutions, 39–40, 75, 92–114; and Kyrgyzstan, 41, 96–97, 108, 125–26, 148, 171; and Ukraine, 19–23, 26, 34, 42, 95–96, 99; and

Russia, (cont'd)
United States, 7, 39–40, 74–75, 92–114, 192–94

Saakashvili, Mikheil, 7–10, 37, 66–67, 140, 186, 190; criticisms of, 116, 129–33; on democratization, 220n9; National Movement Party of, 3, 13–14, 37, 55–58, 83, 205–6; and Putin, 93, 103, 113, 218n12; resignation of, 130–31; after Rose Revolution, 127–29; and Russian-Georgian War, 103–6; United National Movement Party of, 129, 131–32; U.S. support of, 83–84, 98–99, 104, 110–11, 173–74, 217n6; and Zhvania, 14, 67, 68, 208, 216n25
September 11 attacks, 40–41, 74; and Georgia, 80; and Orange Revolution, 93. *See also* terrorism
Serbia, 84, 85; and Kosovo, 98, 107; and Kostunica, 13, 146; and Milosevic, 80, 141–42, 209. *See also* Bulldozer Revolution
Shalikashvili, John, 89
Sharp, Gene, 207, 213n6
Shashkin, Dmitri, 135
Shevardnadze, Eduard, 5, 8, 21, 172–73; and Citizens' Union of Georgia, 3, 36–39, 46–47, 55, 67–68; corruption, 9, 29–31, 30t, 36, 128, 137; election fraud, 29–30, 35–37, 47–48, 56–58, 70–71; foreign policy, 39–41; political opposition, 44–48; political parties, 37–39; regime, 24–26, 28–29, 139, 182; resignation, 57–59, 138, 216n18; U.S. view of, 81, 185–86
Sikorski, Radek, 154
Silitski, Vitali, 12
Skocpol, Theda, 8, 10, 211n3
Skovenia, 101
Slovak Republic, 85, 101, 206
Soros, George, 69, 84, 86, 144, 145
Spain, 139
Spector, Regine A., 33
Stalin, Joseph, 20–21, 214n2
Stern, Henry, 218n13

Symonenko, Petro, 34t, 215n8
Syria, 165

Talbott, Strobe, 89
Tarasyuk, Boris, 67
Tekebayev, Omurbek, 33
terrorism, 74, 192; and Belarus, 154; Georgian measures against, 40, 80, 174; Kyrgyz measures against, 42, 170. *See also* September 11 attacks
Thatcher, Margaret, 16, 188
Timoschenko, Yulia, 14, 35, 60, 67, 118–21, 138, 175–79
Tolstoy, Lev, 32
transitional regimes, 9
Transparency International (TI), 30t
Tucker, J. A., 205
Tudoroiu, Theodor, 209–10
Tuganaliev, Topchubek, 33
Tulip Revolution, 1–5; elections before, 32–34; electoral breakthrough, 44–45, 52–72; expectations, 108–14; exporting of, 141–43; foreign views of, 162–66; foreign policy before, 39–42, 80–81; outcomes, 8, 15–16, 115–18, 122–27, 136–40, 158–59, 188–99; political parties before, 37–39; and Russia, 96–97; scholarship on, 202–10; U.S. role in, 5–7, 78–91, 167–72, 211n2; U.S.-Russian relations during, 92–114; as U.S. plot, 75–79, 81. *See also* Kyrgyzstan
Tunisia, 2, 165, 191
Turkmenistan, 23, 28, 74
Twitter Revolution, 163, 187. *See also* Moldova

Ukraine: corruption, 29–31, 30t; and Crimea, 20, 22, 26, 59, 99, 110; economic problems, 23, 26, 29, 42; elections, 32–35, 34t, 51–52, 59–61, 70–71, 130; EU membership for, 42, 121–22; foreign policy, 39–42, 80–81; Freedom House score, 116t, 117, 122; NATO membership for, 7, 42, 99–103, 109, 110, 112, 192; after Orange

Revolution, 115–22, 136–40; Orthodox Christianity, 17; parliament of, 120–21; political opposition, 14, 37–39, 44–45, 48–52, 55–72, 119–23; and Russia, 19–23, 26, 34, 42, 95–96, 99; Soviet period, 18–20; and United States, 50, 88–89, 152, 175–83. *See also* Orange Revolution

Union of Soviet Socialist Republics (USSR), 73–75, 144, 194–96; breakup of, 1–2, 18–19, 139. *See also* Russia

United Democrats (Georgia), 46

United Kingdom, 16, 111, 188

United National Movement Party (Georgia), 129, 131–32. *See also* National Movement Party

United States, 188; and Belarus, 154–56; civil rights movement, 13; and former USSR territories, 73–75, 194–96; and Georgia, 40–41, 83–84, 98–99, 104, 110–11, 151–52, 191; influence on Color Revolutions, 5–7, 73–91, 211n2; and Kyrgyzstan, 9, 41–42, 167–72; policies after Color Revolutions, 167–86; Revolution, 212n3; and Russia, 7, 39–40, 74–75, 92–114, 192–94; and Ukraine, 50, 88–89, 152, 175–83; and war on terror, 74, 80

U.S. Agency for International Development (USAID), 70, 82–87, 217n6

Ussenov, Daniyar, 33

Uzbekistan, 115, 144–47, 161, 186

Venezuela, 112, 187

Vitrenko, Natalia, 34t

Way, Lucan, 11, 164, 208–9

Wertsch, James, 200

Wheatley, Jonathan, 200, 214n1

Wilson, Andrew, 202, 214n1

Wolchik, Sharon L., 12, 13, 69, 164, 205–6, 210

World Bank, 9–10

Yanukovich, Viktor, 2–4, 122, 191; elections of 2004, 49–52, 59–61, 67, 84–88; elections of 2010, 14–16, 78, 118, 120, 179, 199; and Kuchma, 49, 64–65; and Putin, 4, 49, 75, 85; resurgencef, 108–9; and Timoschenko, 175–79; Yushchenko prime minister, 65

youth organizations, 12–13, 62–63, 69–70, 84–85, 144, 148, 202–6, 213n6

Yushchenko, Viktor, 3–4, 7–9, 13, 138, 140, 186; and Bush, 177; elections of 2004, 49–52, 59–61, 66–67, 84–86, 158; as Kuchma prime minister, 49; Our Ukraine Coalition, 14, 35, 49, 118–21; and Russia, 110; and Timoschenko, 176–79; Yanukovich prime minister of, 65

Zhvania, David, 86, 138

Zhvania, Zurab, 3, 57, 66, 173; death of, 129; after Rose Revolution, 127–29; and Saakashvili, 14, 67, 68, 208, 216n25; and United Democrats, 46; U.S. view, 83–84, 89

Zurabishvili, Salome, 134

Acknowledgments

THIS BOOK AROSE out of several years of observing the Color Revolutions and their aftermath, as well as working with the political leadership of Georgia, Ukraine, and Kyrgyzstan during and after these events. Turning a few thoughts and observations into a book length study required a commitment of time, study, and support. Accordingly, while the ideas, insights, and, of course, mistakes, in this book are mine, I was fortunate to have colleagues, assistants, and interlocutors who helped me along the way.

Several people in New York, Kiev, Tbilisi, and Bishkek provided support and assistance to me. Numerous politicians, scholars, and civil society activists in Ukraine, Georgia, and Kyrgyzstan made themselves available for interviews and discussions, often more than once, during the research and writing. There are too many to name, but David Jijelava in Georgia and Venera Sakeeva in Kyrgyzstan facilitated many of those discussions through their excellent work as research assistants and translators.

This work would not have been possible without the support I received from the Harriman Institute at Columbia University. The Institute gave me travel grants to do research in the region and help with the final stages. In addition, the faculty, staff, and students at Harriman consistently provided assistance and encouragement during the too many years I spent writing this book.

Last, as always, my family Marta, Asher, Reuben, and Isis kept me grounded and often offered a break from thinking of events on the other side of the world from the small island on which we live.